# THE WAGNER ACT CASES

# THE WAGNER ACT CASES

□□□□□□□□□□□□□□□□□□□□□□□□□□□□

## RICHARD C. CORTNER

THE UNIVERSITY OF TENNESSEE PRESS □ KNOXVILLE

# PREFACE

□ □ □ □ □ □ □ □ □ □ □ □ □ □ □ □ □  □ □ □ □ □ □ □ □ □ □ □ □ □ □ □ □ □ □ □

THE STUDY OF CONSTITUTIONAL LAW IN RECENT YEARS HAS COME
more and more to focus on the social, political, and economic context
within which the Supreme Court's decisions are made and on decision-
making by the Court as an exercise of a discretionary power of choice
among the competing claims of interest groups or among policy alternatives. The process of constitutional adjudication is treated as a policy-
making process which differs only in matters of degree from the political
process in the legislative, executive, and administrative areas of government. This concept of judicial decision-making owes much to the growth
of judicial realism and its attack on the traditional, natural-law concept
of the judicial process, and also to such analyses of the governmental
system as David B. Truman's *The Governmental Process*. (New York:
Alfred A. Knopf, 1955.)

In my study of the Wagner Act cases I have generally adhered to this
concept of constitutional adjudication as a form of policy-making. As the
structure of the study implies, I have also made certain specific assump-
tions about this type of analysis generally and the study of the Wagner
Act cases in particular which should be made explicit at the outset. The
state of development of constitutional doctrine at the time any given
litigation arises is, I feel, quite important, since it is the structure of constitutional doctrine that, to a great extent, dictates which tactics pur-
sued by the groups involved will be successful or will fail. Also of course
the claims of such groups must be translated into the language of constitutional or legal doctrine. In addition, an analysis of the constitutional
doctrine will also reveal developmental and intra-court factors which
often in the end determine a decision in a given litigation. In such an
instance, the analysis of the role of interest groups in the process of
constitutional adjudication points up the underlying conflict which the
decision attempts to resolve, reveals the competing claims among

which the Court is asked to choose, and demonstrates the tactics by which the case is brought to the Court, but will not reveal the factors which determine the decision of the case. The legal structure will vary in importance with different cases and may in many cases be of relatively little importance as a factor of decision, whereas the tactics of interest groups may be highly important and perhaps determinative, as for example the role of the National Consumers' League and its use of the Brandeis brief in *Muller* v. *Oregon*.[1]

I have sought to examine the role of a governmental agency, the National Labor Relations Board, in constitutional litigation. Recent studies have illuminated the role of interest groups in the judicial process, but, although agencies of the federal government are engaged in over fifty per cent of the litigation at the Supreme Court level, their role in the judicial process has been largely ignored. I have therefore intensively examined the strategy and tactics of the NLRB as well as those of the interest groups involved in the Wagner Act cases with the hope of shedding some light on the part which federal agencies play as litigants before the Court.

My view is, however, that the Wagner Act cases represented more than a governmental-interest group struggle in the judicial process. The development of the laissez-faire Constitution following the Civil War, and the doctrines of legal realism which formed the language of dissent and the basis of the attack on laissez-faire constitutionalism, resulted in a broader conflict over the role of the Court in the governmental system which reached a crisis in 1937 in the Wagner Act cases and was the most important factor in their being decided as they were. These cases, therefore, determined not only the outcome of the union-employer struggle of the 1930's but also the outcome of the conflict over the constitutional system which had been created in the years since the Civil War. Because the Wagner Act cases ended an era in American constitutional history and marked the beginning of a new constitutional era, I have, in addition to my focus on the group struggle, attempted to set down as accurately as possible the broader aspects of this final battle to preserve the old constitutional order.

### NOTE ON SOURCES

A substantial part of the source material cited herein was derived from the files of the National Labor Relations Board which pertain to the five Wagner Act cases. These files are located in the Labor and Transportation Division of the National Archives, Washington, D.C., and are shelved according to the original case numbers assigned to the Wagner

[1] 208 U.S. 412 (1908).

Act cases by the NLRB. The citation of material from these files will therefore begin with the symbol NA, followed by the case number, folder reference, and the document, along with its date, to which reference is made.

## ACKNOWLEDGMENTS

My indebtedness to Clement E. Vose's study of the restrictive covenant cases in his *Caucasions Only* is I think obvious, and I now acknowledge it. To professors John Leek of the University of Oklahoma, Carl Swisher of The Johns Hopkins University, and David Fellman of the University of Wisconsin, at various times my mentors in constitutional law, and to Professor Lee S. Greene of the University of Tennessee, for his encouragement, I give my special thanks. To Professor Fellman, whose support and criticism aided me immeasurably in preparing this work, I express particular appreciation.

All errors contained herein are of course my own.

R. C. C.

Knoxville, Tennessee
September, 1963

# CONTENTS

□ □ □ □ □ □ □ □ □ □ □ □ □ □ □ □ □ □ □ □ □ □ □ □ □ □ □ □ □ □ □ □ □

# THE WAGNER ACT CASES

"The law is like . . . a single-bed blanket on a double bed and three folks in the bed and a cold night. There ain't ever enough blanket to cover the case, no matter how much pulling and hauling, and somebody is always going to nigh catch pneumonia. Hell, the law is like the pants you bought last year for a growing boy, but it is always this year and the seams are popped and the shankbones to the breeze. The law is always too short and too tight for growing humankind. The best you can do is do something and then make up some law to fit and by the time that law gets on the books you would have done something different."

—WILLIE STARK in *All the King's Men*

# 1

## JUDICIAL POWER IN
## THE POST–CIVIL WAR ERA

□ □ □ □ □ □ □ □ □ □ □ □ □ □ □ □ □ □ □ □ □ □ □ □ □ □ □ □ □ □ □ □ □ □ □ □ □ □

IN THE PERIOD BETWEEN 1886 AND THE TURN OF THE CENTURY, there occurred a veritable slaughter of legislation in the name of liberty of contract on the state court level in the United States. Laws requiring the payment of wages in lawful money, rather than in scrip good only at the company store, were held invalid in Pennsylvania, West Virginia, Kansas, and Missouri,[1] a law prohibiting the charging of laborers a greater per cent than others in company stores was held unconstitutional in West Virginia,[2] and a law outlawing company stores altogether was ruled invalid in Illinois.[3] Efforts to insure the payment of wages at regular intervals met the same fate; such laws were declared unconstitutional in Illinois, Arkansas, and California.[4] Laws prohibiting the screening of coal before weighing, where workers were paid on the basis of the weight of coal mined, were invalidated in Illinois, Colorado, and Ohio.[5] Laws limiting the hours of labor in various classes of occupations were ruled unconstitutional in California, New York, Nebraska, Colorado, and Illinois,[6] while minimum wage laws were invalidated in

[1] Pa.: *Godcharles* v. *Wigeman*, 113 Pa. 431, 6 A. 354 (1886); W.Va.: *State* v. *Goodwill*, 33 W.Va. 179, 10 S.E. 285 (1889); Kans.: *State* v. *Haun*, 61 Kans. 146, 59 P. 340 (1900); Mo.: *State* v. *Loomis*, 115 Mo. 307, 22 S.W. 350 (1893); *State* v. *Mo. Tie & Timber Co.*, 181 Mo. 536, 80 S.W. 933 (1904).

[2] *State* v. *Fire Creek Coal Co.*, 33 W.Va. 188, 10 S.E. 288 (1889).

[3] *Frorer* v. *People*, 141 Ill. 171, 31 N.E. 395 (1892).

[4] Ill.: *Braceville Coal Co.* v. *People*, 147 Ill. 66, 35 N.E. 62 (1893); Ark.: *Leep* v. *St. Louis, I.M. & S. Ry.*, 58 Ark. 407, 25 S.W. 75 (1894); Calif.: *Johnson* v. *Goodyear Mining Co.*, 127 Cal. 4, 59 P. 304 (1899).

[5] Ill.: *Millett* v. *People*, 117 Ill. 294, 7 N.E. 631 (1886); *Ramsey* v. *People*, 142 Ill. 380, 32 N.E. 364 (1892); *Harding* v. *People*, 160 Ill. 459, 43 N.E. 624 (1896); Col.: *In re House Bill*, 21 Col. 27, 39 P. 431 (1895); Ohio: *In re Preston*, 63 Ohio 352, 59 N.E. 101 (1900).

[6] Calif.: *Ex parte Kubach*, 85 Cal. 274, 24 P. 737 (1890); N.Y.: *People* v. *Beck*, 144 N.Y. 225, 39 N.E. 80 (1894); Neb.: *Low* v. *Rees Printing Co.*, 41 Neb. 127, 59 N.W. 362 (1894); Col.: *In re Eight Hour Law*, 21 Col. 29, 39 P. 328 (1895); *In re Morgan*, 26 Col. 415, 58 P. 1071 (1895); Ill.: *Ritchie* v. *People*, 155 Ill. 98, 40 N.E. 454 (1895).

New York and Indiana.[7] Finally, legislation prohibiting the yellow dog contract, whereby an employee agreed to relinquish his union membership or not to join a union as a condition of employment, was held unconstitutional in Georgia, Missouri, Illinois, Wisconsin, and New York.[8]

Many of these state court decisions preceded the 1937 decisions of the Supreme Court in the Wagner Act cases[9] by almost fifty years, but they signified the emergence of a new era in American constitutional law which was to end with the constitutional crisis of the 1930's and the decisions in the Wagner Act cases. For, while the immediate event which led to the Wagner Act cases was the group conflict within the structure of the National Recovery Administration and the halls of Congress after 1933, conditioning, and in a real sense dominating, this conflict was the structure of constitutional law built up over the decades since the Civil War. It was this legal structure which labor and business groups in the 1930's had ultimately to attack or defend and which was inevitably to lead their conflict from the administrative and legislative processes into the process of constitutional litigation. The union-employer struggle was, therefore, joined with a broader conflict over constitutional doctrine and the proper role of the Supreme Court itself in the governmental system.

The basic elements of this broader constitutional conflict can be seen in these post–Civil War state court decisions, since, while the legislation under review differed, the decisions themselves contained common principles. There was first the fusing of the rights of liberty and property in the concept of liberty of contract. The Supreme Court of Arkansas, for example, expressed this principle in declaring invalid a statute requiring the payment of wages at regular intervals. "The right to acquire and possess property," it said, "necessarily includes the right to contract; for it is the principal mode of acquisition, and is the only way by which a person can rightly acquire property by his own exertion. Of all the 'rights of persons' it is the most essential to human happiness."[10] It was also usually assumed by the courts that the economy was operated by

[7] N.Y.: *People* v. *Coler*, 166 N.Y. 1, 59 N.E. 716 (1901); Ind.: *Street* v. *Varney Electrical Supply Co.*, 160 Ind. 338, 65 N.E. 895 (1903).

[8] Ga.: *Wallace* v. *Georgia*, 97 Ga. 213, 22 S.E. 529 (1894); Mo.: *State* v. *Julow*, 129 Mo. 163, 31 S.W. 781 (1895); Ill.: *Gillespie* v. *People*, 188 Ill. 176, 58 N.E. 1007 (1900); Wis.: *People* v. *Kreutzberg*, 114 Wis. 530, 90 N.W. 1098 (1902); N.Y.: *People* v. *Marcus*, 144 N.Y. 225, 39 N.E. 80 (1906).

[9] *National Labor Relations Board* v. *Jones & Laughlin Steel Corp.*, 301 U.S. 1; *National Labor Relations Board* v. *Fruehauf Trailer Co.*, 301 U.S. 49; *National Labor Relations Board* v. *Friedman-Harry Marks Clothing Co.*, 301 U.S. 58; *Associated Press* v. *National Labor Relations Board*, 301 U.S. 103; *Washington, Virginia and Maryland Coach Co.* v. *National Labor Relations Board*, 301 U.S. 142 (1937).

[10] *Leep* v. *St. Louis, I.M. & S. Ry.*, 58 Ark. 408, at 415, 25 S.W. 75, at 77.

"natural" economic laws which were beyond the control of men and that the economy would operate best if let alone. The Supreme Court of Kansas declared that a statute regulating the mode of payment of wages infringed "upon natural rights and constitutional grants of liberty." It reflected on the "dignity and independence of the wage earner" and deceived him "by the promise that legislation can cure all the ills of which he may complain. Such legislation suggests the handiwork of the politician rather than the political economist."[11] A minimum wage of twenty cents an hour, to the Supreme Court of Indiana, interfered with "the operation of natural and economic laws" and "furnishes to those whom it professes to favor few of the advantages expected from its provisions."[12] The Supreme Court of Appeals of West Virginia held unconstitutional a statute which required the payment of wages in lawful money and at regular intervals with the declaration that the "natural law of supply and demand is the best law of trade."[13]

Finally, the courts generally assumed the legal equality of all adults or "persons" in their contractual relations, despite the difference in economic power which might exist between employer and employee or the fact that one of the "persons" contracting might be a corporation.[14] To the West Virginia court, the legislature's requirement that wages be paid in lawful money was "an attempt to degrade the intelligence, virtue, and manhood of the American laborer, and foist upon the people a paternal government of the most objectionable character, because it assumes that the employer is a knave, and the laborer an imbecile."[15] And in *Ritchie* v. *People,* the Supreme Court of Illinois regarded a law establishing the eight-hour day for women as an attempt to deprive a woman of the "right to determine for herself how many hours she can and may work during each day."[16]

It was this concept of equality which was to carry over from these early decisions into the litigation over the constitutionality of the Wagner Act in the 1930's. For even at this early date, state legislatures had begun attempts to protect working men from the employer's use of his superior economic power in forcing them to relinquish their union membership as a condition of employment. But, as noted above, these attempts were usually invalidated by the courts. The Supreme Court of

[11] *State* v. *Haun,* 61 Kan. 146, at 159, 59 P. 340, at 345.

[12] *Street* v. *Varney Electrical Supply Co.,* 160 Ind. 338, at 346, 66 N.E. 895, at 898.

[13] *State* v. *Goodwill,* 33 W.Va. 179, at 186, 10 S.E. 285, at 287.

[14] The Supreme Court in 1886 ruled that corporations were included within the meaning of the term "persons" as used in the fourteenth amendment; *Santa Clara County* v. *Southern Pacific Ry. Co.,* 118 U.S. 394 (1886).

[15] *State* v. *Goodwill,* 33 W.Va. 179, at 186, 10 S.E. 285, at 287–88.

[16] 155 Ill. 98, at 114, 40 N.E. 454, at 459.

Wisconsin, in a typical case, pointed out that a man who had joined a union and "shackled any of his faculties" could be considered "less useful and less desirable by some employers. . . . Whether the workman can find in his membership in such organizations advantages and compensations to offset his lessened desirability in the industrial market is a question each must decide for himself. His right to freedom in so doing is of the same grade and sacredness as that of the employer to consent or refuse to employ him according to the decision he makes."[17] Decisions in at least five other states supported these views.[18]

Of all the theories enunciated during this period of extreme construction of liberty of contract, this theory of the nature of employer-employee relations was to be the most persistent. It was soon adopted by employer groups as an article in their creed of American industrialism. The National Association of Manufacturers, which was established in 1896, began in 1903 its campaign against organized labor under the prodding of its president, David M. Parry. In a speech in that year, Parry declared that "lawless and socialistic unionism" demanded the Association's immediate attention. "Unionism," he said, "denies to those outside its ranks the individual right to dispose of their labor as they see fit—a right that is one of the most sacred and fundamental of American liberty."[19] In response, the Association adopted at its 1903 convention a Declaration of Principles which included the statement that "it is the right of the employee to leave his employment whenever he sees fit, and it is the right of the employer to discharge any employee when he sees fit."[20]

By the early 1900's, therefore, both business groups and an increasing number of American judges had come to look upon liberty of contract as a sacred, natural right and were denying the legitimacy of legislative attempts to regulate contractual relations between employees and employers. The transformation of American constitutional law which resulted may be traced to fears induced in conservative legal circles by the economic and social conflict of the post–Civil War period.[21] Fearing onslaughts upon property rights by an aroused mass electorate, conservative members of the legal profession and propertied interests turned to the courts for protection through the constitutional legitimatization of

[17] *State* v. *Kreutzberg*, 114 Wis. 530, at 541, 90 N.W. 1098, at 1102.
[18] See note 8.
[19] Albion Guilford Taylor, "The Labor Policies of the National Association of Manufacturers," *University of Illinois Studies in the Social Sciences*, Vol. 15 (1927), pp. 35–36.
[20] *Ibid.*, p. 38.
[21] See Arnold M. Paul, *Conservative Crisis and the Rule of Law: Attitudes of Bar and Bench, 1887–1895* (Ithaca, N.Y.: Cornell University Press, 1960).

certain laissez-faire doctrines. Aided by Thomas M. Cooley and Christopher Tiedeman, whose legal treatises encouraged the adoption of new constitutional limitations by the courts, they were able, finally with great success, to persuade the judiciary of the necessity for strengthened constitutional protection of property rights.[22]

Such persuasion by the bar had fallen upon the responsive ears of Justices Field and Bradley in the *Slaughter House* cases[23] in 1873. Although a Supreme Court majority of five rejected ex-Justice John A. Campbell's argument for a broad interpretation of the protections of the fourteenth amendment and refused to strike down a Louisiana statute which conferred a monopoly of slaughtering in New Orleans, Field and Bradley argued tenaciously in dissent that the Louisiana statute violated the right of free labor which the amendment was designed to protect. By the majority opinion upholding the statute, Field argued, citing Adam Smith, "the right of free labor, one of the most sacred and imprescriptible rights of man, is violated."[24]

Both Field and Bradley were able, in the *Butcher's Union* case eleven years later, to express these views in concurring opinions,[25] but it was not until 1897, twenty-four years after the *Slaughter House* cases, that their views were adopted by a majority of the Court in *Allgeyer* v. *Louisiana*[26] and used to declare unconstitutional a legislative enactment regulating the manner in which insurance could be sold. Justice Peckham, speaking for the Court, declared the liberty protected by the fourteenth amendment to include "not only the right of the citizen to be free from the mere physical restraint of his person," but to embrace as well "the right of the citizen to be free in the enjoyment of all his faculties; to be free to use them in all lawful ways; to live and work where he will; to earn his livelihood by any lawful calling; to pursue any livelihood or avocation, and for that purpose to enter into all contracts which may be proper, necessary and essential to his carrying out to a successful conclusion the purposes above mentioned."[27]

This broadening of the concepts of liberty and property which was accomplished by the Court between 1873 and 1897 entailed only the "innocuous generality" that the fourteenth amendment protected the

---

[22] See Clyde E. Jacobs, *Law Writers and the Courts* (Berkeley: University of California Press, 1954), and Benjamin R. Twiss, *Lawyers and the Constitution* (Princeton: Princeton University Press, 1942).

[23] 16 Wall. 36 (1873).

[24] 16 Wall. 36, at 109–10.

[25] *Butcher's Union* v. *Crescent City Co.,* 111 U.S. 746 (1884).

[26] 165 U.S. 578 (1897).

[27] 165 U.S. at 589.

right of the individual to pursue any of the ordinary occupations. Despite the mention by the Court of "the liberty to contract for insurance" in the *Allgeyer* case, the concept of liberty of contract had not yet become a serious threat to state legislation on the Supreme Court level. This was due to the fact that the virtual storm of litigation which had been initiated by business groups seeking a broadened protection of property rights had been diverted from the Supreme Court by a provision of the Judiciary Act of 1789. Under this provision, if the highest appellate state court upheld a state law as being constitutional under the federal Constitution, the aggrieved parties could appeal to the Supreme Court on writ of error; if, however, the state court held a state law unconstitutional under the federal Constitution, there was no right of appeal to the Supreme Court.[28]

Under this statutory umbrella, the state courts, rather than the Supreme Court, were in a negative sense the real interpreters of the Constitution, and the storm of litigation which arose over the tendency of legislatures to intervene in employer-employee relations in behalf of employees was directed for the most part at the state courts. Thus, while by 1897 the Supreme Court had only stated a broadened concept of due process in very general terms, the state courts had seized the initiative and fully developed the right of free contract as an effective instrument of substantive due process.[29]

In the *In re Jacobs* case of 1885, for example, the New York Court of Appeals utilized the concurring opinions of Field and Bradley in the *Butcher's Union* case to declare unconstitutional a statute prohibiting cigar-making in tenement houses which were also used as living quarters.[30] If the statute were valid, the court said, the person who manufactured cigars in his home "must either abandon the trade by which he earns his livelihood for himself and family, or, if able, procure a room elsewhere, or hire himself out to one who has a room upon such terms as, under the fierce competition of trade and the inexorable laws of supply and demand, he may be able to obtain from his employer."[31] Liberty, the court said, "includes the right of one to use his faculties in all lawful ways, to live and work where he will, to earn his livelihood in any lawful calling, and to pursue any lawful trade or vocation."[32] If such

[28] See Carl B. Swisher, *American Constitutional Development* (Boston: Houghton Mifflin Co., 1954), pp. 562–63.
[29] See Roscoe Pound, "Liberty of Contract," 18 *Yale Law Journal* 454, 490 (1908).
[30] 98 N.Y. 98, 50 Am. Rep. 637 (1885).
[31] 98 N.Y. at 104, 50 Am. Rep. at 638.
[32] 98 N.Y. at 106, 50 Am. Rep. at 640.

legislation were allowed to stand, the court predicted a future where the government might regulate the "building of houses, the rearing of cattle, the sowing of seed and the reaping of grain . . . and labor of artisans, the rate of wages, the price of food. . . . Such governmental interferences disturb the normal adjustments of the social fabric, and usually derange the delicate and complicated machinery of industry and cause a score of ills while attempting the removal of one."[33]

Then, in 1886, just one year after the pioneering opinion of the New York Court of Appeals in the *Jacobs* case, the Supreme Courts of Pennsylvania and Illinois held statutes unconstitutional on the ground of interference with liberty of contract.[34] In the Pennsylvania case, *Godcharles* v. *Wigeman,* the statute under review required the payment of wages at regular intervals and in lawful currency. The court ruled that the act was "utterly unconstitutional and void" in that it attempted to prevent "persons who are *sui juris* from making their own contracts." The act, according to the court, violated the rights of both employers and employees and was "an insulting attempt to put the laborer under a legislative tutelage, which is not only degrading to his manhood, but subversive of his rights as a citizen of the United States. He may sell his labor for what he thinks best, whether money or goods, just as his employer may sell his iron or coal, and any and every law that proposes to prevent him from so doing is an infringement of his constitutional privileges, and consequently vicious and void."[35]

Liberty of contract had thus become a constitutionally protected right, and, with the *Jacobs* and *Godcharles* cases as precedents, the state courts began the slaughter of legislation referred to above. This expansion of constitutional protection for property rights signalled the resurgence of judicial power in the United States to a height greater than it had occupied before the Civil War. Along with this increase of judicial power came an emphasis on the natural-law theory of the judicial process. According to this theory, there existed a transcendental body of natural law which could be "discovered" by the use of reason. The decision of cases turned upon the application of these pre-existing principles of law to disputes arising among men. A judge, therefore, did not exercise a policy-making function in deciding cases but merely declared the law as it already existed through a process of deduction

[33] 98 N.Y. at 114–15, 50 Am. Rep. at 647. The principles of the *Jacobs* opinion were reaffirmed in *People* v. *Marx,* 99 N.Y. 377, 2 N.E. 29 (1885), where a statute prohibiting the sale of oleomargarine was held invalid.

[34] Pa.: *Godcharles* v. *Wigeman,* 113 Pa. 431, 6 A. 354 (Oct., 1886); Ill.: *Millett* v. *People,* 117 Ill. 294, 7 N.E. 631 (June, 1886).

[35] 113 Pa. at 437, 6A. at 356.

from the principles of natural justice.[36] On the level of constitutional adjudication, this theory was joined by the conception of the Constitution as the supreme will of the people. Thus the judge in holding a statute unconstitutional was not making policy or overriding the popular will, but only declaring the will of the people as expressed in the Constitution to be contrary to the legislative enactment.[37]

This conception of the judicial process served the function of reconciling policy-making by non-elective judicial institutions with the theory of equal individual participation through voting in the formulation of public policy. There had always existed an ambiguity in democratic natural-law theory concerning the point at which individual rights limited the use of governmental power by legislative majorities. The formation of the Constitution and the establishment of judicial review in a sense institutionalized this ambiguity in the United States. Where theoretically there had been posited the rule of popular sovereignty restrained by inalienable rights, under the Constitution there grew up legislative and executive institutions more or less responsive to the electoral process but restrained by a non-elective judiciary enforcing constitutional limitations on their actions. The theoretical and political conflict which resulted was to an extent screened behind the theory that the judges were not making law but in interpreting constitutional provisions were merely declaring the real will of the people.[38]

Justice David J. Brewer thus declared in 1893 that there was "nothing in this power of the Judiciary detracting in the least from the idea of government of and by the people. The Courts hold neither purse nor sword; they cannot corrupt nor arbitrarily control. They make no laws, they establish no policy, they never enter into the domain of popular action. They do not govern. Their functions in relation to the State are limited to seeing that popular action does not trespass upon right and justice as it exists in written constitutions and natural law."[39]

This theory of the role of the courts could not go unchallenged in the

---

[36] See Fred V. Cahill, *Judicial Legislation* (New York: The Ronald Press Co., 1952), pp. 9–18.

[37] The classic statement here is Hamilton's in Federalist No. 78: "Nor does this conclusion by any means suppose a superiority of the judicial to the legislative power. It only supposes that the power of the people is superior to both; and that where the will of the legislature, declared in the statutes, stands in opposition to that of the people, declared in the Constitution, the judges ought to be governed by the latter rather than the former." *The Federalist* (Modern Library Edition), p. 506.

[38] See Morris R. Cohen, *Law and Social Order* (New York: Harcourt, Brace, and Co., 1933), pp. 136–37.

[39] Quoted in Alpheus T. Mason, *The Supreme Court from Taft to Warren* (Baton Rouge: Louisiana State University Press, 1958), p. 26.

face of judicial frustration of legislative reform efforts throughout the country. A growing body of opinion, both lay and professional, attacked the theory as concealing the true nature of the judicial process and inhibiting a greater degree of realism in dealing with social questions.[40] Oliver Wendell Holmes, who as a judge on the Supreme Judicial Court of Massachusetts had registered one of the few dissents to the laissez-faire rampage on the state court level,[41] had pointed out the policy-making nature of court decisions as early as 1881. The growth of the law, he had said, "is legislative. . . . The very considerations which judges most rarely mention, and always with an apology, are the secret roots from which the law draws all the juices of life. I mean, of course, considerations of what is expedient for the community concerned."[42] Roscoe Pound, in reviewing the liberty of contract decisions in 1908, pointed out the social policy inherent in the decisions and warned that the adoption of extreme laissez-faire by the courts had impaired popular respect for them. "The evil of these cases," he said, "will live after them in impaired authority of the courts long after the decisions themselves are forgotten."[43]

The tide of criticism of the judiciary reached its peak in 1911 when the New York Court of Appeals declared the New York workman's compensation act unconstitutional in *Ives* v. *South Buffalo Railroad Co.*[44] "If such economic and sociologic arguments as are here advanced in support of this statute can be allowed to subvert the fundamental idea of property," the court declared, "then there is no private right entirely safe, because there is no limitation upon the absolute discretion of legislatures, and the guarantees of the Constitution are a mere waste of words."[45] Robert F. Wagner, the thirty-three-year-old legislator who had introduced the legislation in the New York Assembly, declared that "it isn't my law that's wrong, it's the Constitution, and I'll soon fix that." The New York constitution was amended and the law repassed in 1913.[46]

Nevertheless, the harm had been done to the judicial cause. Theodore

[40] See especially, Roscoe Pound, "Mechanical Jurisprudence," 8 *Columbia Law Review* 605 (1908); Morris R. Cohen, "The Process of Judicial Legislation," 48 *American Law Review* 161 (1914).
[41] *Commonwealth* v. *Perry,* 155 Mass. 117, at 123, 28 N.E. 1126, at 1127 (1891).
[42] O. W. Holmes, *The Common Law* (Boston: Little, Brown, and Co., 1881), p. 35.
[43] Roscoe Pound, "Liberty of Contract," *op. cit.* at 487.
[44] 201 N.Y. 271, 94 N.E. 431 (1911).
[45] 201 N.Y. at 295, 94 N.E. at 440.
[46] Owen P. White, "When the Public Needs a Friend," *Colliers,* Vol. 93 (June 2, 1934), p. 18.

Roosevelt called the decision in the *Ives* case "absolutely reactionary" and adopted recall of state judges as an issue in the 1912 campaign.[47] During the campaign, he declared that the Progressives "stand for the Constitution, but we will not consent to make of the Constitution a fetich for the protection of fossilized wrong."[48] The conservative reaction was immediate. Roosevelt's attack on the judiciary alienated the right wing of the Republican Party and hurt his chances of securing the nomination for the presidency.[49] The National Association of Manufacturers reacted by amending its Declaration of Principles in 1913 to pledge its "loyalty to our Judiciary, upon the maintenance of which, unswerved by passing clamor, rest the perpetuation of our laws, our institutions, and our society."[50] The American Bar Association created a Committee to Oppose Judicial Recall which conducted a large-scale campaign and by 1915 was able to report that "this doctrine of lawlessness" had been "beaten to a frazzle."[51]

Probably the most important result of the storm over the *Ives* decision was the passage by Congress in 1914 of an amendment to the Judiciary Act permitting Supreme Court review of state decisions invalidating state legislation through the writ of certiorari.[52] The Supreme Court until almost 1900 had remained comparatively insulated from the frenzy of litigation at the state level. It was not until 1898 that a case involving a labor law challenged on liberty of contract grounds reached the Court. This was *Holden* v. *Hardy,* which involved a Utah statute limiting the hours of labor in mines and smelters to eight hours a day.[53] The majority opinion by Justice Brown offered hope that the Court was not unaware of the economic realities of employer-employee relations and that it might escape contamination by the extreme laissez-faire doctrines developed by the state courts. The Court upheld the legislature's determination that work in mines and smelters might be detrimental to the health of employees and declared that "so long as there are reasonable grounds for believing that this is so, its decision upon this subject cannot be reviewed by the Federal courts."[54] Despite the general right of free contract, the Court recognized that the legislature could interfere "where the parties do not stand upon an equality, or

[47] George E. Mowry, *Theodore Roosevelt and the Progressive Movement* (Madison: University of Wisconsin Press, 1946), pp. 215–16.

[48] *Ibid.*, p. 278.

[49] *Ibid.*, pp. 217–18.

[50] Clarence E. Bonnett, *Employers' Associations in the United States* (New York: The Macmillan Co., 1922), p. 298.

[51] 1915 *American Bar Association Journal*, pp. 276–77.

[52] 38 Stat. 790. See also Swisher, *op. cit.*, p. 563.

[53] 169 U.S. 366 (1898).

[54] *Ibid.* at 395.

where the public health demands that one party to the contract shall be protected against himself." "In other words, the proprietors lay down the rules and the laborers are practically constrained to obey them. In such cases self-interest is often an unsafe guide, and the legislature may properly interpose its authority."[55]

The Court's awareness that contracts between employers and employees were not consummated in an economic vacuum, that employees' bargaining power was unequal to that of employers, and that this inequality could justify intervention by legislatures was a welcome relief from the unreality of the doctrine of equality prevalent on the state court level. Justices Peckham and Brewer dissented, however, indicating that a more rigid liberty of contract doctrine had some support on the Court. In 1899, the Court upheld an Arkansas statute requiring the payment of wages to railroad workers immediately upon discharge,[56] and in 1901, a Tennessee law requiring corporations to redeem store orders or scrip issued to their employees at their face value in currency was sustained.[57] The liberal tendency of the Court was continued when in 1903 it sustained a Kansas law requiring contractors performing work for the state to observe the eight-hour day.[58]

In the latter case, however, Chief Justice Fuller joined Peckham and Brewer in dissent, indicating that the forces favoring a stricter application of liberty of contract were growing. In 1905, the Chief Justice, along with Brewer, Peckham, McKenna, and Brown, joined to form the majority in *Lochner* v. *New York*.[59] For the first time the Court declared a labor law unconstitutional on liberty of contract grounds. Justice Peckham, whose major premise, according to Justice Holmes, was "God damn it," wrote the majority opinion invalidating the New York statute fixing the hours of labor in bakeries at ten hours a day and sixty hours a week. To the majority, the law could be sustained only if bakers were proven less capable than other laborers of exercising their freedom to contract, or if the trade of the baker could be shown to be so unhealthy as to necessitate the intervention of the state for health reasons. On the first point, the majority held that there "is no contention that bakers as a class are not equal in intelligence and capacity to men in other trades or manual occupations, or that they are not able to assert their rights and care for themselves without the protecting arm of the state, interfering with their independence of judgment and of action." Nor could the statute stand as a health measure. To the Court, the

[55] 169 U.S. at 397.
[56] *St. Louis Ry. Co.* v. *Paul,* 173 U.S. 404 (1899).
[57] *Knoxville Iron Co.* v. *Harbison,* 183 U.S. 13 (1901).
[58] *Atkin* v. *Kansas,* 191 U.S. 207 (1903).
[59] 198 U.S. 45 (1905).

occupation of a baker was "not an unhealthy one to that degree which would authorize the legislature to interfere. . . . It is unfortunately true that labor, even in any department, may possibly carry with it the seeds of unhealthiness. But are we all, on that account, at the mercy of legislative majorities?"[60]

In one of the most famous dissents in the history of the Court, Justice Holmes declared that "the 14th Amendment does not enact Mr. Herbert Spencer's Social Statics." The Constitution, he said, "is not intended to embody a particular economic theory, whether of paternalism and the organic relation of the citizen to the state or of *laissez faire.* . . . I think that the word 'liberty' in the 14th Amendment is perverted when it is held to prevent the natural outcome of a dominant opinion, unless it can be said that a rational and fair man necessarily would admit that the statute proposed would infringe fundamental principles as they have been understood by the traditions of our people and our law."[61]

The majority of the Court, however, presumably being "rational and fair men," had decided that the statute did infringe "fundamental principles," and it appears that the legal profession, at least as reflected in the law reviews, approved the decision.[62] With the *Lochner* decision, it became obvious that the doctrine of liberty of contract could not be considered as an ephemeral doctrine developed by the state courts which the Supreme Court would avoid reading into the Constitution. A concerted effort was soon made to mitigate the effects of the decision. The National Consumers' League had been founded in 1899, and by 1908 its leadership was profoundly discouraged by judicial negation of wage and hour legislation. In that year, it reorganized its Committee on Legislation into a Committee on Legislation and Legal Defense of Labor Laws and began to concentrate on the defense of reform legislation in the courts as well as its promotion in legislatures. The new committee was headed by Josephine Goldmark.[63]

The Oregon maximum-hour law for women was then under attack before the Supreme Court, and Miss Goldmark began to search for a lawyer to file a brief *amicus curiae* in behalf of the League in the case. Joseph H. Choate was asked to file the brief, but declined, saying he could see no reason why "a big husky Irishwoman should not work more

---

[60] 198 U.S. at 57, 59.

[61] *Ibid.* at 75–76.

[62] John R. Commons and Associates, *History of Labour in the United States* (New York: The Macmillan Co., 1935), III, 690.

[63] Clement E. Vose, "The National Consumers' League and the Brandeis Brief," *Midwest Journal of Political Science,* Vol. I (Nov., 1957), pp. 274–80.

than ten hours a day in a laundry if she and her employer so desired."[64] Finally, with two weeks remaining in which briefs could be filed, Miss Goldmark persuaded her brother-in-law, Louis Brandeis, to file the League's brief. Brandeis had said in 1905 that the leaders of the bar had "with rare exceptions, been ranged on the side of the corporations, and the people have been represented, in the main, by men of very meager legal ability. . . . This condition cannot continue."[65] Recognizing that the Court in the *Lochner* case had failed to give due consideration to the social realities involved in the review of reform legislation, Brandeis devoted only a few pages of his brief to the legal points involved but covered extensively medical and social studies demonstrating the detrimental effects on women of long working hours. Although a member of the Clerk's Office thought that "that fellow Brandeez has got the impudence of the Devil to bring his socialism into the Supreme Court,"[66] the result of this novel brief was a unanimous decision in *Muller* v. *Oregon* upholding the statute. The Court specially noted and accepted the evidence contained in Brandeis' brief as justifying an interference with liberty of contract.[67]

After the *Muller* victory, the Consumers' League began to use the Brandeis-type brief extensively in winning reversals of extreme liberty of contract decisions on wage and hour legislation. Beginning with the reversal of *Ritchie* v. *People* by the Illinois Supreme Court,[68] other cases involving maximum hours for women were won.[69] In 1917, the League was successful in defending minimum wages for women and maximum hours for both men and women before the Supreme Court.[70]

The liberalizing effect of the League's efforts came too late, however, for organized labor. In 1908, while the League was winning its first victory in the *Muller* case, the Supreme Court in *Adair* v. *United States*

---

[64] Alpheus T. Mason, *Brandeis: A Free Man's Life* (New York: The Viking Press, 1946), p. 248.

[65] *Ibid.,* p. 101.

[66] *Ibid.,* p. 253.

[67] 208 U.S. 412, at 419–20 (1908).

[68] *Ritchie* v. *Wayman,* 244 Ill. 509, 91 N.E. 695 (1910).

[69] *Ex parte Hawley,* 85 Ohio 494, 98 N.E. 1126 (1911), *affirmed, Hawley* v. *Walker,* 232 U.S. 718 (1914); *In re Miller,* 162 Cal. 687, 124 P. 427 (1912), *affirmed, Miller* v. *Wilson,* 236 U.S. 373 (1915).

[70] *Stettler* v. *O'Hara, affirmed* by an evenly divided Court, 243 U.S. 629 (1917); *Bunting* v. *Oregon,* 243 U.S. 426 (1917). The Court during this period also upheld state laws regulating the screening of coal, *McLean* v. *Arkansas,* 211 U.S. 539 (1909); requiring payment of wages in currency, *Keokee Coke Co.* v. *Taylor,* 234 U.S. 227 (1914); and requiring the payment of wages semi-monthly, *Erie Ry. Co.* v. *Williams,* 233 U.S. 685 (1914). For other League cases see Vose, *loc. cit.,* p. 277.

ruled for the first time on the power of the federal government to protect labor unions under the commerce power.[71] The *Adair* case, in which the doctrine of liberty of contract intermeshed with the power of Congress to regulate interstate commerce, was to become one of the most important constitutional obstacles to the Wagner Act. Congress attempted for the first time to adjust labor disputes on the railroads with the Arbitration Act of 1888.[72] It provided for voluntary arbitration and investigation of railway labor disputes. The arbitration provisions were never used; and the investigatory provisions were used only once, in the case of the Pullman strike.[73] William Howard Taft, then a federal circuit judge in Ohio, welcomed news during the Pullman strike that "thirty men have been killed by the federal troops. Though it is a bloody business, everyone hopes it is true."[74] Congress, however, reacted differently and passed the Erdman Act in 1898.[75] It provided for voluntary arbitration and government mediation, and section 10 prohibited a carrier from requiring "any employee or any person seeking employment as a condition of such employment, to enter into an agreement, either written or verbal, not to become or remain a member of any labor corporation, association, or organization." Violations were made misdemeanors punishable by fines of from one hundred to one thousand dollars.

William Adair, as an agent of the Louisville and Nashville Railroad, fired O. B. Coppage in 1906 solely because of his membership in the Order of Locomotive Firemen. A federal district court in Kentucky found Adair guilty of a violation of section 10 of the Erdman Act and fined him one hundred dollars.[76] The question on appeal to the Supreme Court was whether section 10 constituted a valid regulation of commerce. Relying on the Court's decisions under the Sherman Anti-Trust Act of 1890, counsel for Adair argued that the employer-employee relationship affected commerce only indirectly, if at all.[77] In interpreting the Sherman Act, the Court had held in *United States* v. *E. C. Knight Co.* that the American Sugar Refining Company's control of the refining of ninety-eight per cent of the sugar refined in the United States did not affect commerce to the degree necessary to subject it to the congressional

---

[71] 208 U.S. 161 (1908).

[72] 25 Stat. 501.

[73] Glenn Miller, *American Labor and the Government* (New York: Prentice-Hall, Inc., 1948), p. 397.

[74] Henry F. Pringle, *The Life and Times of William Howard Taft* (New York: Farrar & Rinehart, Inc., 1939), Vol. I, p. 128.

[75] 30 Stat. 424.

[76] *United States* v. *Adair*, 152 F. 738 (E.D. Ky., 1907).

[77] 26 Stat. 209.

power to regulate commerce.[78] "Doubtless the power to control the manufacture of a given thing involves in a certain sense the control of its disposition," Chief Justice Fuller had written, "but this is a secondary and not the primary sense; and although the exercise of that power may result in bringing the operation of commerce into play, it does not control it, and affects it only incidentally and indirectly. Commerce succeeds to manufacture, and is not a part of it."[79]

Three years later, in *Hopkins* v. *United States* and *Anderson* v. *United States*,[80] the Court had held that an agreement among stock brokers of the Kansas City Live Stock Exchange not to buy or sell stock from persons not members of the exchange did not affect commerce, despite the fact that most of the cattle bought and sold arrived in Kansas City from outside the state. The services of the brokers, the Court had held, operated "in furtherance and in aid of commerce by providing for its facilities, conveniences, privileges or services," but they did "not directly relate to charges for its transportation, nor to any other form of interstate commerce."[81]

From these cases, counsel for Adair argued that in order for Congress to regulate validly any activity under the commerce clause, the effects of that activity upon commerce must be "direct" and not merely "indirect" or "collateral." Activity which affected commerce only indirectly was subject to state, not congressional, power, and section 10 of the Erdman Act, it was argued, was "a bold attempt to regulate an ordinary relation of life—of master and servant—one hitherto supposed to be entirely within state control." The second basic objection urged against section 10 was, of course, that it interfered with liberty of contract as guaranteed by the fifth amendment. To support this argument, counsel for Adair cited the state decisions declaring similar legislation invalid.[82]

The government argued that the outlawing of yellow dog contracts was a valid protection of interstate commerce, Congress having "recognized the fact that discrimination against employes because of their membership in a labor organization was calculated to bring on . . . disturbances."[83] The government could also rely on anti-trust cases in support of its argument, for in 1905, the Court in *Swift & Company* v. *United States* had sustained a prosecution of packing companies which had agreed not to bid against one another at stockyards, to fix prices of sales of cattle, and to receive less than lawful shipping rates from rail-

[78] 156 U.S. 1 (1895).
[79] *Ibid.* at 12.
[80] 171 U.S. 578 (1898); 171 U.S. 604 (1898).
[81] 171 U.S. at 592.
[82] 208 U.S. at 166.
[83] *Ibid.* at 164.

roads.[84] Justice Holmes, writing for the Court, described commerce as "not a technical legal conception, but a practical one, drawn from the course of business." To the Court, the trade in cattle was a "typical, constantly recurring" course of trade, "a current of commerce among the states, and the purchase of the cattle is a part and incident of such commerce."[85] The Court thus seemed to be saying that commerce could not be considered solely as transportation, as was implied from the *Knight* case, but that it also embraced trade, and that Congress could regulate activity which, although essentially local in nature, affected such trade.

Further bolstering the government's case was the Court's opinion in the *Employers' Liability* case, decided in the 1908 term.[86] As early as 1888, the Court had said that Congress could "legislate as to the qualifications, duties, and liabilities of employes and others on railway trains engaged in . . . commerce,"[87] and in the *Liability* case the Court upheld the Federal Employers' Liability Act of 1906 as a valid regulation of commerce, although its application to employees in what the Court considered intrastate commerce was declared invalid.[88] "We think," the Court said, in the devious language of Justice White, "the unsoundness of the contention, that because the act regulates the relation of master and servant, it is unconstitutional, because under no circumstances and to no extent can the regulation of such subject be within the grant of authority to regulate commerce, is demonstrable."[89]

In the *Adair* case, then, the Court had to determine whether the question of union organization in the "local" relations of master and servant could directly affect commerce, as the sales of cattle did in the *Swift* case or the compensation for injuries to employees did in the *Employers' Liability* case; or whether the unionization could have only an indirect effect on interstate commerce, as the virtual monopoly of sugar refining did in the *Knight* case. The Court concluded that there was no direct relation to commerce. "Manifestly," it said, "any rule prescribed for the conduct of interstate commerce, in order to be within the competency of Congress under its power to regulate commerce among the States, must have some real or substantial relation to or connection with the commerce regulated. But what possible legal or logical connection is there between an employe's membership in a labor organization and the carrying on of interstate commerce? Such relation to a labor organization

[84] 196 U.S. 375 (1905).
[85] *Ibid.* at 398–99.
[86] 207 U.S. 463 (1908).
[87] *Nashville, C. & St. Louis Ry. Co.* v. *Alabama,* 128 U.S. 96, at 99 (1888).
[88] 34 Stat. 232 (1906).
[89] 207 U.S. at 495.

cannot have, *in itself* and in the eye of the law, any bearing upon the commerce with which the employe is connected by his labor and services."[90]

According to the Court, section 10 was invalid not only because it represented an improper exercise of the commerce power but because it interfered with liberty of contract under the fifth amendment. Justice Harlan, who spoke for the majority, declared that "the right of the employee to quit the service of the employer, for whatever reason, is the same as the right of the employer, for whatever reason, to dispense with the services of such employee. It was the legal right of the defendant . . . to discharge Coppage because of his being a member of a labor organization, as it was the legal right of Coppage . . . to quit the service in which he was engaged. . . . In all such particulars the employer and the employee have equality of right, and any legislation that disturbs that equality is an arbitrary interference with liberty of contract which no government can legally justify in a free land."[91]

The decision was six to two, Justice Moody taking no part. Justice Holmes dissented, seeing in section 10 "a very limited interference with the freedom of contract. . . . The section simply prohibits the more powerful party to exact certain undertakings, or to threaten dismissal or unjustly discriminate on certain grounds against those already employed."[92] Justice McKenna, also dissenting, thought the decision in the *Liability Act* Case was sufficient precedent for congressional regulation of employer-employee relations under the commerce power. As for liberty of contract, he thought liberty to be "an attractive theme, but the liberty which is exercised in sheer antipathy does not plead strongly for recognition."[93]

Although, as we have seen, the Court weakened in the rigidity of its position in regard to liberty of contract in other areas of labor relations beginning with the *Muller* case, it persisted in adhering to the strict application of the doctrine in regard to the protection of labor unions. Thus, in 1915, while the Court was sustaining an eight-hour law for women,[94] it reaffirmed the principle of the *Adair* case by holding invalid a Kansas anti-yellow dog contract law in *Coppage* v. *Kansas*.[95] Liberty of contract, the Court said, "does not include a liberty to procure employment from an unwilling employer, or without a fair understanding. Nor may the employer be foreclosed by legislation from

[90] 208 U.S. at 178.
[91] 208 U.S. at 174–75.
[92] *Ibid.* at 191.
[93] *Ibid.* at 183, 186.
[94] *Miller* v. *Wilson*, 236 U.S. 373 (1915).
[95] 236 U.S. 1 (1915).

exercising the same freedom of choice that is the right of the employee."[96] To the contention that this "freedom of choice" attributed to the employee did not exist, given the position of economic inequality the employee occupied in relation to his employer, the Court said that "since it is self-evident that, unless all things are held in common, some persons must have more property than others, it is from the nature of things impossible to uphold freedom of contract and the right of private property without at the same time recognizing as legitimate those inequalities of fortune that are the necessary result of the exercise of those rights."[97]

Again in 1917 the yellow dog contract issue was before the Court, and again the Court adhered to the doctrine of the *Adair* case. In *Hitchman Coal Company* v. *Mitchell*,[98] the Court sustained an injunction prohibiting organizing activities by the United Mine Workers on the grounds that such activities were a conspiracy to induce the employees of the Hitchman Coal Company to disregard yellow dog contracts they had signed with the company. The Court again reaffirmed the right of employers to make non-membership in unions a condition of employment, such right being "a part of the constitutional rights of personal liberty and private property, not to be taken away even by legislation, unless through some proper exercise of the paramount police power."[99]

As pointed out by Justice Brandeis, who was joined in his dissent by Justices Holmes and Clark, the *Hitchman* decision meant that the employer could exert his economic power against unionization and force his employees to sign yellow dog contracts, while the union could not attempt to exert economic power against the employer where such contracts existed.[100] The *Hitchman* case combined the three most powerful legal weapons used against labor in the United States—the conspiracy doctrine, the injunction, and liberty of contract—and, despite Brandeis' criticism, it was long to plague the organizing efforts of unions.[101]

In contrast to the *Adair-Coppage-Hitchman* line of decisions, in other areas the Court found ample room within the commerce clause for

---

[96] *Ibid.* at 21–22.
[97] *Ibid.* at 17.
[98] 245 U.S. 229 (1917).
[99] *Ibid.* at 251.
[100] *Ibid.* at 271–72.
[101] See Homer F. Carey and Herman Oliphant, "The Present Status of the Hitchman Case," 29 *Columbia Law Review* 441 (1929). The Hitchman doctrine was modified later to permit unionization by peaceful means if the employees, after joining the union, quit their jobs in accordance with their contracts. *International Organization* v. *Red Jacket C. C. & C. Co.,* 18 F.2d 839 (CCA 4th, 1927).

broad congressional regulation of employer-employee contractual relations. In 1911, the Court upheld the railroad Safety Appliance Act,[102] declaring that the commerce power was "plenary, and competently may be exerted to secure the safety of persons and property transported therein and of those who are employed in such transportation, no matter what may be the source of the dangers which threaten it."[103] It was upon this broad conception of commerce that the Court in the same year sustained the Hours of Service Act,[104] which regulated hours of employment on railroads.[105] The length of hours of service, the Court said, "has direct relation to the efficiency of the human agencies upon which protection to life and property necessarily depends."[106] The following year, the Court in the second *Employers' Liability* case sustained the amended liability act which included a provision invalidating contracts whereby the employee agreed to forego the benefits of the act.[107]

Finally, in 1916, while Charles Evans Hughes (who had written the opinion of the Court in the *Hours of Service* case) was engaged in a close contest with Woodrow Wilson for the presidency, Congress prevented a nationwide railroad strike by passing the Adamson Act.[108] The act provided not only for the eight-hour day on the railroads but also, pending a report by a commission appointed by the President, for the maintenance of wage scales at the standard daily rate. This meant, given the eight-hour day, that about eighty-five per cent of the railroad workers would be paid the same wages for eight hours of work as they previously had been paid for ten hours.[109] The act was at the time the most far-reaching regulation of labor relations ever attempted by Congress. Although Hughes denounced Wilson's demand for the act as "a shocking abandonment of principle,"[110] a closely divided Court sustained the act in *Wilson v. New* in 1917.[111]

Both the contention that the Adamson act was an invalid regulation under the commerce clause and the contention that it interfered with liberty of contract were rejected by the Court. Chief Justice White, writing for the majority, declared that while emergency could not cre-

---

[102] 27 Stat. 531 (1903).

[103] *Southern Ry. Co.* v. *United States,* 222 U.S. 20, at 27 (1911).

[104] 34 Stat. 1415 (1907).

[105] *Baltimore & Ohio Ry. Co.* v. *I.C.C.,* 221 U.S. 612 (1911).

[106] 221 U.S. at 619.

[107] 223 U.S. 1 (1912). The "contract out" provision was sustained in *Phila., Balt., Wash., Ry. Co.* v. *Schubert,* 224 U.S. 603 (1912).

[108] 39 Stat. 721.

[109] Glenn Miller, *op. cit.,* pp. 82–83.

[110] Merlo J. Pusey, *Charles Evans Hughes* (New York: The Macmillan Co., 1951), Vol. I, pp. 352–53.

[111] 243 U.S. 332 (1917).

ate power, "nevertheless emergency may afford a reason for the exertion of a living power already enjoyed." "If acts which, if done, would interrupt, if not destroy, interstate commerce, may be by anticipation legislatively prevented," he said, "by the same token the power to regulate may be exercised to guard against the cessation of interstate commerce, threatened by a failure of employers and employees to agree as to the standard of wages, such standard being an essential prerequisite to the uninterrupted flow of interstate commerce." "The capacity to exercise the private right free from legislative interference," the Chief Justice said, "affords no ground for saying that legislative power does not exist to protect the public interest from the injury resulting from a failure to exercise the private right."[112]

The victory of the government was on the narrowest of grounds, since Justice McKenna, the fifth member of the majority, concurred in the decision only on the ground that the act could be sustained as an hour law. Nevertheless, *Wilson v. New* established an important precedent on congressional power to regulate employer-employee relations in order to protect interstate commerce. The opinion of the Chief Justice had shown recognition of the necessity of the use of congressional power to eliminate labor disturbances interrupting commerce, a recognition which could not be found in the Court's opinion in the *Adair* case. Moreover, *Wilson v. New* culminated the line of railroad cases which, taken together with the erosion of liberty of contract begun with the *Muller* case, seemed to have carried the Court well beyond the rigidity of the *Lochner* decision.

The period between 1900 and 1920 for the Supreme Court may be viewed as comparable to the period from 1886 to 1900 on the state court level. On the whole the Court had done much better than the state courts in dealing with the issues of industrialism. Despite the *Adair-Coppage-Hitchman* line of cases, the doctrine of liberty of contract appeared by 1920 to be in eclipse, and in the railroad cases the Court seemed to have at last grasped the importance of the effects of labor relations on interstate commerce. After the election of 1920, however, the personnel of the Court altered considerably, and the continuation of these liberal tendencies was in doubt as the Court, under Chief Justice Taft, entered a final decade of choice in labor cases before the crucial period of the 1930's.

[112] 243 U.S. at 348–53.

# 2

# LABOR AND THE TAFT COURT

□ □ □ □ □ □ □ □ □ □ □ □ □ □ □ □ □ □ □ □ □ □ □ □ □ □ □ □ □ □ □ □ □ □ □ □ □ □ □ □ □ □

THE DECADE OF THE TWENTIES OPENED WITH WIDESPREAD EVIDENCE OF a reaction against the Progressive idealism of the Wilson administrations and of the war years. The election of Warren Harding in 1920 coincided with a trend toward both social and political reaction. Organized labor's gains during the war were generally counteracted by the start of an open shop drive by business groups,[1] and such anti-unionism was only part of a general hysteria over what were thought to be "radical" machinations aimed at undermining American institutions. Of particular concern to conservatives were the growing attacks of "agitators" on constitutional rigidity and the conservative judiciary. The president of the American Bar Association in 1922 warned that governmental power "in recent years has gone far in the direction of the communistic state," and condemned those who attacked the attempts of the judiciary to prevent further use of governmental power. He asked that "the vast influence of the American bar" be used to show the people "the value of that liberty under the law which our forefathers established." "Upon the rostrum, in the press, and above all in our schools of every grade," he declared, "our people should be taught that our constitution and laws and the courts that interpret them do not destroy but preserve their liberties."[2]

In response to this appeal, the Association established a committee which drafted a "program for promoting American ideals." In its report this committee concluded that many Americans believed the Constitution "was intended as an aid to the rich and the powerful" and that "a large number of our citizens would vote in favor of abolishing the Constitution entirely." In regard to the courts, the committee felt that many

[1] See Albion Guilford Taylor, "Labor Policies of the National Association of Manufacturers," *University of Illinois Studies in the Social Sciences,* Vol. 15, pp. 82–94.

[2] Cordenio A. Severance, "The Constitution and Individualism," 8 *American Bar Association Journal* 535, 539–42 (1922).

people had the "mistaken notion that judges in deciding cases have full power to do as they please," never having learned "the great truth expressed by Chief Justice Marshall, that this is a 'government of laws and not of men.' "[3] The remedy, the committee felt, was education in patriotism in the schools. No college should award a degree to anyone, it said, "until such person understands and feels that under our Constitution this is a government by the people, with self-imposed limitations based upon a recognition of inalienable rights. . . ." "The schools of America," the report continued, "should no more consider graduating a student who lacks faith in our government than a school of theology should consider graduating a minister who lacks faith in God."[4]

The result of this analysis was the creation by the Bar Association of a Committee on American Citizenship for the purpose of re-establishing "the Constitution and the principles and ideals of our government in the minds and hearts of the people." Co-ordination was established with local bar associations, and a nation-wide campaign to rehabilitate the legitimacy of judicial decision-making was begun.[5]

With this atmosphere prevailing in the legal profession, William Howard Taft assumed the center chair of the Supreme Court, where during 1922–23 he was joined by three new appointees—Justices Sutherland, Butler, and Sanford. While the generally recognized conservatism of these appointments was disheartening for those favoring a more liberal construction of the Constitution, there were elements of hope for labor at least in the character and experience of the new Chief Justice. Probably no man of his generation loved the Court more than did the former President. To him, it was always the "sacred shrine,"[6] and it might have been hoped that to preserve the Court from criticism he would steer it away from unpopular constitutional rigidity. A source of hope for labor even more important than Taft's love of the Court was the liberalizing influence which his service on the War Labor Board had exerted upon him. During his term on the Board he had gone so far as to violate the doctrine of the *Adair* and *Coppage* cases when he sanctioned a rule of the Board guaranteeing the right of labor to organize free from interference by employers.[7]

Whatever hope these factors may have aroused in pro-labor circles was soon dashed by Taft's performance on the Court. The only mani-

---

[3] *Ibid.*, pp. 585–86.
[4] *Ibid.*, p. 587.
[5] See M. Louise Rutherford, "The Influence of the American Bar Association on Public Opinion and Legislation" (Phila.: Ph.D. Dissertation, University of Pennsylvania, 1937), pp. 117–30.
[6] Pringle, *op. cit.*, Vol. II, p. 951.
[7] *Ibid.*, p. 918.

festation of the effect of the Labor Board experience on the Chief Justice was his dissent in *Adkins* v. *Childrens' Hospital,*[8] a case in which a majority of the Court revived the rigid liberty of contract doctrine of the *Lochner* case. In invalidating the federal act establishing a commission to set a living wage for women in the District of Columbia, the majority rejected a Brandeis-type brief filed by Felix Frankfurter in behalf of the Consumers' League. According to Justice Sutherland, writing for the Court, the materials presented by this brief would have been properly considered by Congress when it enacted the law, but "they reflect no legitimate light upon the question of its validity, and that is what we are called upon to decide. The elucidation of that question cannot be aided by counting heads."[9] The act, to the majority, interfered with liberty of contract, and such liberty was "the general rule and restraint the exception; and the exercise of legislative authority to abridge it can be justified only by the existence of exceptional circumstances."[10]

Taft, in dissent, thought that the *Lochner* case, upon which the majority relied, had been overruled *sub silentio.* It was not the function of the Court, he thought, "to hold Congressional acts invalid because they are passed to carry out economic views which this court believes to be unwise or unsound."[11] Justice Holmes also was unconvinced by the majority's reasoning. Sutherland's argument that the elevation of women to a legal status equal to that of men ended the need for special legislative treatment of women, failed to convince Holmes that "there are no differences between men and women, or that legislation cannot take those differences into account." Since the Court had sustained maximum hours for both men and women in *Bunting* v. *Oregon,* Holmes "had supposed . . . *Lochner* v. *New York* . . . would be allowed a deserved repose."[12]

Taft's dissent in the *Adkins* case seems to have dissipated any liberal inclinations he may have had, and his love of the Court led not to a more liberal view of the Constitution but to a conception of the Court as the great bastion standing between the people and socialism.[13] Thus he could write for a majority of the Justices in *Truax* v. *Corrigan,*[14] a

[8] 261 U.S. 525 (1923). See Mason, *The Supreme Court from Taft to Warren,* p. 51.
[9] 261 U.S. at 259–60.
[10] *Ibid.* at 546.
[11] *Ibid.* at 562.
[12] 261 U.S. at 568.
[13] By 1929, Taft was writing his brother that although older, "as long as things continue as they are, and I am able to answer in my place, I must stay on the court in order to prevent the Bolsheviki from getting control. . . ." See Pringle, *op. cit.,* Vol. II, p. 967.
[14] 257 U.S. 312 (1921).

case in which an Arizona law limiting the use of the labor injunction was invalidated by the Court on the grounds that it weakened the constitutional protection of property. Criticism of the Court's decisions by dissenting Justices or by outside groups came to have for Taft sinister and subversive implications. Holmes was to Taft "a poor constitutional lawyer, lacking experience of affairs in government that would keep him straight on constitutional questions." Brandeis, the other persistent dissenter in the court's laissez-faire decisions, also aroused suspicions, especially when he changed his vote in a case after a trip to Harvard where Taft assumed he "communed with Frankfurter and that crowd." Frankfurter seemed to Taft "to be closely in touch with every Bolshevik, Communist movement in the country."[15]

To these threats from within the Court was added, Taft felt, the threat from organized labor from the outside. "The only class which is distinctly arrayed against the court," the Chief Justice wrote his brother, "is a class that does not like the courts at any rate, and that is organized labor. That faction we have to hit every little while, because they are continually violating the law and depending on threats and violence to accomplish their purpose."[16] It was only a matter of time, therefore, before Taft joined the *Adkins* majority in reviving the liberty of contract doctrine. Indeed, two months after the *Adkins* case, he wrote the opinion in *Wolff Packing Company* v. *Industrial Court*,[17] accepting Sutherland's dictum that liberty of contract "was the rule, and restraint the exception."

The statute under review in the case classified certain businesses as being "affected with the public interest" and created a commission to set wages and other labor standards when the employers and employees in such businesses failed to agree. Over the dissents of Holmes and Brandeis, Taft declared that the act "curtails the right of the employer, on the one hand, and the employee, on the other, to contract about his affairs." "While there is no such thing as absolute freedom of contract, and it is subject to a variety of restraints," he said, "they must not be arbitrary or unreasonable. Freedom is the general rule, and restraint the exception. The legislative authority to abridge can be justified only by exceptional circumstances."[18]

Taken together, the *Adkins* and *Wolff* cases turned the tide again toward the strict reading of liberty of contract which had been undermined mainly through the efforts of the Consumers' League between 1900

---

[15] Pringle, *op. cit.,* Vol. II, pp. 969–71, 1047.
[16] *Ibid.*, p. 967.
[17] 262 U.S. 522 (1923).
[18] 262 U.S. at 534.

and 1920. Following the principles enunciated in the *Adkins* and *Wolff* cases, the Court again in 1925 and 1927 invalidated minimum wage laws for women in memorandum opinions[19] and invalidated the fixing of hours of labor under the Kansas industrial relations statute when it was again before the Court in 1925.[20] This resurgence of liberty of contract under Chief Justice Taft insured its survival as an impediment to labor legislation and as a defensive doctrine of business groups in the 1930's.

Although governmental regulation of labor relations was discouraged by the Taft Court's revival of the liberty of contract doctrine, governmental power in the area of commerce decisions was considerably broadened under the Taft Court. Indeed, in the very process of "hitting" labor every little while, as Taft put it, the Court provided a line of valuable precedents which National Labor Relations Board attorneys were to use in the defense of the Wagner Act. The Sherman Anti-Trust Act had first been applied to labor in *Loewe* v. *Lawler*[21] (The *Danbury Hatters'* case) in 1908, the same year as the *Adair* decision. Involving an indictment against the United Hatters of America for conspiracy to restrain interstate trade by a nationwide boycott of the Loewe Company's product, the case upheld the application of the Sherman Act to the union even though the pressure of the union was applied before and after interstate transportation of the product had occurred. Relying on the doctrine of the *Swift* case, the Court had found that while some of the activity was "beyond the scope of Federal authority, . . . the acts must be considered as a whole, and the plan is open to condemnation, notwithstanding a negligible amount of intrastate business might be affected in carrying it out."[22]

The Court in the *Danbury Hatters'* case placed emphasis on the fact that the Hatters' conspiracy had involved an intent to restrain commerce.[23] It seemed to be saying that the purpose or intent of persons forming a combination determined whether or not they were subject to congressional regulation under the commerce clause. That is, a conspiracy could be held subject to the provisions of the Sherman Act if those conspiring did so with the intent to restrain interstate commerce. If the Court had continued to espouse this doctrine of intent, the power of Congress over labor disputes affecting commerce would have been seriously weakened, but as the Taft Court came to apply the

---

[19] *Murphy* v. *Sardell,* 269 U.S. 530 (1925); *Donham* v. *West–Nelson Mfg. Co.,* 273 U.S. 657 (1927). In 1924, however, a law prohibiting night work for women was upheld in *Radice* v. *New York,* 264 U.S. 292 (1924).

[20] *Wolff Packing Co.* v. *Industrial Court,* 267 U.S. 552 (1925).

[21] 208 U.S. 274 (1908).

[22] 208 U.S. at 301.

[23] *Ibid.* at 297.

Sherman Act to strikes as well as boycotts, the doctrine of intent became of obscure application.[24]

In 1914, after a long campaign by labor, Congress amended the Sherman Act by the passage of the Clayton Act, which many thought specifically exempted labor disputes from the anti-trust laws, except where irreparable injury to property was threatened.[25] The Supreme Court, however, in *Duplex Printing Press Company* v. *Deering*[26] virtually ignored this widely accepted opinion of the purpose and intent of the Clayton Act and applied the anti-trust laws to a boycott instituted by the International Association of Machinists against the presses of the Duplex Company. The Court held that the Clayton Act's restriction of the equity powers of the federal courts in labor cases was "in the nature of a special privilege or immunity to a particular class" and thus had to be construed narrowly. The Court said that Congress, in enacting the Clayton Act, "had in mind particular labor controversies, not a general class war."[27] The boycott was held to be a conspiracy with the intent to restrain interstate commerce and therefore subject to the anti-trust acts.

Brandeis, in a memorable dissent, pointed out that the Clayton Act was the result of over twenty years of "unceasing agitation" and "was designed to equalize before the law the position of workingmen and employers as industrial combatants." To Brandeis, the result of the Clayton Act was to allow employees and employers "to push their struggle to the limits of the justification of self-interest," although he attached no "constitutional or moral sanction to that right. All rights are derived from the purposes of the society in which they exist; above all rights rises duty to the community. The conditions developed in industry may be such that those engaged in it cannot continue their struggle without danger to the community. But it is not for judges to determine whether such conditions exist, nor is it their function to set the limits of permissible contest, and to declare the duties which the new situation demands. This is the function of the legislature, which, while limiting individual and group rights of aggression and defense, may substitute processes of justice for the more primitive method of trial by combat."[28]

For a majority of the Taft Court, however, it was the judiciary

[24] For a fuller discussion of the anti-trust cases, see Charles O. Gregory, *Labor and the Law* (New York: W. W. Norton & Co., 1949), pp. 211–19.

[25] See Edward Berman, *Labor and the Sherman Act* (New York: Harper & Brothers, 1930), pp. 99–101.

[26] 254 U.S. 443 (1921).

[27] *Ibid.* at 471–72.

[28] 254 U.S. at 484–88.

rather than the legislature which should have the last word on the rules of industrial combat. Nevertheless, in the very process of exerting this power of decision, the conservative majority enlarged the area of power of the federal government in labor disputes. This increase in federal power was especially evident in the *Coronado Coal* cases, which arose out of the attempt of the Bache-Denman Coal Company to expel the United Mine Workers from its mines in Arkansas and to operate on an open shop basis. The resistance of the union miners led to bloodshed and the destruction of property. The company instituted injunction proceedings and a damage suit against the UMW on the grounds that the activities of the union constituted a conspiracy to restrain trade under the anti-trust laws. A trial in the district court resulted in a verdict against the union and damages totaling about $750,000.[29]

On appeal to the Supreme Court in 1922, the decision was unanimously reversed on the grounds that the anti-trust act had not been violated.[30] The evidence, according to the opinion by Taft, failed to prove an intent to obstruct interstate commerce. But in discussing the question of intent, he declared that "coal mining is not interstate commerce, and obstruction of coal mining, though it may prevent coal from going into interstate commerce, is not a restraint of that commerce unless the obstruction to mining is intended to restrain commerce in it, *or has necessarily such a direct, material and substantial effect to restrain it that the intent reasonably must be inferred.*"[31] There being no intent shown, the Court then considered the effect of the union's activities and found that the mines involved produced only 5,000 tons of coal per week. This amount, the Court concluded, was not enough to affect commerce if production should cease.[32]

From Taft's opinion it appeared that congressional power over labor disputes included, not only the right to remove restraints imposed by *intent* to restrain or obstruct commerce, but also the power to remove restraints which, although without intent, had a "direct, material and substantial effect" on commerce. This dual basis for congressional power was carried over into the second *Coronado* case in 1925.[33] In this case new evidence had been introduced which indicated that the strike and violence were intended by the UMW district officials to keep nonunion coal out of competition with union-mined coal in interstate com-

[29] See the case on appeal, *United Mine Workers* v. *Coronado Coal Co.,* 258 F. 829 (CCA 8th, 1919).
[30] *United Mine Workers* v. *Coronado Coal Co.,* 259 U.S. 344 (1922).
[31] *Ibid.* at 410–11 (italics mine).
[32] *Ibid.* at 412.
[33] *Coronado Coal Co.* v. *United Mine Workers,* 268 U.S. 295 (1925).

merce.[34] In addition, however, the Court discovered that the mines involved produced 5,000 tons of coal per day rather than that amount per week as it had appeared in the first case. It was clear from the language of the Court that this factor, combined with the new evidence of intent, justified the conviction of the union under the anti-trust act.[35]

It appeared from the *Coronado* cases, then, that the doctrine of intent had been joined by the doctrine that a conspiracy, even without intent to restrain interstate commerce, could be subject to the Sherman Act if such a conspiracy produced a "direct, material, and substantial effect" on commerce. Justice Sutherland seemed to confirm this in a discussion of the first *Coronado* case in *Industrial Association* v. *United States.*[36] The Court failed to find a conspiracy to restrain commerce in the first *Coronado* case, he said, because there was "the absence of proof of an intention to restrain it or proof of such a direct and substantial effect upon it, that such intention reasonably must be inferred."[37] National Labor Relations Board attorneys were thus able to argue later that a labor dispute in a highly integrated manufacturing enterprise was likely to involve such a "direct, material, and substantial effect" on commerce that an intention to restrain commerce could be inferred and federal jurisdiction over such disputes be justified.

This rationale for possible extension of federal power was largely overlooked partly because of the Court's finding, in the first *Coronado* case, that unions were suable under the anti-trust laws.[38] Taft noted that the ruling "seems to have called forth great denunciation by Gompers and LaFollette and other demagogues, and to have suggested a movement to deprive the court of the power of holding laws . . . unconstitutional." The Chief Justice was calm, however, because he believed "the supporters of an amendment to the Constitution will find arrayed against them a conservative strength that in their blatant mouthings they do not realize the existence of."[39] Demonstrating this attitude of calmness, Taft attempted to "mass" the Court in *Bedford Cut Stone Company* v. *Journeymen Stone Cutters*[40] wherein the Court found that a refusal of members of the Stone Cutters' Union to work on stone quarried under nonunion conditions was a violation of the anti-trust act. Despite the fact that the stone against which the strike was directed had ceased its interstate transportation, the Court found the activities

[34] *Ibid*. at 306–308.
[35] *Ibid*. at 310.
[36] 268 U.S. 64 (1925).
[37] *Ibid*. at 81.
[38] 259 U.S. at 391.
[39] Pringle, *op. cit.*, Vol. II, p. 1041.
[40] 274 U.S. 37 (1927).

of the union "were not in pursuit of a local motive,—they had for their primary aim restraint of the interstate sale and shipment of the commodity."[41]

Taft, writing to Sutherland, had said that unless the Court found a violation of the anti-trust laws "we should be imposing on interstate trade a burden that would be intolerable, and every national labor union could at once adopt it as a means of establishing a closed shop . . . in every center of business in the country."[42] But Taft failed in his attempt to mass the Court on the issue. Brandeis, with Holmes concurring, thought the restraint on commerce a reasonable one in pursuance of the union's "struggle for existence."[43] Stone and Sanford concurred only because they felt bound by the *Duplex* case. The Chief Justice was particularly disappointed in Stone's failure to join the majority, and soon thereafter Stone ceased to meet the Chief Justice, Sutherland, Van Devanter, Sanford, and Butler on Sunday afternoons at Taft's home,[44] where "plans were made to block the liberal machinations of Holmes and Brandeis."[45]

Apart from the anti-trust cases, the decisions of the Court during the 1920's perpetuated the conflict of the formulas used to gauge congressional power over commerce which had begun in the *Knight* and *Swift* cases. The conception of the commerce power in the *Knight* case, that it extended primarily to traffic and could be brought to bear only upon activities which directly burdened such traffic, had been seriously eroded by the *Swift* case and subsequent decisions. But in 1918, in *Hammer* v. *Dagenhart*,[46] the Court revived the doctrine of the *Knight* case to invalidate the child labor act passed by Congress in 1916. The act prohibited the shipment of goods manufactured by child labor in interstate commerce. To the Court, however, this was not a regulation of commerce but in fact a regulation of production, and "the production of articles, intended for interstate commerce, is a matter of local regulation."[47] The commerce power could not be used, the Court said, to "destroy the local power always existing and carefully reserved to the States by the Tenth Amendment to the Constitution."[48] The Taft Court, in 1922, reaffirmed

[41] *Ibid*. at 46.

[42] Pringle, *op. cit.,* Vol. II, p. 1043.

[43] 274 U.S. at 56.

[44] Alpheus T. Mason, *Harlan Fiske Stone: Pillar of the Law* (New York: The Viking Press, 1956), p. 260.

[45] Pringle, *op. cit.,* Vol. II, pp. 1043–44.

[46] 247 U.S. 251 (1918).

[47] 247 U.S. at 272.

[48] *Ibid*. at 274. Holmes, with whom McKenna, Brandeis, and Clarke concurred, dissented: "It is not for this Court to pronounce when prohibition is necessary—to say that it is reasonable as against strong drink but not as against the product of ruined lives." *Ibid*. at 280.

the *Child Labor* case when it invalidated an act imposing a ten per
cent tax on establishments employing child labor.[49] But in two other
decisions, *Stafford* v. *Wallace*[50] and *Chicago Board of Trade* v. *Olsen*,[51]
the Court provided two major precedents which provided hope for the
power to govern.

The victory of the government in the *Swift* case in 1905 had confirmed its power over the meat packing industry, and in 1921 this power
was exercised in the passage of the Packers and Stockyards Act[52] which
regulated the rates of commission marketing agencies and prohibited
various unfair or deceptive practices by such agencies as well as by
packers. The act was fully sustained by the Court in the *Stafford* case.
"The application of the commerce clause of the Constitution in the
Swift Case," Chief Justice Taft wrote, "was the result of the natural
development of interstate commerce under modern conditions. It was
the inevitable result of the great central fact that such streams of commerce from one part of the country to another which are ever flowing
are in their very essence the commerce among the States. . . ."[53] As
to the regulation of the activities of market agencies and packers which
were primarily local, the Court held that Congress could regulate such
activity if it found it threatened commerce. "Whatever amounts to more
or less constant practice, and threatens to obstruct or unduly to burden
the freedom of interstate commerce," the Court said, "is within the regulatory power of Congress under the commerce clause, and it is primarily
for Congress to consider and decide the fact of the danger and meet
it. This court will certainly not substitute its judgment for that of Congress in such a matter unless the relation of the subject to interstate
commerce and its effect upon it are clearly non-existent."[54] Finally, the
Court held that the finding of Congress that these intrastate practices
"will probably and more or less constantly be used in conspiracies
against interstate commerce or constitute a direct and undue burden on
it, . . . serves the same purpose as the intent charged in the Swift
indictment to bring acts of a similar character into the current of interstate commerce for federal restraint."[55]

A finding by Congress could, then, be a substitute for intent in regard
to practices which probably would be used in conspiracies against com-

[49] *Bailey* v. *Drexel Furniture Co.,* 259 U.S. 20 (1922).
[50] 258 U.S. 495 (1922).
[51] 262 U.S. 1 (1923).
[52] 42 Stat. 159.
[53] 258 U.S. at 518–19.
[54] *Ibid.* at 521.
[55] 257 U.S. at 520.

merce, and, remembering the application of the Sherman Act to labor disputes, it could be argued from the *Stafford* case that the power of Congress to regulate commerce could reach labor disputes which "more or less" constantly threatened "to obstruct or unduly burden" interstate commerce. This promising extension of federal power was reaffirmed a year later in the *Olsen* case. Again in this case, the government had first been successful in an anti-trust prosecution against traders in grain futures.[56] Congress in its attempt to regulate trading in grain futures, however, first adopted a tax on the grain futures held by those boards of trade which were not complying with the regulations imposed by the Sherman Act. The Court invalidated the act, following the precedent of the *Child Labor Tax* case, but it hinted that such regulations might be upheld under the commerce clause.[57] "There is not a word in the act," the Court said, "that it is confined in its operation to interstate commerce. The words 'interstate commerce' are not to be found in any part of the act from the title to the closing section."[58]

Congress, taking the hint, passed the Grain Futures Act,[59] basing it clearly on the commerce power as defined in the *Stafford* case.[60] When the act was challenged in the *Olsen* case, the Court sustained it, using reasoning similar to its rationale for sustaining the Packers and Stockyards Act. The *Swift* case, the Court said, had "recognized the great changes and development in the business of this vast country" and "refused to permit local incidents of great interstate movement, which, taken alone, were intrastate, to characterize the movement as such. The Swift Case merely fitted the commerce clause to the real and practical essence of modern business growth. It applies to the case before us just as it did in Stafford v. Wallace."[61] Again the Court gave great weight to the findings of Congress. The Court was prevented "by reason and authority," the Chief Justice wrote, "from questioning the conclusion of Congress that manipulation of the market for futures on the Chicago Board of Trade may, and from time to time does, directly burden and obstruct commerce between the States in grain, and that it recurs and is a constantly possible danger. For this reason, Congress has the power to provide the appropriate means adopted in this act by which this abuse may be restrained and avoided."[62]

---

[56] *United States* v. *Patten,* 226 U.S. 525 (1913).
[57] *Hill* v. *Wallace,* 259 U.S. 44 (1922).
[58] *Ibid.* at 68.
[59] 42 Stat. 998 (1922).
[60] *Ibid.* at 998–99.
[61] 262 U.S. at 35.
[62] 262 U.S. at 40.

The opinions in the *Stafford* and *Olsen* cases were both written by Chief Justice Taft and were, in addition to the Judges bill of 1925,[63] probably his greatest contributions to constitutional law in the United States. His concept of commerce, if his bias against labor could have been excised, was broad and liberal. "The power of Congress in this respect," he wrote privately, "is exactly what it would be in a government without states."[64] In addition to the regulatory power sanctioned for Congress in these cases, the legislative experience gained in bringing grain futures under effective regulation was also to prove of value to Congress in the 1930's. The Wagner Act was to be based not only upon the concept of the flow of commerce and the power of Congress to prevent recurrent local practices which had a substantial effect on commerce, but also on the adoption of the Court's concept of commerce in a congressional declaration of policy which had proven successful in overcoming constitutional objections in the *Olsen* case.[65]

The decision of the Taft Court on child labor, the revival of liberty of contract in the *Adkins* and *Wolff* cases, and the extensive application of the anti-trust laws to labor, however, gave impetus to criticisms of the courts in general and the institution of judicial review and the role of the Supreme Court in American government in particular. Since Holmes had first pointed out the policy-making role of the courts in 1881, the myth of judicial impotence had been slowly undermined by a steadily growing body of professional opinion which subjected court decisions to critical analysis and condemned the making of laissez-faire policy by the courts.

This growth of judicial realism[66] constituted part of the broader pragmatic attack on a natural-law philosophy which not only in the law, but also in economics and philosophy itself, appeared to the pragmatists to have been bypassed by a modern industrial society. In opposition to the logic of deduction and the emphasis upon immutable principles which characterized the older approach, the new philosophy emphasized inductive logic and the basis of social reality upon which philo-

[63] This act allowed the Court to control its docket through the writ of certiorari and thus confine its decisions more to issues of major public importance than previously had been the case.

[64] Pringle, *op. cit.*, Vol. II, p. 1015.

[65] See Chapter IV.

[66] I use the term generally to include those who agreed that there was no immutable, transcendental body of law which the judge "discovered" in rendering a decision and that judges made law by choosing between policy alternatives in deciding cases. Thus, I use the term in its most general sense and do not attempt what the "realists" themselves cannot do, that is, to determine who is and who is not *really* a realist.

sophic postulates ought to rest.[67] Holmes, until his retirement from the Court, continued to be the foremost representative in the legal field of the new criticism. He rejected the notion that cases were decided by judges through the discovery and application of immutable principles of justice and frankly admitted that the law was composed not of immutable principles but was simply "the prophesies of what the courts will do in fact. . . ."[68] He raised the policy-making role of judges to the level of conscious scrutiny, instead of submerging it, as the older theory had done, in the myth of legal immutability and judicial impotence. To Holmes, the judge's responsibility was constantly to re-examine legal rules in the light of their history and social utility under modern conditions. "A body of law is more rational and more civilized," he said, "when every rule it contains is referred articulately and definitely to an end which it subserves."[69]

In the area of constitutional law, Holmes' skepticism of general principles and his emphasis on the constant reference of the law to social realities led to an insistence on judicial restraint in the exercise of judicial review. The legislatures were more closely subjected to the political processes than were the courts and were more likely to reflect the social conditions to which the law, and particularly constitutional law, must continually readjust. It was thus incumbent upon the Court in reviewing legislative policy to substitute its judgment for the legislative judgment on social policy only in the most extreme cases. Asked his judicial philosophy, Holmes said, "Long ago I decided that I was not God. When a state came in here and wanted to build a slaughter house, I looked at the Constitution and if I couldn't find anything in there that said a state couldn't build a slaughter house I said to myself, if they want to build a slaughter house, God dammit, then let them build it."[70]

This was of course an over-simplification of his philosophy of the role of the Court, but Holmes did believe profoundly that the American system should permit a majority to use legislation to adapt the law to its views. The judicial veto was not abandoned, but should be exercised only when, as he said in his *Lochner* dissent, "a rational and fair man necessarily would admit that the statute proposed would infringe funda-

[67] See Morton White, *Social Thought in America: The Revolt Against Formalism* (Boston: Beacon Press, 1957).

[68] O. W. Holmes, Jr., "The Path of the Law," *Collected Legal Papers* (New York: Harcourt, Brace and Co., 1920), p. 173.

[69] Holmes, *op. cit.*, p. 186.

[70] Quoted in Eric F. Goldman, *Rendezvous with Destiny* (New York: Vintage Books, 1956), p. 105.

mental principles as they have been understood by the traditions of our people and our law."[71] This was an admittedly ambiguous formula to guide the role of the Court (as the followers of Holmes, judicial and otherwise, were to discover), but within the context of the *Lochner* and other laissez-faire decisions it served a purpose. As long as the primary question in constitutional law was the extent to which the legislature should be allowed to enact social and economic reform legislation, the Holmesian attitude of deference to the legislative judgment served the cause of those who desired to adapt the law through such legislation to the complexities of a modern industrial society.

This theory of the judicial role, which Brandeis and Stone shared in general with Holmes, was embodied in their long line of dissents during the 1920's, and, coupled with their continuing charge that the conservative majority of the Court was reading a policy of laissez-faire into the Constitution, provided to groups hostile to the doctrines of the Court powerful political ammunition. Even by 1931, however, a writer could state that Holmes "seems to have exerted remarkably little influence on the actual development of American law." "Carrying to the bench the soldierly spirit of loyal and disciplined acceptance of the task assigned to him," the writer continued, "he has nevertheless suffered the ironic fate of becoming most popularly known as a writer of dissenting opinions."[72] This was of course true in constitutional law itself; on the Court conservatism was still dominating. Holmes' influence, as well as that of his fellow dissenters, Brandeis and Stone, was felt, however, when in 1930 Chief Justice Taft's resignation and Justice Stanford's death left two vacancies on the Court. Continuing a fight which had begun in 1925 with the appointment of Stone who was then considered a conservative, Senate liberals launched an attack on the nomination of Charles Evans Hughes as Chief Justice and managed to delay his confirmation.[73]

President Hoover's nomination of Court of Appeals Judge John J. Parker to succeed Sanford was the occasion for a demonstration of power by two groups, labor and the Negroes, whose objectives had been largely frustrated by the nature of constitutional development since the Civil War. The American Federation of Labor charged Parker with sanctioning yellow dog contracts in deciding a case on the precedent of the *Hitchman* case.[74] The National Association for the Advancement

[71] 198 U.S. 45, at 76.

[72] Morris R. Cohen, "Justice Holmes and the Nature of Law," 31 *Columbia Law Review* 352 (1931).

[73] Mason, *The Supreme Court from Taft to Warren*, pp. 70–77.

[74] *International Organization v. Red Jacket Coal Co.*, 18 F.2d 839 (CCA 4th, 1927).

of Colored People charged that Parker in a campaign for governor of North Carolina in 1920 had opposed Negro suffrage.[75]

William Green, president of the American Federation of Labor, charged before the Senate Judiciary Committee that if Parker were confirmed "the power of reaction will be strengthened, and the broad-minded, humane, progressive influence so courageously and patriotically exercised by the minority members of the highest judicial tribunal of the land will be weakened. There is the kernel in the nut."[76] Senator Norris, leading the opposition to the nomination along with Senator Borah, referred in his opening speech to Brandeis' appointment and the fight against it by conservative interests. "Time has passed, Mr. President," he declared, "and now every liberty-loving man, woman, and child, not only in this country but the world prays nightly to God to spare the lives of Justices Brandeis and Holmes, famous for their dissenting opinions."[77] The effects of the depression which then had almost immobilized the nation were reflected in Senator Borah's attack on Parker. The Senate had "a high and almost sacred obligation" to scrutinize appointments to the Court, he said, especially at a time when the "political atmosphere is almost fevered with fright over the break-down, as it is called, the failure of representative government." The fault, he declared, "is not in the form of our institutions; the fault, if any may arise, will be in the failure to find men with the intelligence to appreciate the obligations imposed and the courage to execute the powers of Government." To Borah, the confirmation of Parker would be "in moral effect a decision of the Senate in favor of the 'yellow dog' contract."[78]

Defending Parker, Senator Fess of Ohio charged that the question of Parker's nomination was only an incident and that the opposition's real object was to undermine the judiciary.[79] "Mr. President," Senator Norris replied, "I agree with the Senator from Ohio . . . that Judge Parker is only an incident. I go further than that, and say that the Supreme Court is only an incident. The thing that is important and the issue that is here is the preservation of human liberty. It is to keep burning the fires of human freedom that our forefathers laid upon the altars of our country. It is not the Supreme Court. It is something greater than the Supreme Court. . . . It is the liberty that we ought to endow upon the children that are yet in the womb of time. Human liberty is at stake.

[75] Joseph P. Harris, *The Advice and Consent of the Senate* (Berkeley: University of California Press, 1953), p. 128.

[76] *Ibid.*

[77] 71 *Cong. Rec.* 8182, 71st Cong. 2d sess.

[78] *Ibid.*, pp. 7938–39.

[79] *Ibid.*, p. 7949.

Human slavery is showing its hideous face in front of our institutions. We can not permit such things to continue. The very stability of our Government will not permit it."[80]

The Senate rejected Parker's appointment by a vote of 39 to 41, the first time in thirty-six years a nomination to the Court had been rejected by the Senate.[81] For the Negroes, whose protection by federal legislation and the Civil War amendments had been gutted by Court interpretation, and for labor, whose protection by the government had been retarded by liberty of contract and a restricted interpretation of the commerce clause, the victory was "necessary to demonstrate their strength and influence."[82] It was significant in that two major groups whose objectives had been blocked by the conservative interpretation of constitutional law since the post–Civil War era had achieved sufficient strength to launch an effective attack on the Court. In 1930 the Court may fairly be said to have been more responsive to the claims of business groups than to those of any other groups, and the labor-Negro alliance which defeated Judge Parker signified the emergence of political forces whose constitutional claims were, when recognized, to erect almost a new Constitution.[83]

Of more immediate significance to labor at least was the fact that during the debate on Parker's nomination the question of the constitutionality of the Railway Labor Act of 1926[84] was being argued before the Court. The result of an agreement between the railroad unions and carriers, the act was the federal government's first peacetime attempt to guarantee the right to bargain collectively to non-governmental employees.[85] The act declared that its purpose was in part to "avoid any interruptions to commerce or to the operation of any carriers engaged therein" and "to forbid any limitations upon the freedom of association among employees or any denial, as a condition of employment or otherwise, of the right of employees to join a labor organization. . . ." This declaration clearly violated the doctrine of the *Adair* and *Coppage* cases

[80] *Ibid.*, p. 8190.

[81] Harris, *op. cit.*, p. 127.

[82] *Ibid.*, p. 132.

[83] It is interesting to note, however, that the claims of labor and the Negroes were in a sense contradictory as far as the role of the Court within the political system was concerned. Capable of marshalling strong legislative forces especially during the 1930's, labor's major objective was for the Court to step aside and simply recognize as accomplished facts the validity of its legislative victories. The Negroes, however, faced with discrimination in voting and other handicaps in the political process, were unable to marshal such legislative forces and thus depended upon the Court to assume a positive legislative role to meet their claims. Labor could accept the Holmesian concept of judicial restraint; Negroes could not.

[84] 44 Stat. 577.

[85] See Miller, *op. cit.*, pp. 401–402.

by prohibiting the yellow dog contract. The act also provided for a National Mediation Board and boards of adjustment which could mediate disputes subject to the agreement of the parties. If a dispute threatened substantially to interrupt commerce, the Board of Mediation could notify the President who was authorized to appoint a board of investigation which was to survey the dispute and publish its findings. During such an investigation, and for thirty days thereafter, the status quo was to be maintained between the disputants. There were, however, no penalties for violations of the act's provisions.

The act had been challenged in *Texas & New Orleans Railroad Company* v. *Brotherhood of Railway and Steamship Clerks,*[86] and its constitutionality was being argued before the Supreme Court during the fight over Parker's nomination. Senator Borah had attacked Parker's alleged position favoring yellow dog contracts and asserted that in case of his confirmation "it is possible that Judge Parker would be permitted to sit in that case and help determine it before it is finally decided."[87] ". . . I would not myself vote to put a man upon the Supreme Court," Borah declared, "who was committed to the doctrine, regardless of how he became committed. I think this is so fundamental, so righteous in and of itself that I could not get my consent to put upon the Supreme Court a man who had already declared his position upon the question. The court is divided; the controversy is there again. . . ."[88]

It is impossible to tell what effect, if any, the Senate debates on Parker's nomination had on the Court's unanimous decision sustaining the Railway Labor Act in the *Texas and New Orleans* case. The case was argued on May 1 and 2 while the debates were in progress, and the opinion came down May 26, after Parker had been rejected on May 7. It was nonetheless labor's greatest victory in constitutional litigation since *Wilson* v. *New* and was to be the most important single precedent urged in behalf of the validity of the Wagner Act. The case grew out of a wage dispute which took place in 1925 between the Brotherhood and the Texas & New Orleans Railroad. The Brotherhood had gained recognition as the representative of the railroad's employees during the government's control of the railroads during the war. The railroad denied the Brotherhood's demand for a raise in wages, and the controversy was referred to the Board of Mediation. While the dispute was pending before the Board, the railroad sought to establish a company union and grant recognition to it as the representative of its employees.[89]

---

[86] 281 U.S. 548 (1930).
[87] 71 *Cong. Rec.* 7930.
[88] *Ibid.*, p. 7938.
[89] 281 U.S. 548, at 555.

The Brotherhood obtained an injunction in a federal district court against the railroad's actions. The railroad challenged the injunction on constitutional grounds, but the court denied a motion to vacate the order, and the injunction was made permanent in 1928.[90] The district court relied on the provision of the Railway Labor Act which provided that representatives, "for the purposes of this Act, shall be designated by the respective parties in such manner as may be provided in their corporate organization or unincorporated association, or by other means of collective action, without interference, influence, or coercion exercised by either party over the self-organization or designation of representatives by the other."[91] The injunction restrained the railroad from "in any way or manner interfering with, influencing, intimidating, or coercing plaintiffs . . . with respect to their free and untrammeled right of selecting or designating their representatives for the purpose of considering and deciding any and all disputes between said clerical employees and the Railroad Company" and from "interfering with, influencing, intimidating, or coercing plaintiffs or any of said clerical employees . . . [in] their free and untrammeled right of self-organization."[92]

After this injunction had been granted, the railroad proceeded to recognize the company union and discharge several employees who were members of the Brotherhood. The court held the railroad in contempt of court and ordered the disestablishment of the company union and the recognition of the Brotherhood until a secret ballot was held under court direction. The railroad was also ordered to reinstate the discharged employees.[93] In the contempt proceedings the court relied on *Wilson* v. *New* on the commerce question and brushed aside objections based on the fifth amendment by quoting Justice McKenna's remark in his *Adair* dissent that "liberty which is exercised in sheer antipathy does not plead strongly for recognition."[94] The railroad's motion to vacate or modify the contempt order especially attacked that part of the order requiring reinstatement of the discharged employees. The court, in answer, said that nothing "in the order attempted to, nor could it, fix any time or conditions to the continuing in place of these persons," and that it merely declared that "the severance of these relations and the disturbance of the status quo as to them, which the court found from the evidence had been brought about through a deliberate violation of the injunction order of the court must be undone,

90 25 F.2d 873 (N.D. Tex. 1928).
91 281 U.S. at 556–57.
92 *Ibid.* at 555–56, note 1.
93 24 F.2d 426.
94 24 F.2d 426, at 430–32.

and inferentially that it should not occur again for the same or similar reasons."[95]

On appeal by the railroad, the Circuit Court of Appeals, with one dissent, upheld the order of the district court on the grounds that because of the "situation created by violations of the injunction, it was permissible for the court to provide for the restoration of the status quo." The Railway Labor Act itself was upheld on the basis of *Wilson* v. *New*.[96]

In argument before the Supreme Court, counsel for the railroad challenged the act as beyond the power of Congress under the commerce clause and as a violation of liberty of contract on the basis of the *Adair* and *Coppage* cases. In addition, it was argued that the act was a mere declaration of public policy and not meant to be judicially enforced. Here the railroad counsel relied on two cases in which the Taft Court had held the labor provisions of the Transportation Act of 1920 to be legally unenforceable.[97]

The Court, in an opinion by Chief Justice Hughes, rejected these contentions. "We entertain no doubt," Hughes wrote, "of the constitutional authority of Congress to enact the prohibition. The power to regulate commerce is the power to enact 'all appropriate legislation' for its 'protection and advancement'. . . ; to adopt measures 'to promote its growth and insure its safety . . .' ; to 'foster, protect, control and restrain. . . .' Exercising this authority, Congress may facilitate the amicable settlement of disputes which threaten the necessary agencies of transportation." It had been long recognized, the Court said, that workers could organize and "Congress was not required to ignore this right of the employees but safeguard it and seek to make their appropriate collective action an instrument of peace rather than strife. Such collective action would be a mockery if representation were made futile by interferences with freedom of choice. Thus the prohibition by Congress of interference with the selection of representatives for the purpose of negotiation and conference between employers and employees, instead of being an invasion of the constitutional rights of either, was based on the recognition of the rights of both."[98]

On the liberty of contract objections to the act, the Court held that the *Adair* and *Coppage* cases "are inapplicable." "The Railway Labor Act of 1926 does not interfere with the normal exercise of the right of

[95] 25 F.2d 876, at 877.
[96] 33 F.2d 13, at 16–17 (CCA 5th, 1929).
[97] 281 U.S. at 551. The cases were *Penn. Ry. Co.* v. *U.S. Railway Labor Board*, 261 U.S. 72 (1923); *Penn. System Federation* v. *Penn. Ry. Co.*, 267 U.S. 203 (1925).
[98] 281 U.S. at 570.

the carrier to select its employees or to discharge them. The statute is not aimed at this right of employers, but at interference with the right of employees to have representatives of their own choosing. As the carriers subject to the act have no constitutional right to interfere with the freedom of the employees in making their selections, they cannot complain of the statute on constitutional grounds."[99]

Justice Van Devanter, writing on the proofs of Hughes' opinion, said it was "as near perfect as is humanly possible." Brandeis, too, approved. "You have made this matter entirely clear," he wrote.[100] Although the Court had not specifically overruled the *Adair-Coppage* doctrine, it was clear from the majority opinion that these cases had been either overruled or seriously qualified as far as carriers engaged in interstate transportation were concerned. The authority of the *Texas and New Orleans* case as a precedent for federal regulation of labor relations was undermined, however, by several circumstances. The Court conservatives—Sutherland, Van Devanter, and Butler (McReynolds did not participate)—who normally were adamant in their zeal to protect liberty of contract, had joined the majority. It can be guessed that they did so because they were more willing to sustain an interference with liberty of contract in the field of interstate transportation where the regulatory power of the federal government had been long recognized. A second reason for the unanimity of the Justices may have been that the conservatives felt the district court's power to enforce its order justified its ordering the reinstatement of the discharged employees and the disestablishment of the company union as a means by which the carrier could purge itself of contempt.[101] Aside from these considerations, the *Texas and New Orleans* case was to be a rather shaky precedent because of personnel changes on the Court. When the case was decided, there was one vacancy and McReynolds failed to participate. The vacancy was filled by Owen J. Roberts, after Judge Parker's rejection. Roberts, along with the four conservatives, could form a majority of the Court after 1930, and this was precisely what was to occur in the major cases testing the constitutionality of New Deal legislation.

The *Texas and New Orleans* case, plus the passage of the Norris-LaGuardia Act,[102] which restricted the injunctive powers of the federal courts in labor disputes and declared the yellow dog contract to be

[99] *Ibid.* at 570–71.

[100] Pusey, *op. cit.*, Vol. II, p. 713.

[101] This had been the reason the district court had given for its order of reinstatement and partially the basis upon which the Circuit Court had sustained it; 25 F.2d 876, at 877; 33 F.2d 13, at 17. This was to be the argument of the companies in the Wagner Act cases; see below, Chapter VIII.

[102] 47 Stat. 70 (1932).

against public policy, gave some basis for hope that federal power could deal effectively with labor disputes. But the legacy of the decades during which labor had felt that its objectives had been frustrated by the constitutional doctrines of the Court was not easily forgotten, especially in a time of acute unemployment brought on by the greatest depression the American economy has yet sustained. The laissez-faire constitutionalism created by the Court in the post–Civil War era still retained powerful adherents on the Court, and many persons both on and off the bench believed that this persistence of constitutional anachronism was forcing the nation to the brink of disaster. "Today the unemployed walk the streets and securities belie their very name," Walton Hamilton wrote. "Against an unplanned and undirected industrialism, and its imminent hazards to life, liberty, and property, we have no constitutional rights. But thanks to John Locke—or to the thinkers, statesmen, warriors, business men, and jurists who put punch in his words—we have adequate safeguards against the resort by any state to the kind of stuff the Stuart kings used to pull."[103]

To another writer, it was apparent during this period that labor groups were "smarting with a sense of injustice at the hands of the courts." Respect for the courts and the law was "growing less and less every year. The situation calls for constructive efforts to meet the growing danger, not only on the part of labor leaders, but on the part of all who believe in American law and American traditions."[104]

With the election of Franklin Roosevelt as President and the inauguration of the New Deal in 1933, these frustrations of labor and the conflict over federal protection of the right to organize were to be diverted for a time into the administrative complex composing the National Recovery Administration and then into the legislative struggle over the passage of the Wagner Act. Nevertheless, the ambiguity of constitutional doctrine on the issue assured that the final policy choice was to be made by the Court and that the administrative and legislative struggle was but a prelude to a return to constitutional adjudication.

[103] Walton H. Hamilton, "Property—According to Locke," 41 *Yale Law Review* 879, 880 (1932).

[104] Francis B. Sayre, "Labor and the Courts," 39 *Yale Law Review* 682 (1930).

# 3

# LABOR, EMPLOYERS, AND NRA

□ □ □ □ □ □ □ □ □ □ □ □ □ □ □ □ □ □ □ □ □ □ □ □ □ □ □ □ □ □ □ □ □ □ □ □ □ □ □ □ □ □ □ □

WHEN FRANKLIN ROOSEVELT WAS INAUGURATED IN MARCH OF 1933, the nation had already entered its fourth year of depression. The number of unemployed had reached thirteen to fifteen million, and national income was down 53 per cent from 1929 levels. The repudiation of business leadership and the criticism of the ideology of laissez-faire which the economic crisis entailed might reasonably have been expected to have resulted in significant gains for organized labor. The labor movement, however, battered by depression and weakened in membership and resources, only slowly recognized the opportunities created by new and changing conditions.[1]

The American Federation of Labor continued to draw its strength largely from the craft unions, which had in the past secured for the federation reasonably stable membership and financial support. But the failure of the federation to penetrate the mass production industries to any significant degree meant that by 1933 it spoke for a membership of less than three million, or about 10 to 15 per cent of the organizable laborers in the country.[2]

By its adherence to the philosophy of voluntarism with its suspicion of governmental reform, the A.F. of L. had also alienated the political support of many non-labor social workers and liberal reformers who were labor's natural allies. This separation between unionists and the rest of the liberal movement was the major political factor which conditioned the relationship between the administration of Franklin Roosevelt and organized labor. Roosevelt himself was not interested in the problems of unionism, was not sympathetic to efforts to guarantee the right of labor to organize, and was generally suspicious of labor lead-

[1] See Louis Stanley, "The Collapse of the A.F. of L.," *The Nation,* Vol. 131 (Oct. 8, 1930), p. 367.
[2] Harry A. Mills and Emily C. Brown, *From the Wagner Act to Taft-Hartley* (Chicago: University of Chicago Press, 1950), p. 19; see also Edward Levinson, *Labor on the March* (New York: Harper & Brothers, 1938).

ers.[3] His Secretary of Labor, Frances Perkins, was a former social worker and interested more in a program of social reform than in the issue of organization. Her program, presented to Roosevelt before her acceptance of the position, included unemployment compensation, public works, minimum wages, maximum hours, federal employment agencies, and abolition of child labor, but there was no mention of protection of the right to organize or other problems peculiar to unions themselves.[4] These attitudes of Roosevelt and Perkins meant that organized labor's principal means of access to the administration was not to be in the executive branch. It was rather to be in the Congress, principally in the person of Senator Robert F. Wagner of New York.[5]

Wagner had been born in Nastätten, Germany, in 1878, and had come to the United States at the age of eight. His family had settled in New York City, where it eked out a living on his father's earnings of $3.75 per week. Wagner, however, graduated from high school as valedictorian of his class, and, with the help of his brother, graduated from City College of New York in 1898. He completed his legal education which was financed by the father of one of his friends, and began to practice law in 1900.

The law, however, was not to be his career. He had joined the Democratic party through Charley Murphy's Tammany Hall in 1898, and in 1904 was sent to the New York Assembly, two years after the election of his friend and roommate at Albany, Al Smith. As the result, in part, of the veto of Wagner's popular five-cent fare bill by Governor Charles Evans Hughes, the Democrats swept the state in 1909, and Wagner was elected to the New York Senate, where he became majority leader as Al Smith became leader of the Assembly. As a legislator, Wagner introduced the resolution creating the commission to investigate the Triangle Shirtwaist Factory fire, an investigation which resulted in the passage of fifty-six bills on factory safety. Wagner also introduced the New York workmen's compensation act which was invalidated by the New York Court of Appeals in the notorious *Ives* case.

In 1919, Wagner was elected to the New York Supreme Court. He served there until 1925 when he announced his candidacy for the United States Senate against James W. Wadsworth, despite Al Smith's attempt to induce him to run for mayor of New York City. Defeating

[3] Rexford G. Tugwell, *The Democratic Roosevelt* (Garden City: Doubleday & Company, Inc., 1957), pp. 336–37; Frances Perkins, *The Roosevelt I Knew* (New York: The Viking Press, 1946), p. 152.

[4] Perkins, *ibid.*

[5] Irving Bernstein, *The New Deal Collective Bargaining Policy* (Berkeley: University of California Press, 1950), p. 130.

Wadsworth, Wagner entered the Senate in 1926 and by the beginning of the New Deal was recognized as one of the outstanding friends of labor in that body. His interest in the plight of the workingman, and his belief in unionism as a force of economic democracy, which he believed to be a necessary complement of political democracy, were determining factors in labor's rise to power in the 1930's.[6]

Wagner insisted on the inclusion of Section 7(a) in the National Industrial Recovery bill in 1933.[7] The NIRA was aimed primarily at economic recovery, and to this end the anti-trust acts were relaxed to allow employer groups to formulate codes restricting production and controlling prices in exchange for provisions regulating minimum wages, maximum hours, and child labor. Section 7(a), which guaranteed the right of labor to organize, was the price which organized labor and its supporters were able to extract from the administration's desire for business-labor unity in the recovery effort. Employer groups, however, attacked the inclusion of the section in the bill. The National Association of Manufacturers proposed amendments which would have protected individual bargaining, and the Iron and Steel Institute, speaking through Robert P. Lamont, declared that the open shop steel industry was "opposed to conducting negotiations . . . otherwise than with its own employees; it is unwilling to conduct them with outside organizations of labor or with individuals not its employees."[8]

As a result of this employer opposition, the Senate Committee on Finance inserted a provision in Section 7(a) declaring that "nothing in this title shall be construed to compel a change in existing satisfactory relationships between the employees and employers of any particular plant, firm or corporation. . . . "[9] This proposed change would have protected company unions organized by employers to prevent unionization of their employees. The A.F. of L. declared it would attempt to defeat the whole NIRA bill if this provision remained, and with Senator Norris leading the opposition to it the Senate defeated the provision.[10] As finally passed, Section 7(a) provided that "employees shall have the right to organize and bargain collectively through representatives of their own choosing, and shall be free from the interference, restraint or

[6] This biographical sketch of Wagner is based on: Owen P. White, "When the Public Needs a Friend," *Colliers,* Vol. 93 (June 2, 1934), p. 18; I. F. Stone, "Robert F. Wagner," *The Nation,* Vol. 159 (Oct. 28, 1944), p. 507; Oswald G. Villard, "Pillars of Government: Robert F. Wagner," *Forum and Century,* Vol. 96 (Sept., 1936), p. 124.

[7] I. F. Stone, *loc. cit.*

[8] National Industrial Recovery, Hearings on S. 1712 and HR 5755, Senate Committee on Finance, 73rd Cong., 1st sess., pp. 288–89, 395.

[9] 77 *Cong. Rec.* 5257.

[10] 77 *Cong. Rec.* 5284.

coercion of employers of labor, or their agents, in the designation of such representatives or in self-organization or in other concerted activities for the purpose of collective bargaining or other mutual aid or protection." The provision declared further that "no employee and no one seeking employment shall be required as a condition of employment to join any company union or to refrain from joining, organizing, or assisting a labor organization of his own choosing."[11]

Thus outlawing the yellow dog contract and prohibiting discrimination against union members, Section 7(a), if strictly enforced, meant a major shift of economic power to unions and a limitation of employer control of industry. NIRA required the inclusion of the language of Section 7(a) in all codes of "fair competition," but employer groups, having lost the fight to qualify the section in the Senate, focused their attention on the formulation of codes under NIRA as a means of diluting its effects. The National Industrial Conference, meeting in Chicago in June, 1933, urged all employer groups to insist on a "clarifying" declaration to follow Section 7(a) in the codes. This declaration should state, the Conference resolved, that Section 7(a) "does not impair in any particular the constitutional rights of the employer and employee to bargain individually or collectively" and that nothing in the code "is to prevent the selection, retention, and advancement of employees on the basis of their individual merit, without regard to their affiliation or nonaffiliation with any labor organization."[12] At the same time funds from employer groups were collected and administered by the NAM to publicize employee representation plans, or company unions, in an attempt to offset the expected organization efforts of the A.F. of L.[13]

With the major concern of the administration directed toward recovery efforts, it soon became clear that the success of labor in securing benefits under codes as well as the retention of the language of Section 7(a) would be determined by the relative strength of union organization in particular industries. The organization machinery of the A.F. of L., however, was slow to move to take advantage of the benefits of NIRA. John L. Lewis, president of the United Mine Workers, had attended early planning sessions on NIRA and had insisted on the protection of the right to organize. Later, he contacted William Green and pointed out the opportunity such a provision would have for labor. To Lewis' insistence that the A.F. of L. start organizing drives in

---

[11] Section 7(a), NIRA, 49 Stat. 195 (1933).

[12] Hearings before a Subcommittee of the Committee on Education and Labor, U.S. Senate, 75th Cong., 2nd sess., pt. 17, p. 7427. (Hereinafter cited as LaFollette Committee, *Hearings*.)

[13] *Ibid.*, p. 7572.

steel, autos, rubber and other mass production industries, Green responded by pointing out the cost and saying, "Now, John, let's take it easy."[14] Lewis, however, refused Green's counsel of caution and launched a UMW organizing drive immediately after the passage of NIRA. The argument that because of Section 7(a) "the President wants you to join a union" was used to full effect, and by the time of the code hearings for the coal industry, the UMW was stronger in the industry than it had been for a decade.[15] The Mine Workers were thus able to balance to a degree the influence of the employer's association in the drafting of the coal code.[16]

Other unions also were in relatively strong positions and were able to extract better terms in the codes than was generally the case in most industries. The Amalgamated Clothing Workers, under the leadership of Sidney Hillman, was one of these. The ACW had broken from the A.F. of L.–affiliated United Garment Workers in 1914 and had achieved considerable success in organizing an industry which had been largely open shop until 1910.[17] Amicable relations had long existed between the ACW and many employers, and employer associations such as the New York Clothing Manufacturers' Association, plus union firms such as Hart, Schaffner and Marx of Chicago, could be counted on to support the union's standards in the code hearings. In opposition were the Industrial Recovery Association of Clothing Manufacturers, an anti-union group, and the A.F. of L. United Garment Workers. Through negotiations between the rival unions, however, the rift in union ranks was healed, and the ACW rejoined the A.F. of L. in August of 1933.[18] The result was that the men's clothing code, providing for twenty per cent wage increases and the thirty-six-hour week, was recognized as being, "from labor's point of view, . . . among the best established for American industry."[19]

The Amalgamated Clothing Workers' strong position in the industry thus won improved conditions for unorganized as well as organized workers and alleviated the competitive advantage nonunion firms held over unionized firms. The nature of the men's clothing industry, however, posed a continuous threat to the union and forced almost continuous organization efforts. In 1933, there were over two thousand firms

[14] Saul Alinsky, *John L. Lewis* (New York: G. P. Putnam's Sons, 1949), pp. 67–68.

[15] *Ibid.*, p. 72.

[16] *Ibid.*, pp. 71–72.

[17] Matthew Josephson, *Sidney Hillman: Statesman of American Labor* (Garden City: Doubleday & Company, Inc., 1952), pp. 96–100.

[18] *Ibid.*, p. 369.

[19] Joel Seidman, *The Needle Trades* (New York: Farrar & Rinehart, Inc., 1942), p. 199.

employing about 120,000 workers in the industry.[20] These establishments were highly mobile and easily moved to communities desiring to attract new industry. By the 1930's, the movement of many firms to the South and other nonunion employment areas had begun, forcing the union to maintain constant organizing efforts to prevent the undermining of the competitive positions of unionized firms in the North. An example was the Friedman–Harry Marks Company, a manufacturer of men's summer clothing and overcoats, which had been established at Richmond, Virginia, in 1931. Employing about nine hundred workers, the Friedman–Harry Marks Company operated on a nonunion basis and belonged to the "Curley group" of nonunion clothing manufacturers in Virginia. The company adhered to the provisions of the men's clothing code, but later was to meet with tenacious resistance the attempts of the Amalgamated Clothing Workers to organize its employees.[21]

The success of the Amalgamated Clothing Workers in the code hearings was not to be repeated, however, in most other industries. In the automobile industry, the employees were largely unorganized, and the drafting of the automobile code was dominated by the Automobile Chamber of Commerce. The Chamber submitted a draft code in July, 1933, which affirmed the industry's determination "to continue the open-shop policy heretofore followed. . . . " Because of objections from the officials of NRA, references to the open shop were eliminated, but the automobile code as finally approved contained a provision following Section 7(a) which stated that "without in any way attempting to qualify or modify, by interpretation, the foregoing requirements of the NIRA, employers in this industry may exercise their right to select, retain, or advance employees on the basis of individual merit, without regard to their membership or non-membership in any organization."[22]

This was a major breakthrough for employer groups in their attempt to amend and qualify the meaning of Section 7(a). After Roosevelt approved the automobile code containing this language, business groups loosed a barrage of demands for such qualifying language in codes for other industries. General Johnson, the Administrator of NRA, confessed that he had allowed the inclusion of the so-called "merit clause" in the automobile code "in an unguarded moment," and,

[20] *Ibid.,* Table VI, p. 340.

[21] The information on the Friedman–Harry Marks Company is based on NA–Case No. C-40, Friedman–Harry Marks Clothing Co., Folder No. 1, NLRB memorandum dated Sept. 30, 1935.

[22] Lewis L. Lorwin and Arthur Wubnig, *Labor Relations Boards* (Washington: The Brookings Institution, 1935), pp. 65–66.

after the Labor Advisory Board—labor's watchdog in the NRA administrative apparatus—declared opposition to qualifications of Section 7(a) in the codes, Johnson promised that in future instances such qualifying language would not be permitted.[23]

The auto industry, however, having won its "merit clause," was able to continue its traditional open shop policy and its opposition to the organization of its employees. The A.F. of L. instituted an organizing drive in the industry, and by early 1934 its federal locals, based on the industrial principle of organization, claimed a membership of 40,000 and were threatening a strike. In order to head off a recovery-crippling strike, the President created the National Automobile Labor Board to hear complaints from auto employees. The order creating the NALB, however, sanctioned the principle of proportional resspresentation of union, company union, and unorganized employees, and the board would recognize ballots cast only for individuals in representation elections. As a result of these policies, plus effective espionage and strike-breaking efforts by the industry, membership and employee interest in unions declined.[24]

The A.F. of L. organizing efforts and the desire to escape adverse publicity during the early days of NRA, however, led some companies in the auto industry to at least meet with union representatives and to avoid open and blatant anti-union discrimination. The Fruehauf Trailer Company was one of these. The company had grown out of a blacksmith shop and wagon works founded by August C. Fruehauf in Detroit in 1897. This operation was converted to the manufacture of truck trailers and incorporated in 1918. By the 1930's, with August Fruehauf's sons, Harvey and Harry, as president and vice president, the company owned a factory covering nine acres and employing about seven hundred workers.[25] When A.F. of L. organizers penetrated the plant after the passage of NIRA, the company met with union representatives as long as NRA was in effect.[26] An employee who had been laid off and had charged anti-union discrimination before the NRA Detroit Regional Labor Board was rehired at the suggestion of the Board.[27]

To counter the unionization of its employees, however, the Board of Directors of the Fruehauf Company decided to contact the Pinkerton

[23] *Ibid.*, pp. 67–68.

[24] William Heston McPherson, *Labor Relations in the Automobile Industry* (Washington: The Brookings Institution, 1940), pp. 16–17.

[25] NA–Case No. C-2, Fruehauf Trailer Co., Extra Papers Folder, Statement of Earl L. Vosler, Vice President of Fruehauf Trailer Co. (no date).

[26] Official Report of the Proceedings before the NLRB, in the Matter of Fruehauf Trailer Co., p. 300.

[27] *Ibid.*, pp. 590–602.

Detective Agency, which in early 1934 supplied an operative to the company at the cost of $175 per month. The operative was hired by the company under the name of J. N. Martin and reported to a company vice president, Earl L. Vosler, several times a week on union activities in the plant.[28] Martin joined the union, eventually becoming treasurer of the local, and was known at union meetings as a "queer man of some kind or another. He was always reciting poetry or saying something like, 'You can catch more flies with molasses than you can with vinegar.' "[29] As a result of Martin's activities, unionization in the Fruehauf plant, as in the auto industry generally, failed to be very effective during 1934–35.

One of the industries most reluctant to join the NRA recovery effort was the newspaper industry. The unionization of the mechanical trades in the newspaper industry had been established as early as the 1890's.[30] A minority of the members of the American Newspaper Publishers' Association, however, had begun agitation for an open shop policy in the mechanical departments following World War I, charging that unionization threatened freedom of the press. The ANPA had condemned these charges, but the minority was effective enough to force the creation of an open shop division within the Association in 1922.[31] The result was that during the 1930's the ANPA maintained both a Standing Committee on Labor, which aided union publishers in negotiations with unions, and the Open Shop Division, which aided nonunion publishers in breaking strikes.[32]

The ANPA recommended in July, 1933, that publishers refrain from "subscribing to a code under the recovery act at the present time," but the pressure to join the recovery effort led the ANPA to draft a code which was submitted to NRA during the following month.[33] Particular emphasis in the Association's draft code was placed on the question of the freedom of the press and the right of labor to organize. The draft provided that "because of the limitations of the first amendment to the Constitution of the United States nothing in this code shall be construed as authorizing the licensing of publishers and/or newspapers or as permitting injunction proceedings which would restrain the publication of newspapers." The draft code also qualified Section 7(a) by stating that "no employee shall be required to join any organization

[28] *Ibid.*, pp. 260–355.
[29] *Ibid.*, pp. 613, 648.
[30] National Labor Relations Board, Division of Economic Research, *Collective Bargaining in the Newspaper Industry*, Bulletin No. 3 (Oct., 1936), p. 68.
[31] *Ibid.*, pp. 82–83.
[32] *Ibid.*, p. 88.
[33] *Editor & Publisher*, Vol. 66 (July 22, 1933), p. 5; (Aug. 12, 1933), p. 3.

to secure or retain employment or to secure the benefits of the code, and the right of every individual to refrain from joining any organization, and the right of employe and employer to bargain together, free from interference by any third party, is hereby recognized."[34]

General Johnson objected particularly to the ANPA's attempt to qualify Section 7(a), and a process of negotiation, which was to last several months, began. The labor provisions soon became of criticial importance to the publishers because of the rapid organization of editorial and reportorial employees into "guilds." Heywood Broun, then a columnist for the New York *World-Telegram,* announced in August, 1933, that he would begin attempts to organize editorial employees.[35] The same month editorial employees of the Cleveland press organized into the Editorial Employees' Association and announced opposition to the ANPA draft code. They asserted it would allow publishers "to fly the Blue Eagle while at the same time evading the economic burden strict adherence to the letter and spirit of the act required of other industries." Editorial employees, they said, were squeezed "between the pressures of advertisers and stockholders, between exorbitant tolls of syndicates and press services, and the unionized requirements of the mechanical trades" and were "the most notoriously exploited of all producer groups in this country which require similar standards of intelligence, skill and industry." "It is time," they said, "that local room staffs start living and working for something more than the byline and pat-on-the-back. NRA holds out to them their first bona fide opportunity to go after realities."[36]

Conferences among New York reporters were held at Heywood Broun's apartment during the summer of 1933,[37] and in late September about three hundred reporters met to form the Guild of New York Newspaper Men and Women. They demanded that minimum wage and maximum hour standards for reporters be included in the newspaper code and elected a committee to represent them at the NRA code hearings. The committee was headed by Heywood Broun, and included Morris Watson, the star reporter for the Associated Press in New York.[38] Other editorial and reportorial employees across the country, inspired by the passage of Section 7(a), were soon organizing into similar organizations.

There was, however, no agreement on the part of these employees

[34] *Ibid.* (Aug. 12, 1933), p. 5.
[35] *Editor & Publisher,* Vol. 66 (Aug. 12, 1933), p. 31.
[36] *Ibid.* (Aug. 26, 1933), p. 6.
[37] Levinson, *op. cit.,* p. 246.
[38] *Editor & Publisher,* Vol. 66 (Sept. 23, 1933), p. 7.

as to the type of organization the "guilds" should be. Many supported the guilds only as a form of professional society, while others, notably Heywood Broun, early favored the trade union principle.[39] This lack of organizational identity alienated many members during the early days of the guilds. Several New York reporters resigned from the New York Guild in early 1934, asserting that its meetings "are devoted to mammy palaver, Utopia in Gotham, and the price of drinks at the nearest bar. The Guild is riding hell-for-leather to nowhere." Many, like H. L. Mencken, didn't "think it will ever accomplish anything, but it will be a hell of a lot of fun."[40] The voice of the ANPA, *Editor & Publisher,* approved the early organizational activities of editorial employees. It editorially admitted the abuses of which the writers complained "are real and should be cleaned up whether there is unionization or not. Not the least of these is ruthless and unjustified dismissal, without notice. The obvious dissatisfaction of news writers commands the attention of the newspaper field. After all, they remain the backbone of the structure."[41]

Despite this endorsement, the ANPA and the guilds soon clashed over the provisions of the newspaper code. Elisha Hanson, counsel for the ANPA, asserted in the code hearings that the qualification of Section 7(a) in the Association draft code was "vital if this code is to be signed by publishers of daily newspapers." The qualifying provision, he said, protected publishers against "racketeering." Heywood Broun challenged the publishers' attempt to qualify the section and said that reporters who organized might be subject to "penalties." "The penalty may not be dismissal. All newspapermen know of an institution known as the Chinese Torture room. A reporter who incurs the displeasure of his boss by organizing activity may find himself writing obits for the rest of his life." Morris Watson also appeared at the code hearing and asked for the inclusion of the press association employees in the code.[42]

The ANPA was also adamant on the inclusion of a guarantee of freedom of the press in the newspaper code. Colonel Robert R. McCormick was chairman of the Free Press Committee of the ANPA and was the author of the free press provision in the draft code. It is possible that the Committee's recent successful fight against the Minnesota censorship statute had focused attention on the issue,[43] but whatever the

---

[39] *Ibid.* (Dec. 9, 1933), p. 9.
[40] *Editor & Publisher,* Vol. 66 (April 7, 1934), pp. 11, 38.
[41] *Ibid.* (Sept. 23, 1933), p. 24.
[42] *Editor & Publisher,* Vol. 66 (Sept. 30, 1933), pp. 6, 14.
[43] See *Near* v. *Minnesota,* 283 U.S. 697 (1931).

reason, as *Editor & Publisher* stated, there had seldom "been such a unified and insistent demand from newspapers that their constitutional rights be reaffirmed officially."[44] The Inland Daily Press Association, meeting in October, 1933, demanded the inclusion of a free press and open shop guarantee in the code. The Association passed a resolution pointing out that a free press could be abolished by repealing the first amendment, signing the NRA code without a free press provision, or by the "establishment of censorship, made possible by the unionization of all departments of a newspaper."[45] The issue of the freedom of the press was thus joined at an early stage with the issue of unionization, and this fusion of the two issues was to continue in the publisher-union struggle throughout the 1930's.

General Johnson called the free press issue a "synthetic dead cat," but the publishers were able to gain the support of the American Civil Liberties Union on the issue and succeeded in their efforts to have it remain in the code. The qualification of Section 7(a) was eliminated, but on all other issues the publishers were largely successful in the code hearings. The only major addition to the ANPA draft was the provision for a Newspaper Industrial Board to hear complaints arising under Section 7(a); otherwise, as Charles Howard, president of the International Typographical Union, said, "The employers wrote their own code."[46]

The organizing impetus of the guilds had in the meantime culminated in the creation of the American Newspaper Guild by a convention of guild representatives from twenty-one cities. Heywood Broun, although opposed by some because of his advocacy of trade unionism, was elected president. Morris Watson was elected to head the Press Association Committee of the Guild, and, after addressing the convention, handed General Johnson a proposed press association code providing for a five-day, thirty-five-hour week, and notice before dismissal. Although *Editor & Publisher* editorialized that the Guild "bids fair to play an important and decidedly helpful role in American journalism,"[47] most publishers were reluctant to enter into negotiations with Guild representatives on wages and hours. When the New York Guild attempted to break the ice and invited the New York Publishers' Association to negotiate, the Association replied that there was no evidence that the Guild represented any of its members' employees. "With-

---

[44] *Editor & Publisher,* Vol. 66 (Nov. 4, 1933), p. 3.

[45] *Ibid.* (Oct. 21, 1933), pp. 7–9.

[46] National Labor Relations Board, Division of Economic Research, *op. cit.,* p. 143. For a copy of the Newspaper Code see *Editor & Publisher,* Vol. 66 (Feb. 24, 1934), p. 36.

[47] *Editor & Publisher,* Vol. 66 (Dec. 23, 1933), pp. 7, 22.

out such credentials," it said, "the Association has no authority to meet your representatives."[48]

The New York Guild replied that it was "amazed and regretful at the apparent decision of a majority of members of the Publishers' Association of New York to refuse to meet employee representatives except on a 'strictly legalistic basis,' "[49] but this was to be the fairly uniform pattern of reaction by publishers throughout the country. The result was that the American Newspaper Guild slowly moved toward the organizational form and tactics of a trade union. By September, 1934, *Editor & Publisher* was denouncing the ANG, declaring that editors and publishers "need no longer regard the American Newspaper Guild as an independent body of responsible professional news writers and editors, a 'guild' with an economic program. It is a radical trades union. . . . " The Guild was a "pitiful wreck" and its failure "shameless."[50]

There still existed public pressure to preserve recovery unity, however, and many publishers resorted to covert tactics against troublesome Guildsmen. Morris Watson, a vigorous proponent of the Guild, soon was made to pay the price for his activities by his superiors in the Associated Press. Watson was a native of Joplin, Missouri, had served in the army in World War I, and had been gassed in France. While recuperating, he had begun newspaper work, first for the Omaha *World-Herald* and later the Denver *Morning Post*. He joined the Associated Press in Chicago in 1928 and was transferred to the New York office in 1930, where he rapidly became one of the AP's star reporters.[51] His superiors in the AP duly noted and filed in his personnel record his appearance in the NRA code hearings in behalf of the inclusion of the press associations under the code.[52] Later, Watson, as head of the Press Association Committee, signed an open letter to NRA which was published in the *Guild Reporter* and *Editor & Publisher* demanding a press association code and charging labor abuses by the associations. Watson was forced by his superiors to sign a retraction in so far as the Associated Press was concerned.[53]

By April of 1934, the Guild membership at the New York AP office totaled about eighty,[54] and in the fall the AP was requested to negoti-

[48] *Ibid.* (March 17, 1934), p. 10.
[49] *Ibid.* (March 24, 1934), p. 11.
[50] *Editor & Publisher,* Vol. 67 (Sept. 13, 1934), p. 24.
[51] *Ibid.,* Vol. 70 (April 17, 1937), p. 12.
[52] NA–Case No. C-84, The Associated Press, Folder No. 1, memorandum dated Nov. 27, 1935, from Regional Office, Dist. II, to NLRB.
[53] *Editor & Publisher,* Vol. 66 (March 24, 1934), p. 11; also memorandum referred to in note 52.
[54] *Ibid.* (April 14, 1934), p. 14.

ate. When the AP responded by adopting the five-day week, the Guild hailed the move as a victory, but charged that the AP management was attempting to intimidate Guild members. Watson, who was by then treasurer of the New York Guild, said, "We made a move toward collective bargaining, and then came the five-day week." Over his objections, the AP Guild members rescinded their request for a bargaining conference.[55]

Watson had been warned in the meantime by an AP executive that "he would quit his job rather than bargain with an outsider," and that a foreign assignment, which Watson had requested, would not be granted as long as he remained in the Guild.[56] In September, 1934, Watson was transferred to a less desirable job, but was recalled to his old post to cover the Hauptman trial.[57] Shortly after the beginning of 1935, he suffered a nervous breakdown which he attributed to the transfer from his old job. He did not return to work until midsummer, 1935.[58]

The technique of "Chinese torture" was obviously not unknown to the management of the Associated Press. By the use of similar tactics, plus threats and in some cases outright dismissal, the publishers retained the commanding position they had gained during newspaper code hearings throughout 1933 and 1934. By the end of 1934, *Editor & Publisher* could declare with some truth that the "labor union threat of six months ago has not materialized. It is not going to materialize, and certain highly emotional young men of the newsroom who sought to force newspapers into a class-conscious affiliation with one side of the boiling politico-economic controversy, contravening all journalistic idealism, know today that their cause has been licked to a standstill."[59]

Unionization efforts in the newspaper industry could have been called successful, however, when compared to the position of unions in the steel industry under NRA. Except perhaps for the auto industry, steel was the most notoriously anti-union industry in the country. Not since the great steel strike of 1919 had there been any substantial union threat to complete employer control of steel.[60] Anti-unionism was so ingrained in steel executives that when Secretary of Labor Perkins called leading steel executives together for a steel code conference with

[55] *Editor & Publisher,* Vol. 67 (Sept. 8, 1934), p. 9; Official Report of the Proceedings before the NLRB, In the Matter of the Associated Press and American Newspaper Guild, p. 255.

[56] *Ibid.,* pp. 250–52.

[57] *Ibid.,* pp. 260–68.

[58] *Ibid.,* pp. 271–78.

[59] *Editor & Publisher,* Vol. 67 (Nov. 17, 1934), p. 14.

[60] See Robert R. R. Brooks, *As Steel Goes . . . Unionism in a Basic Industry* (New Haven: Yale University Press, 1940).

A.F. of L. president Green in early 1933, most of them backed into a corner and refused even to shake hands. They were afraid, they said, that it would get back to the steel towns that they had talked with Green.[61]

Meetings on the steel code were begun even before NIRA had passed Congress. The Iron and Steel Institute submitted a draft code which formed the basis of hearings in July, 1933, and which, like most codes submitted by other industrial groups, attempted to qualify Section 7(a). The draft code endorsed company unions and restricted representatives of employees to the employees of individual companies. General Johnson objected to the provisions in the public hearings and Robert P. Lamount, representing the Institute, agreed to their withdrawal.[62] The Institute made it clear, however, that the withdrawal of the qualifying provisions did "not imply any change in the attitude of the industry on the parts therein"; unions were denounced as fomenters of class antagonism which were of "no profit to anyone concerned, unless it be the many racketeers who have fastened themselves on to the unions. . . . "[63]

President Michael Tighe of Amalgamated Association of Iron, Steel, and Tin Workers, the A.F. of L. union having jurisdiction over the steel industry, was hardly a racketeer, but, as many believed, hardly a union leader either. After the passage of NIRA, William Green had telegraphed Tighe urging an intensive organization drive in steel to head off the industry's efforts to establish company unions, but Tighe replied that he was busy negotiating a contract with a small Kansas City company where two of the Amalgamated's locals were located. He promised, however, to take the matter up with the union's executive board and pointed out that he had written an article on the company union threat in the union's journal.

It was not until late summer, 1933, that the Amalgamated's executive board authorized a full-scale drive in steel. The union's membership in 1933 was 4,852, but during 1933 and 1934 the union spent over $177,000 on organizational work, and membership reached a peak of over 18,000 in 1934. Nevertheless, the all-out resistance of the industry, plus the lack of full backing from the A.F. of L. and the failure of the government to make good the promise of Section 7(a), meant eventual failure of these efforts for effective unionization of steel

---

[61] Frances Perkins, *op. cit.,* pp. 221–22.

[62] Carroll R. Daugherty, Melvin G. DeChazeau, and Samuel S. Stratton, *The Economics of the Iron and Steel Industry* (New York: McGraw-Hill Book Co., 1937), Vol. I, pp. 260–63.

[63] *Ibid.,* Vol. II, pp. 984–85.

workers. By the end of 1934, all organizing activities by the Amalgamated were stopped and membership began to decline.[64]

The tactics of the Jones & Laughlin Steel Corporation in its resistance to the union's organizing drive were not atypical of the steel industry as a whole. The firm had been founded by B. F. Jones, who had begun with a small rolling mill in Brownsville, Pennsylvania, and had later moved to what was to be South Pittsburgh. The company followed the rest of the steel industry in eliminating unionism in its works after the disastrous Homestead strike in 1892. The company was reorganized and incorporated in 1902, and with new capital it decided to construct a new works in addition to the South Pittsburgh plant. For this purpose, Jones & Laughlin in 1907 bought Woodlawn Park, an area twenty-six miles below Pittsburgh along the Ohio River. A company town and plant were constructed, and the site was later renamed Aliquippa, after Queen Aliquippa, an Indian woman famous in the early history of Pennsylvania.[65]

In 1914, Jones & Laughlin hired Tom M. Girdler as assistant superintendent of the Aliquippa works. W. L. Jones, who hired Girdler, told him the company wanted Aliquippa "to be the best steel town in the world. We want to make it the best possible place for a steelworker to raise a family." The town was laid out in "plans," each "plan" containing a nationality or racial group, including Italians, Poles, Serbians, Greeks, Russians, and Negroes. Girdler soon hired an ex-state policeman, Harry Mauk, who established a company police, the efficiency of which was proven when the plant failed to lose a single manhour during the 1919 steel strike. "There was," Girdler wrote later, "in Aliquippa, if you please, a benevolent dictatorship."[66]

By the 1930's Aliquippa was known to union organizers as "little Siberia."[67] Jones & Laughlin owned the city transportation facilities, the water company, and 674 of its employees' houses.[68] Beaver County, in which Aliquippa was located, was dominated politically by former state senator David Craig, who reportedly was retained by Jones & Laughlin as an attorney. The sheriff was Charles O'Laughlin, a former Aliquippa police officer; the warder of the county jail, Hamilton Brown, was a

[64] Daugherty, DeChazeau, and Stratton, op. cit., pp. 944–53.

[65] Tom M. Girdler, Boot Straps: The Autobiography of Tom M. Girdler (Charles Scribner's Sons, 1943), pp. 163–68. Jones & Laughlin eliminated unionism in its plants in 1897; see NLRB, Division of Economic Research, Written Trade Agreements in Collective Bargaining, Bulletin No. 4 (Nov., 1939).

[66] Girdler, op. cit., pp. 166–77.

[67] Brooks, op. cit., p. 111.

[68] Official Report of Proceedings before the NLRB, In the Matter of Jones & Laughlin Steel Corporation and Amalgamated Association of Iron, Steel and Tin Workers, p. 127.

former Aliquippa police chief; the Aliquippa chief of police was W. L. Ambrose, a former Jones & Laughlin police officer; and all company police held commissions as special borough policemen.[69]

In anticipation of new unionization efforts, Jones & Laughlin in June, 1933, established a company union,[70] but also prepared for trouble by purchasing more than $4,000 worth of tear and sickening gas in the period 1933–1935.[71] By the summer of 1934, several of its employees had joined the national steel-workers' union, however, and a local was chartered on August 4.[72] Union members soon paid the price for their activities. Angelo Volpe had his house raided and was constantly shadowed, after refusing a company police offer to work against the union. Martin Gerstner, another union member, met with three friends at his home to discuss union business, but company police posted themselves outside the house and threatened the men when they left. Harry V. Phillips, the president of the local, was assaulted by two men on August 31st.[73] When he asked for protection from the Aliquippa police, he was told to get "the hell out of here. You don't deserve protection."[74]

The union continued its organizing efforts, despite these attempts at intimidation. It hired George Isaski, a former Jones & Laughlin employee, as an organizer, but Isaski was arrested on September 11 and charged with being drunk and disorderly. He was jailed for thirty days and his wife was refused permission to visit him. Finally, upon petition by the Sheriff, the County Judge appointed a lunacy commission composed of an attorney, James Knox Stone, who was known to be violently anti-union, Dr. Margaret Cornelius, who was employed by the County Commissioners, and Dr. M. M. Mackall, the jail physician. Although there was no record of any testimony or witnesses heard by the commission, Isaski was committed to the Torrence State Hospital for the Insane on September 19, and neither his wife nor friends were informed of his whereabouts. It was some time before an investigation ordered by Governor Pinchot was launched, a state psychologist had certified Isaski as sane, and his release from the institution was obtained.[75] These tactics of Jones & Laughlin resulted in a hearing by the

[69] Report of the Pennsylvania Department of Labor and Industry on the Relations between the Jones & Laughlin Steel Corp. and its Workers, Submitted at the request of the National Steel Labor Relations Board, Charlotte E. Carr, Sec. of Labor and Industry, Commonwealth of Pennsylvania (Nov. 10, 1934), p. 1.

[70] Brooks, *op. cit.*, p. 112.

[71] LaFollette Committee, Report No. 6, pt. 3, p. 202.

[72] Off. Rep. of Proceedings before NLRB—Jones & Laughlin, p. 149.

[73] Report of the Pennsylvania Department of Labor and Industry, pp. 6–7.

[74] Off. Rep. of Proceedings before NLRB—Jones & Laughlin, p. 155.

[75] Report of the Pennsylvania Department of Labor and Industry, pp. 11–13.

National Steel Labor Relations Board in October, 1934, on alleged violations of Section 7(a). The hearings were at first scheduled in Pittsburgh on October 4, but were postponed. The union members who had been prepared to testify, however, asked the Board for safe conduct when they returned to Aliquippa. This request aroused the Board's interest and Governor Pinchot was requested to send state police into Aliquippa. Pinchot complied, and seven state policemen arrived and established headquarters at the Woodlawn Hotel. Tension and the intimidation of union members immediately lessened, and on October 14 Pinchot's wife, Cornelia, addressed the first open, public labor meeting ever held in Aliquippa. The Amalgamated was also able for the first time to rent space for a union headquarters.[76]

The resistance of Jones & Laughlin to the unionization of its employees at the Aliquippa works typified the resistance of the steel industry as a whole to granting full recognition of the rights theoretically guaranteed by Section 7(a). In September, 1934, Roosevelt called for a truce between the industry and the union for the benefit of the recovery effort, and during the fall and winter, the industry and organized labor, acting through the National Steel Labor Relations Board, attempted to compromise on a formula on organization rights. In its first proposal, the steel industry offered to meet with representatives of any of its employees and attempt to adjust grievances, but refused to enter into any contract or to recognize the union. Because the proposal avoided the issue of representation elections and did not grant the legitimacy of the jurisdiction of the NSLRB, the union rejected it. Union leaders demanded that the industry accept both representation elections, which would determine the sole bargaining agents for steel workers, and also the jurisdiction of the NSLRB in cases of anti-union discrimination. The industry would not accept both of these conditions, and, despite many proposals and counter-proposals and a White House conference, throughout the NRA period there was no basic change in the industry's anti-union position which it had announced during the hearings on NIRA and the code hearings.[77]

The failure of the steel negotiations was characteristic of the failure generally, despite some successes, of the NRA labor board system to effect full recognition by industry of the right to organize. In an administrative apparatus focused primarily on economic recovery and relying largely on the good will of industry for compliance, the labor boards

[76] Report of the Pennsylvania Department of Labor and Industry, p. 3; Daugherty, DeChazeau, and Stratton, *op. cit.*, p. 1000, note 1; and Brooks, *op. cit.*, pp. 111–13.

[77] Daugherty, DeChazeau, and Stratton, *op. cit.*, pp. 1041–46.

were in important respects peripheral both from a policy and administrative standpoint. Under the chairmanship of Senator Wagner, the National Labor Board was created in August, 1933, to enforce compliance with Section 7(a), but neither its legitimacy nor jurisdiction was supported by an executive order until December. In addition to the handicap of early conflict with the labor boards established under the codes, the NLB was weakened administratively by its lack of enforcement powers. It had to rely on the Compliance Division of NRA to remove the Blue Eagles of truculent employers and on the Justice Department to proceed legally against such employers. Enforcement of Section 7(a) was thus subject to the Compliance Division's desire to avoid alienating the good will of employer groups and the Justice Department's hesitance to test what was widely considered an unconstitutional statute on the basis of a Section 7(a) case.[78]

The constitutional and legal difficulties in enforcing Section 7(a) became apparent within a few months of the NLB's creation. In the process of settling early representation cases, the Board adopted the election principle and ruled that employees should not be restricted to voting for fellow employees in such elections. This allowed voting for bona fide unions against company unions, which industry in general was promoting in an attempt to escape the full effects of Section 7(a). The NAM and the Iron and Steel Institute attacked the Board on the election issue, as well as on the rule that a majority should determine the sole bargaining agent for all employees. The Board met early success in settling many threatened strikes on the basis of these principles, but in early December the Weirton Steel Company, repudiating an earlier agreement to allow an NLB election, refused to accept the NLB's procedures and determined to hold its own election on the issue of its company union. Despite an appeal by General Johnson, who warned the company that it was "about to commit a deliberate violation of federal laws," the company persisted in its refusal to accept the NLB's jurisdiction and proceeded with its own election. Senator Wagner asked the Attorney General to take charge of the case.[79]

The government's prosecution of the case failed when the federal district court of Delaware refused to issue an injunction against the company in May, 1934. In an opinion handed down later, the court fully sustained the Weirton Steel Company's position and rejected a government supervised election as a "revolutionary suggestion."[80] Relying on

---

[78] Lorwin and Wubnig, *op. cit.*, pp. 134–37.

[79] Lorwin and Wubnig, *op. cit.*, pp. 102–104. See also, "Weirton and 7(a)," *New Republic*, Vol. 77 (Dec. 27, 1933), p. 183.

[80] *United States* v. *Weirton Steel Co.*, 10 F. Supp. 55 (D.C., Del., 1935), at 71.

the line of Supreme Court decisions holding manufacturing not to be interstate commerce, the court rejected the government's flow of commerce argument as "devious." "The manufacturing operations conducted by defendant in its various plants or mills," the court declared, "do not constitute interstate commerce. The relations between defendant and its employees do not affect interstate commerce." The government had also argued that employees must be allowed to organize to balance the economic power of the employer and that the Weirton company union did not permit this. This argument, the court said, was "based on the assumption of an inevitable and necessary diversity of interests. This is the traditional old world theory. It is not the Twentieth Century American theory of that relation as dependent upon mutual interest, understanding and good will. This modern theory is embodied in the Weirton plan of employee organization. Furthermore, the suggestion that recurrent hard times suspend constitutional limitations or cause manufacturing operations to so affect interstate commerce as to subject them to regulation by Congress borders on the fantastic and merits no serious consideration." Section 7(a), as applied to the Weirton Steel Company, was therefore unconstitutional.[81]

The NLB had determined to stake its prestige on the prosecution of the *Weirton* case, and the court's refusal to enjoin the company was a solid blow to the enforcement of Section 7(a). An additional blow came in March when Roosevelt and Johnson negotiated the auto settlement to head off a strike in that industry. The settlement provided for an Automobile Labor Board and endorsed the principle of proportional representation, which contradicted the majority rule principle recommended by the NLB for representation elections.[82] These events as well as other difficulties in the enforcement of Section 7(a) which Senator Wagner observed as chairman of the NLB led him to introduce his labor disputes bill on February 28, 1934. The bill was based on the theory that continuing strikes interrupted and affected the flow of interstate commerce and harmed the general welfare. It proposed to establish a permanent labor board to prevent unfair labor practices which interfered with the right of employees to organize or discriminated against union members. The board was to be composed of employer, employee, and public members and was given powers to arbitrate labor disputes as well as prevent unfair labor practices.[83] Wagner argued in a speech in the Senate that the bill would raise purchasing power by guaranteeing the

[81] 10 F. Supp. at 86.

[82] Lorwin and Wubnig, *op. cit.*, pp. 111–14.

[83] *Legislative History of the National Labor Relations Act,* The National Labor Relations Board (Washington: Government Printing Office, 1949), Vol. I, pp. 1–10.

right to organize and the right to union recognition, would destroy company unions, which did not permit true collective bargaining, and would prevent individual bargaining where the majority of the workers desired a collective agreement.[84]

Hearings on the bill began before the Senate Committee on Education and Labor during March, 1934. The proponents of the bill, who appeared first, argued generally that NIRA had allowed almost unrestricted employer organization, but because of the failure in the enforcement of Section 7(a), employees had not been able to organize effectively to counterbalance the power of the employers. The ranks of the bill's proponents were thin, however; besides Wagner and A.F. of L. leaders, only a few professors appeared in the bill's behalf, and Frances Perkins was the only administration official who appeared.[85]

In contrast to the two days of testimony by those favoring the bill, employer groups conducted a massive attack over a period of almost a month. Leading off the attack was James A. Emery, general counsel of the National Manufacturers' Association, who focused his argument on the bill's unconstitutionality. According to the NAM's brief, the bill was void on commerce grounds because manufacturing and production were not a part of interstate commerce; it was void as an interference with liberty of contract as guaranteed by the fifth amendment; and finally, it violated the fifth amendment and article III of the Constitution by conferring judicial power on an administrative agency whose procedure violated due process of law.[86] "It will thus be observed," Emery said, "that the power of Congress is hung upon a hypothetical conjecture, resting in the unrestrained imagination of administrative authority, surmising a relationship between a local complaint and its probable influence upon interstate commerce."[87]

Following the NAM's presentation came chambers of commerce and manufacturers' associations from all sections of the country to protest against the Wagner bill on constitutional and policy grounds. On April 5, the steel industry opened its arguments with Arthur H. Young of U.S. Steel assuring the committee that the company union plan was "a supplement to the Golden Rule."[88] Tom Girdler, by then president of Republic Steel, testified that there had been no labor troubles at the Jones & Laughlin plant at Aliquippa because of the "direct personal contact between our management and our men." The Wagner bill, he

[84] *77 Cong. Rec.* 3443.
[85] Hearings before the Committee on Education and Labor on S. 2926, pt. 1, U.S. Senate, 73rd Cong. 2nd sess., pp. 1–337.
[86] *Ibid.,* pp. 397–400.
[87] *Ibid.,* p. 353.
[88] *Ibid.,* p. 729.

said, would by encouraging unionization interfere with these direct relations.[89]

Despite this picture of peaceful employer-employee relations presented by the steel executives, the industry was faced in April with both a demand by a "progressive" rank and file movement within the Amalgamated Association for recognition and a threat of strike in mid-June, 1934.[90] The industry uniformly turned down the demand for union recognition, but the threat of a strike won for the dissident unionists an invitation to visit Washington to confer with NRA and NLB officials. Offers by the Iron and Steel Institute to settle the issue along the lines of the auto settlement or to agree to a tripartite steel labor board were refused by the unionists. They denounced the NRA as the "National Run Around" and threatened "bloody war" unless the steel industry bargained. In a letter to Roosevelt, they declared that they had "lost faith in your administration, which promised justice and a new deal to the workers of the nation."[91]

The Wagner bill had in the interim been reported favorably by the Senate committee on May 26, but, faced with the threatened steel strike, Roosevelt decided on the expedient of temporary labor boards based upon a congressional resolution.[92] Public Resolution No. 44, authorizing the President to create impartial boards which would mediate disputes, hold representation elections, and hear discrimination cases under Section 7(a), was introduced in the Senate on June 14, but quickly aroused opposition from pro-labor Senators. Senator LaFollette offered the Wagner bill as an amendment and spoke eloquently for its passage. Wagner, declaring that it was "one of the most embarrassing moments of my whole political life," was forced to ask LaFollette to withdraw his amendment. LaFollette complied, but Senator Cutting of New Mexico declared that the "new deal is being strangled in the house of its friends."[93] On June 15, William Green persuaded the steel unionists to accept a National Steel Labor Relations Board to be appointed by the President under Public Resolution No. 44 and to cancel the threatened strike.[94] A new National Labor Relations Board, composed entirely of public members, was also soon established in place of the old NLB.[95]

Public Resolution No. 44 could not, however, cure the difficulties the old board system had encountered. As one corporation executive put it, the resolution "means that temporary measures, which cannot last more

[89] *Ibid.*, pp. 773–74.
[90] Daugherty, DeChazeau, and Stratton, *op. cit.*, Vol. II, p. 1059.
[91] *Ibid.*, pp. 1060–61.
[92] Lorwin and Wubnig, *op. cit.*, p. 258.
[93] 78 *Cong. Rec.* 12024–52.
[94] Daugherty, DeChazeau, and Stratton, *op. cit.*, 1062–63.
[95] See "Goodbye Section 7(a)," *New Republic,* Vol. 80 (Oct. 31, 1934), p. 325.

than a year, will be substituted for the permanent legislation proposed in the original Wagner bill. I do not believe that there will again be as good a chance for the passage of the Wagner Act as exists now, and the trade is a mighty good compromise."[96] After a brief tenure as chairman of the new NLRB, Lloyd K. Garrison was writing that "Section 7(a) of the Recovery Act can never be thoroughly enforced with even-handed justice, under the existing administrative machinery. The powers of the Board, which is the chief governmental agency dealing with 7-a cases, are quite inadequate for the proper discharge of its responsibilities."[97] Although the congressional resolution bolstered the basis of the labor board system, it did not alter the basic reliance of the NRA administrative structure on the cooperation and good will of business groups, and, just as the constitutional weakness of the old NLB had been demonstrated by the *Weirton* case, the inability of the new NLRB to enforce Section 7(a) against determined employer pressure on the Recovery Administration was soon demonstrated in a case involving the newspaper industry.

Dean Jennings, a reporter for the San Francisco *Call-Bulletin,* was fired in June, 1934. Jennings charged he was removed because of his activities in the American Newspaper Guild.[98] The case was first referred to the Newspaper Industrial Board which had been established under the newspaper code.[99] Composed of equal numbers of publisher and mechanical trade union representatives, the NIB had remained in deadlock on the question of selecting an impartial chairman throughout 1933 and 1934. In addition, the American Newspaper Guild was not represented on the board, and the publishers refused to expand the board for the purpose of allowing an ANG representative.[100] In view of these circumstances, the NLB reassigned the case to one of its regional boards, and in the winter of 1934 it came before the new NLRB.[101]

Despite the contention of the American Newspaper Publishers' Association that the case could only be considered by the Newspaper Board, the NLRB announced its decision ordering Jennings reinstated on December 3, 1934, while hearings on revision of the newspaper code were in progress.[102] A spokesman for the ANPA declared that the decision was "a threat to the free press in the United States. It nullifies the freedom of the press reservation contained in the daily newspaper code. . . ."[103] The decision sent NRA officials "scurrying into conferences,"

[96] *79 Cong. Rec.* 7569.
[97] "7(a) and the Future," *Survey Graphic,* Vol. 24, No. 2 (Feb., 1935), p. 53.
[98] *Editor & Publisher,* Vol. 67 (June 9, 1934), p. 13.
[99] *Ibid.,* Vol. 67 (June 16, 1934), p. 14.
[100] NLRB, *Collective Bargaining in the Newspaper Industry,* pp. 145–49.
[101] *Editor & Publisher,* Vol. 67 (June 30, 1934), p. 24.
[102] 2 NLRB 1 (1934).
[103] *Editor & Publisher,* Vol. 67 (Dec. 8, 1934), p. 7.

and the following day the NLRB was requested by NRA General Counsel Donald Richberg to reopen the case. Richberg's action caused the Newspaper Guild representatives to walk out of the hearings on the code. Heywood Broun declared that "as long as the corridors of Mr. Richberg are filled with mysterious, high-pressure representatives of the publishers, we feel that we belong elsewhere." Morris Watson, who had planned to attempt again to procure the inclusion of the press associations under the code, denounced the code as "apparently a sham to cover special privileges for publishers."[104]

The NLRB complied with Richberg's request and reconsidered the Jennings case, but on December 13 reaffirmed its original decision and recommended that the NRA Compliance Division remove the *Call-Bulletin*'s Blue Eagle when the paper failed to reinstate Jennings.[105] Howard Davis, president of the ANPA, stated that the "issue raised by the National Labor Relations Board has precipitated the gravest problem with which the press of the country has yet been confronted."[106] The ANPA scheduled an emergency convention for January and threatened withdrawal from the recovery effort. Before the publishers could act, however, Roosevelt intervened with a letter to the chairman of the NLRB requesting that the Board not assume jurisdiction of cases arising under codes which provided for their own labor boards.[107] The publishers had won. Heywood Broun denounced the President, saying that his letter "means that the Jennings case becomes no more than a pressed flower in our memory book. And we will remember. We feel that it is impossible to dodge the fact that the newspaper publishers have cracked down on the President of the United States, and that Franklin D. Roosevelt has cracked up."[108]

The President's order to remove from the NLRB's jurisdiction all cases arising in industries whose codes provided for labor boards and the resultant blow to the jurisdiction and prestige of the NLRB culminated with the announcement of the district court's opinion in the *Weirton Steel* case, declaring the federal government's jurisdiction over labor relations in manufacturing enterprises unconstitutional. By the end of February, 1935, the NLRB had thus been reduced to a position of almost complete impotence. It was already a "voice crying in the wilderness" when in *Schechter Poultry Corporation* v. *United States*[109] the Supreme Court delivered the *coup de grace* to the whole recovery effort.

[104] *Ibid.* (Dec. 8, 1934), p. 5.
[105] *Ibid.* (Dec. 15, 1934), p. 17.
[106] *Ibid.* (Dec. 29, 1934), p. 1.
[107] *Ibid.* (Jan. 26, 1935), p. 1.
[108] *Ibid.*, p. 11.
[109] 295 U.S. 495 (1935); Lorwin and Wubnig, *op. cit.*, pp. 327–29.

For an administration whose major policy efforts had from the beginning existed under the shadow of unconstitutionality, the Roosevelt administration showed a singular lack of preparation to meet judicial challenges of its program. During the early days of the administration, Frances Perkins had pointed out to Roosevelt that her program would entail legislation which could well be unconstitutional. "Well, that's a problem," he had said, "but we can work out something when the time comes."[110] This ambivalent attitude was reflected in the quality of the legal personnel recruited to policy positions during the early part of the New Deal. The Attorney General was Homer Cummings, who had served as a Democratic national committeeman from Connecticut for twenty-five years and who had been an early Roosevelt supporter. While most of the Connecticut delegation had supported Al Smith, Cummings had served as a Roosevelt floor manager at Chicago in 1932, and his reward was the governorship of the Philippines. The candidate for Attorney General, Tom Walsh, had died suddenly, however, and Cummings, passing through Washington for instructions before leaving for the Philippines, found himself in the cabinet post. Under Cummings, the Justice Department was staffed by many with first-rate political credentials but with second-rate legal ability.[111]

One of these was J. Crawford Biggs, the Solicitor General. A North Carolina Democrat, it was rumored that Biggs had been appointed to the government's most important policy post on constitutional issues because Cummings opposed the appointment of Dean Acheson to the post.[112] Biggs did only mediocre work and is generally blamed for the poor representation the administration received on constitutional issues before the Supreme Court. Chief Justice Hughes on one occasion had to admonish Biggs to present more clearly "what you want this court to do." It was not until mid-March, 1935, that Biggs resigned and was replaced by Stanley Reed, who began a reorganization of the Solicitor General's office. The downfall of the NIRA, however, was already rapidly approaching.[113]

The Recovery Administration had from the beginning met with some resistance from business against the enforcement of the codes and had resorted in many instances to litigation in the lower federal courts. By early 1935, there had resulted a growing stream of decisions declaring

[110] Perkins, *op. cit.*, p. 152.

[111] Joseph Alsop and Turner Catledge, *The 168 Days* (Garden City: Doubleday, Doran and Co., 1938), pp. 25–26; Arthur Schlesinger, Jr., *The Politics of Upheaval* (Boston: Houghton Mifflin Co., 1960), pp. 261–62.

[112] Eugene C. Gerhart, *America's Advocate: Robert H. Jackson* (New York: The Bobbs-Merrill Co., Inc., 1958), p. 85.

[113] Schlesinger, *op. cit.*, pp. 261–62.

NIRA unconstitutional and resulting in increased difficulties of enforcement. In addition, the terms in which the act was denounced by federal judges no doubt encouraged resistance to code enforcement by businessmen already chafing under the myriad of NRA regulations. According to one such judge, the procedure of the Recovery Administration was "enough to shock the sensibilities of a person trained in the belief that we are living under a constitutional government where the citizen is governed by laws and not by men." It would, the judge continued, "cause any citizen to wonder whether he is still living under and is protected by the Constitution of the United States or whether he is in the country of a Stalin, a Mussolini, or a Hitler."[114] Speeches such as this from the lower courts denouncing NRA reminded some of the political involvement of Federalist judges in the early years of the Republic.[115]

In the face of the rising tide of constitutional doubt, the Justice Department was faced in the *Schechter* case with making its defense of NIRA on the basis of a prosecution under the live poultry code, one of the least tenable of the codes. On the Circuit Court level the government's prosecution had been sustained in part, but the Schechter Corporation had petitioned the Supreme Court for a writ of certiorari and the Justice Department was forced to prepare for the test.[116] The case was not, however, entirely hopeless. A year earlier, the government had successfully prosecuted under the Sherman Act a combination of New York live poultry wholesalers, slaughterers, and a local union for conspiring to control the market and to raise prices. The Court had found that the "control of the handling, the sales and the prices at the place of origin before the intended journey begins or in the State of destination where the interstate movement ends may operate directly to restrain and monopolize interstate commerce."[117] From this language, it could reasonably have been assumed that at least some aspects of the live poultry industry were subject to NRA regulation under the commerce clause.

This anti-trust case, plus the *Swift, Olsen,* and *Stafford* cases, were the primary precedents relied on by the government in its commerce argument in the *Schechter* case, but to no avail.[118] The Court found that NIRA was an unconstitutional delegation of legislative power and an exertion of power beyond the commerce clause. "So far as the poultry here in question is concerned," Chief Justice Hughes wrote on the com-

---

[114] *Table Supply Stores* v. *Hawking,* 9 F. Supp. 888 (S.D. Fla., 1935), at 889–90.

[115] Robert H Jackson, *The Struggle for Judicial Supremacy* (New York: Alfred A. Knopf, 1941), pp. 115–16.

[116] *Ibid.,* p. 113.

[117] *Local 167* v. *United States,* 291 U.S. 293, at 297 (1934).

[118] 295 U.S. 495, at 510.

merce question, "the flow in interstate commerce had ceased. . . . Hence, decisions which deal with a stream of interstate commerce— where goods come to rest within a State temporarily and are later to go forward in interstate commerce—and with the regulations of transactions involved in that practical continuity of movement, are not applicable here."[119] The fact that the defendants had violated code provisions on wages, hours, and sales, the Court held, could not constitute practices "affecting" interstate commerce. "In determining how far the federal government may go in controlling intrastate transactions upon the ground that they 'affect' interstate commerce," the Chief Justice wrote, "there is a necessary and well established distinction between direct and indirect effects. The precise line can be drawn only as individual cases arise, but the distinction is clear in principle." The NIRA's regulation of wages, hours, and prices was an attempt to control practices which only indirectly affected interstate commerce and were thus beyond the power of the federal government. To the Court, the restriction of federal regulatory power to the power granted by the commerce clause meant that "the distinction between direct and indirect effects of intrastate transactions upon interstate commerce must be recognized as a fundamental one, essential to the maintenance of our constitutional system."[120]

With Justices Cardozo and Stone concurring in the opinion, the decision of the Court was unanimous. In one blow, the Court had knocked out what had constituted the administration's principal domestic program since 1933.[121] Section 7(a) and the restraint imposed by the recovery effort on employers desiring to discriminate against union members collapsed along with the Recovery Administration and the labor boards. The effect in some businesses was immediate. In Detroit, the Fruehauf Trailer Company ceased to meet with union representatives, and soon foremen were circulating around the plant firing union members on the basis of a list furnished by the company's spy in the union.[122] In Aliquippa, the Jones & Laughlin Corporation resumed the pressure against unionization of its employees to the point that some believed it was greater than before the enactment of NIRA.[123]

Some unions, however, prepared to resist losing any of the ground

[119] 295 U.S. at 543.

[120] *Ibid*. at 546–48.

[121] On the same day the Court also invalidated the Frazier-Lemke Act in *Louisville Bank* v. *Radford*, 295 U.S. 555, and rebuked the President in his attempt to remove a conservative member of the Federal Trade Commission in *Humphrey's Executor* v. *United States*, 295 U.S. 602.

[122] NA–Case No. C-2, Fruehauf Trailer Co., Folder No. I, Memorandum from G. L. Patterson to NLRB, Sept. 24, 1935; Off. Rep. of Proceedings before NLRB —Fruehauf, pp. 19, 513.

[123] Off. Rep. of Proceedings before NLRB—Jones & Laughlin, p. 391.

gained during the NRA period. Sidney Hillman, president of the Amalgamated Clothing Workers, had been warned by his friend Justice Brandeis that NIRA was unconstitutional, and upon hearing a broadcast report of the *Schechter* decision, rolled off a couch laughing, finally recovering enough to say that he "knew this would happen all along." Later, while preparing to leave Washington, Hillman declared that he was "going to raise a war chest of a million dollars through my union to see to it that we hold onto the gains labor has won."[124] The union's general executive board, called into special session, authorized a National Emergency Defense Fund of a million dollars, and organizers were soon being sent into action.[125] By June, 1935, organizers had reached the employees of the Friedman–Harry Marks Company in Richmond, and union meetings were beginning to be held.[126]

Roosevelt expressed surprise at the *Schechter* decision and at the fact that the Court liberals had joined in the opinion. When notified of the decision by telephone, he had asked, "Well where was Ben Cardozo? How did he stand? And what about old Isaiah (Brandeis)?"[127] Four days after the decision, the President attacked the opinion in his press conference for an hour and a half. It contained, he said, "a horse-and-buggy definition of interstate commerce." He had already been forced by events to throw his support behind another policy based on the broad conception of the commerce clause which the Court had rejected. In February, Senator Wagner had reintroduced his bill guaranteeing the right to organize and providing for its enforcement, and it had passed the Senate by a vote of 63–12 eleven days before the *Schechter* decision. Faced with the likelihood that the bill would pass the House with strong labor support, Roosevelt endorsed the bill three days before the Court invalidated NIRA.[128]

With Roosevelt's belated support, the Wagner bill promised to succeed where Section 7(a) and NRA had failed; that is, in effecting a fundamental shift of power between employers and employees. The recovery effort had been based on the recognition of the dominance of employer groups, and in every important test of strength on the issue of the enforcement of Section 7(a), these groups had won. While union membership had increased by almost a million under NRA, the effectiveness of employer countermeasures was demonstrated by the fact that

[124] Josephson, *op. cit.*, pp. 377–80.
[125] Seidman, *op. cit.*, p. 203.
[126] NA–Case No. C-40, Friedman–Harry Marks Co., Folder No. 1, Memorandum from Gerhard Van Arkel to Charles Fahy, Sept. 30, 1935.
[127] Gerhart, *op. cit.*, p. 99.
[128] James MacGregor Burns, *Roosevelt: The Lion and the Fox* (New York: Harcourt, Brace and Co., 1956), pp. 219–23.

membership in company unions had almost doubled since 1933.[129] With the Wagner bill close to passage in Congress, the employers' position of dominance was seriously threatened, and in the spring of 1935, employer groups across the country mobilized for the legislative battle ahead.

---

[129] In 1932 it was estimated that the workers under company union plans numbered about one and a quarter million; by 1934, this number had grown to about two and a half million. See Robert R. R. Brooks, *When Labor Organizes* (New Haven: Yale University Press, 1937), p. 90.

# 4

# PASSAGE OF THE WAGNER ACT

□ □ □ □ □ □ □ □ □ □ □ □ □ □ □ □ □ □ □ □ □ □ □ □ □ □ □ □ □ □ □ □ □ □ □ □ □ □ □ □ □ □ □

WITH MUCH OF THE PRESTIGE OF BUSINESS DESTROYED BY THE economic debacle of 1929, employer groups during the 1930's found themselves reeling under the frenetic pace of the New Deal and the complexity of the anti-depression measures. As the mood of the country shifted to the left and the administration abandoned the business-labor-government unity once symbolized by NIRA, businessmen were placed on the defensive, and feelings of confusion, fear, and anger became common in the business community. "We feel there should be a cessation of more of the so-called reform legislation," one businessman testified in 1934. "We have got mental indigestion, trying to keep up."[1] Senator Wagner's fight to remedy the weaknesses of the NRA labor board system and to provide effective enforcement of labor's right to organize only sent another of a series of chills through employer groups. In January, 1934, William F. Long of the Associated Industries of Cleveland expressed the mood of business in a letter to James A. Emery, general counsel of the NAM. Long feared that "organizations such as yours and mine are not doing all that should be done to fight the determined effort that is certainly going to be made in the present Congress to have the Government actively encourage unions and to make the formation of 'company unions' difficult, if not impossible." In addition, he doubted that the leadership of business groups had adequately warned industrialists of the danger of governmental encouragement of unions and "told them frankly that industry must either put up the financial sinews of war or see the Open Shop destroyed." He suggested that representatives of the National Metal Trades Association, National Founders Association, the Illinois and Michigan Manufacturers' Associations, the Employers' Association of Detroit, and the NAM meet "at least once every fortnight as a sort of war council, for the purpose of

[1] Hearings before the Committee on Education and Labor on S. 2926, 73rd Cong., 2nd sess., p. 577.

72

exchanging opinions and if possible correlating our efforts. I cannot avoid the feeling that we are drifting."[2]

The threat of governmental action against industry and the loss of prestige by business was also worrying others. During the winter and spring of 1934, a retired vice president of the Du Pont corporation and John J. Raskob, a vice president of Du Pont and ex-chairman of the Democratic party, corresponded on the subject of the loss of business prestige and the political threat this entailed. Raskob finally suggested that his correspondent "take the lead in trying to induce the Du Pont and General Motors groups, followed by the other big industries, to definitely organize to protect society from the sufferings which it is bound to endure if we allow communistic elements to lead the people to believe all businessmen are crooks."[3] The result was the formation of the American Liberty League in August of 1934.

During the League's formative stages, a confidential memorandum was circulated among prospective supporters which suggested that "however efficient such an organization may be, it will have great difficulty in accomplishing its work unless it has a moral or emotional purpose, and thereby creates a moral or emotional issue." "Nor do I believe," the author of the memorandum continued, "that many issues could command more support or evoke more enthusiasm among our people than the simple issue of the 'Constitution.' The public ignorance concerning it is dense and inexperienced, but, nevertheless, there is a mighty, though vague, affection for it. The people, I believe, need merely to be led and instructed, and this affection will become almost worship."[4] This was a succinct statement of what was to become one of the principal tactics of the Liberty League and other business groups in their opposition to governmental regulation during the 1930's. In choosing this tactic, these groups could identify their cause with the conception of the Constitution as an immutable document enforced by a powerless, but impartial, judiciary. The traditional theory of the judicial function, sponsored by both bench and bar, had long inculcated in the people this view of an unchanging fundamental law and a passive judiciary. Once again the traditional theories of judicial impotence and conservatism were to travel hand in hand.

Against no other piece of New Deal legislation were business'

---

[2] LaFollette Committee, *Hearings*, pt. 17, p. 7573.

[3] Frederick Rudolph, "The American Liberty League, 1934–1940," *American Historical Review*, Vol. 55, No. 1 (Oct., 1950), p. 19.

[4] Alpheus T. Mason, *Harlan Fiske Stone: Pillar of the Law* (New York: The Viking Press, 1956), p. 443. See also George Wolfskill, *The Revolt of the Conservatives, A History of the American Liberty League 1934–1940* (Boston: Houghton Mifflin Co., 1962), pp. 110–13.

polemics of unconstitutionality directed more urgently than the Wagner Act. Although he had suffered defeat at the hands of the administration when Public Resolution No. 44 was adopted in 1934, Wagner reintroduced his bill in the Senate in February, 1935. The bill had been drafted by Wagner, his staff assistants, and the legal staff of the NLRB. The President, the NRA, and the Department of Labor were not participants, and even the A.F. of L. played only a minor role.[5] The bill guaranteed the right of employees "to self-organization, to form, join, or assist labor organizations, to bargain collectively through representatives of their own choosing, and to engage in concerted activities, for the purpose of collective bargaining or other mutual aid or protection." Employers were forbidden to "interfere with, restrain or coerce" employees in the exercise of this right of self-organization, to "discriminate or interfere with the formation of any labor organization or to contribute financial or other support to it," to discriminate in regard to "hire or tenure of employment or any terms or condition of employment" for the purpose of discouraging membership in unions, and to "discharge or otherwise discriminate" against any employee because he filed charges under the act. It was provided, however, that none of these "unfair labor practices" should prevent an employer from agreeing to a closed shop.

To prevent these unfair labor practices, the bill provided for a National Labor Relations Board composed of three members appointed by the President and serving staggered five-year terms. The Board was empowered to issue complaints against employers charged with committing unfair labor practices, to subpena witnesses and evidence and hold hearings to determine the merits of such charges, and to issue cease and desist orders against employers found to be committing unfair practices. If the order were not obeyed, the Board could petition the federal circuit courts for orders requiring compliance under penalty of contempt, after the court had reviewed the record of the Board's hearing on points of law. The findings of the Board on points of fact, if supported by evidence, were made conclusive.

In addition to prohibiting unfair labor practices, the bill authorized the NLRB to hold representation elections and certify the union selected by a majority of employees concerned as the exclusive bargaining agent for all employees within the bargaining unit. For the purposes of such elections, power was lodged in the Board to determine whether the "unit appropriate for the purposes of collective bargaining shall be the employer unit, craft unit, plant unit, or other unit." Individual employees or groups of employees, however, were permitted to present grievances

[5] Irving Bernstein, *The New Deal Collective Bargaining Policy* (Berkeley: University of California Press, 1950), p. 88.

to their employer. Finally, the Board was given the power to arbitrate labor disputes upon agreement of the parties involved and to file arbitration awards in federal district courts for enforcement.[6]

The drafters of the Wagner bill attempted to hurdle the issue of constitutionality through the use of careful language in a "Declaration of Policy" and in their definition of the terms "commerce" and "affecting commerce." The Declaration of Policy stated two general bases for the policy embodied in the bill. First, it was pointed out that the inequality of bargaining power between employers and employees led to failure "to maintain equilibrium between the rate of wages and the rate of industrial expansion," a condition which "impairs economic stability and aggravates recurrent depressions, with consequent detriment to the general welfare and to the free flow of commerce." Secondly, it was stated that denials "of the right to bargain collectively lead also to strikes and other manifestations of economic strife, which create further obstacles to the free flow of commerce." It was declared to be the policy of the United States to "remove obstructions to the free flow of commerce and to provide for the general welfare by encouraging the practice of collective bargaining. . . ."[7] The interstate commerce aspect of the Declaration of Policy was based on the experience of Congress in drafting the Packers and Stockyards and Grain Futures acts, as well as on the language used by the Supreme Court sustaining these acts in *Stafford* v. *Wallace* and *Chicago Board of Trade* v. *Olsen*.[8] In both cases the Court had stated that it was bound by a declared finding by Congress that certain practices were recurringly utilized in conspiracies which affected commerce, and, in the *Stafford* case, it had held that such a congressional finding could be considered the same as proof of intent to restrain commerce in an anti-trust prosecution.[9]

The Wagner bill defined interstate commerce as "trade or commerce, or any transportation or communication relating thereto, among the several States . . . ," and the term "affecting commerce" was defined as "in commerce, or obstructing the free flow of commerce, or having led or tending to lead to a labor dispute that might burden or affect commerce or obstruct the free flow of commerce."[10] The Board provided for in the

[6] For a copy of the original bill, S. 1958, see National Labor Relations Board, *Legislative History of the National Labor Relations Act* (Washington: Government Printing Office, 1949), Vol. I, pp. 1295–1310. (Hereinafter cited as, NLRB, *Legislative History*.)

[7] *Ibid.*, p. 1295.

[8] 258 U.S. 495 (1922); 262 U.S. 1 (1923).

[9] NLRB, *Legislative History*, Comparison of S. 2926 and S. 1958, pp. 1338–42. See above, Chapter II.

[10] *Ibid.*, 1297–98.

bill was given jurisdiction over any unfair labor practice which affected commerce as described in this definition. Here again the drafters of the bill relied on similar language in the Packers and Stockyards and the Grain Futures acts and the fact that these statutes had been sustained by the Court.[11]

With the drafting of his bill completed, Wagner decided that the best strategy would be to make the major effort for its passage in the Senate, which, because of the election of 1934, had become the more liberal body in Congress.[12] The result was that both the proponents and opponents of the bill concentrated their efforts on the Senate Committee on Education and Labor during the hearing stage and on the Senate itself after the bill reached the floor. The National Association of Manufacturers became the general co-ordinator of the opposition efforts of business groups, and as the date for the hearings approached, letters were sent to leaders of business groups calling for witnesses to appear in Washington "to meet the onslaught of union fostered attacks on industry. . . . This is the most important cooperation the NAM ever asked of you."[13]

The opposition was weakened by the fact that their arguments were simply reiterations of the arguments used in the 1934 hearings and by the fact that an opposition mail campaign directed at Congress reached its peak too soon and faltered before congressional action was taken.[14] As in the 1934 hearings, however, the opponents of the Wagner bill occupied most of the time before the committee. James A. Emery, general counsel of the NAM, opened industry's attack on March 21. "The first day of spring, Mr. Chairman," he said, "is marked by consideration of an exotic in legislation, which we trust will find little favor in your cultivated consideration."[15] Emery's arguments against the bill were again based principally on constitutional considerations. He argued that the bill contravened the tenth amendment by attempting to confer on the federal government jurisdiction over manufacturing and production enterprises which were local in nature and subject only to state regulation; that the bill violated the fifth amendment by interfering with liberty of contract and by authorizing a procedure for the Board which violated the guarantees of due process; and that the bill further violated the fourth and seventh amendments, as well as article III of the Constitution, by delegating judicial power to the Board and by conferring on it an arbitrary

[11] NLRB, *Legislative History*, pp. 1347–48, 1357–58.
[12] Bernstein, *op. cit.*, pp. 88, 100.
[13] LaFollette Committee, *Hearings*, pt. 17, p. 9059.
[14] LaFollette Committee, *Hearings*, p. 14194.
[15] Hearings before the Senate Committee on Education and Labor on S. 1958, 74th Cong., 1st. sess., p. 241.

power of investigation and the power to order reinstatement and back pay for discriminatorily discharged workers.[16]

Following Emery's presentation came a phalanx of opposition from representatives of all types of business and industry. The attacks on the bill, other than constitutional objections, centered on the provision outlawing company unions and the provision authorizing a majority of workers to determine the exclusive bargaining agent for all employees in a collective bargaining unit. It was contended that company unions were generally useful instruments of industrial peace and that the majority rule provision arbitrarily denied the rights of individuals or minority groups of employees.

One of the most effectively organized industrial groups to appear was the steel industry, which began its appearance in opposition on March 26. Appearances by representatives of the Iron and Steel Institute and executives from the individual steel companies were followed by testimony of representatives of the company unions in the steel industry. These representatives testified on the effectiveness of their organizations and the preference of a majority of the steel workers for such representation. The representative of the Jones & Laughlin Employees' Representation Plan at Aliquippa, for example, testified that a majority of workers there preferred the company union and that the Amalgamated Association local was defunct. According to the company union's spokesman, an Amalgamated organizer had been sent to Aliquippa, "but he was withdrawn when the Pittsburgh papers published a story showing that he had been guilty of a criminal assault on his ten-year-old stepdaughter. Two weeks ago one of their members was found guilty of felonious assault and battery in the Beaver Court, after he had stabbed one of our employees because he refused to join the Amalgamated. It is not surprising that our workmen have shown their preference to our plan."[17]

To counter this testimony, the A.F. of L. transported representatives of the Aliquippa local to Washington a few days later. They testified that the local had organized a majority of Jones & Laughlin's employees at Aliquippa, but that there were "men fired just lately for the least little thing, without any reason whatsoever. Our men are scared; and they have—the company—spies all over the street following us."[18]

Despite this protest, the roll call of industry continued. The Automobile Manufacturers' Association[19] entered strong objections to the bill,

---

[16] *Ibid.*, pp. 1629–30.
[17] *Ibid.*, p. 459.
[18] *Ibid.*, p. 665.
[19] Formerly the Automobile Chamber of Commerce.

as did the American Newspaper Publishers' Association, whose representative denounced it as "unfair and one-sided legislation, which amounts, in practical application, to a labor dictatorship."[20] Finally, on April 2, James A. Emery again appeared to round out industry's case on the last day of hearings. Again he attacked the bill on the grounds that its application to production or manufacturing enterprises would be unconstitutional, citing twenty cases in which the lower federal courts had ruled that NIRA could not be applied to such enterprises under the commerce clause.[21] And he reiterated that the bill arbitrarily interfered with liberty of contract, the "right of a man to make a contract to enter into engagements for the sale of his labor or for the sale of his goods or for the sale of his talent or for the sale of his services in any way he pleases. . . ." "Freedom of contract is the rule," Emery declared, "restraint the exception."[22]

Frances Perkins had thought that the leadership of the A.F. of L. would oppose the Wagner bill because of its objections to the basing of recognition on elections and majority rule.[23] Wagner, however, had sold the bill to the federation, and it lobbied effectively for its passage, counteracting the massive assault by industry. On April 29, the A.F. of L. held a conference of four hundred representatives of its international unions who divided into state groups and called upon congressmen urging the passage of the bill.[24] These efforts were rewarded when on May 2 the Senate committee reported the bill favorably with few basic amendments. The committee rewrote the declaration of policy to eliminate any reference to the general welfare in order to base the act wholly on the commerce clause. The rationale that inequality of bargaining power between employers and employees reduced purchasing power, thus tending to produce depressions, was retained, however, and was a constitutional basis for the act at least as important as the theory that the denial of the right to organize tended to lead to strikes affecting commerce.[25] The committee also eliminated the provisions of the original bill giving arbitration powers to the NLRB.[26]

Wagner and his assistants wrote the committee report accompanying the bill, using language which they hoped would guide the courts in ruling

[20] Hearings before the Senate Committee on Education and Labor on S. 1958, 74th Cong., 1st sess., pp. 593, 637.

[21] Ibid., pp. 840–44.

[22] Ibid., p. 853.

[23] Frances Perkins, The Roosevelt I Knew (New York: The Viking Press, 1946), p. 243.

[24] Bernstein, op. cit., p. 111.

[25] NLRB, Legislative History, Vol. II, pp. 2285–86.

[26] Ibid., pp. 2295–97.

on the act.[27] In the section of the report dealing with constitutional issues, the *Texas and New Orleans* case upholding the Railway Labor Act was relied on to rebut objections based on the liberty of contract. On the commerce question, the anti-trust cases involving labor, mainly the *Coronado, Duplex,* and *Bedford* cases, and *Wilson* v. *New, Stafford* v. *Wallace,* and *Chicago Board of Trade* v. *Olsen* were relied upon. "While this bill of course does not intend to go beyond the constitutional power of Congress," the report stated, "as that power may be marked out by the courts, it seeks the full limit of that power in preventing these unfair labor practices. It seeks to prevent them, whether they burden interstate commerce by causing strikes, or by occurring in the stream of interstate commerce, or by overturning the balance of economic forces upon which the full flow of commerce depends."[28]

The Wagner bill failed to attract the support of the administration despite the Senate committee's favorable report. Both the NRA and the Department of Labor were unenthusiastic, as was the Senate majority leader, Joe Robinson. This did not prevent, however, attempts by the administrative agencies to add the powers conferred on the NLRB to their own domains. General Johnson, although opposed to the bill, hoped the Board would be attached to the NRA if it passed. Frances Perkins also hoped the Board would be added to the Labor Department,[29] while the Justice Department, through Senator Robinson, sought to attach an amendment transferring the control of the Board's litigation to the local district attorneys.[30] The Justice Department's attempt at amendment, if it had succeeded, would have had serious consequences in the litigation testing the act's constitutionality, since the Board's ultimate success in this area was based to a great extent on its ability to select its test cases and control their preparation and legal defense from the hearing stage to the Supreme Court.

More important to the bill's chances than this administrative infighting, however, was the failure of Roosevelt to give it his support. He had hardly been consulted on the subject during the early drafting stages,[31] and when Wagner had asked for his support before the bill's introduction, the President had refused.[32] Roosevelt was still adhering to a middle political position which included the NRA concept of business-labor

[27] Bernstein, *op. cit.,* p. 112.
[28] Senate Report No. 573, Committee on Education and Labor, 74th Cong., 1st sess., pp. 17–19.
[29] Perkins, *op. cit.,* pp. 239–40.
[30] NLRB, *Legislative History,* Vol. II, pp. 2319–20.
[31] Perkins, *op. cit.,* p. 239.
[32] Bernstein, *op. cit.,* p. 89.

cooperation, and in the face of the approaching presidential election in 1936 he may have been afraid to lose business support by backing the Wagner bill. In addition, according to Rexford Tugwell, Roosevelt was appealing over the heads of labor leaders, whom he continued to distrust, "on issues other than those having to do with organization. Such matters were absorbing to leaders but not to the rank and file, and Franklin could take advantage of this." The President's sponsorship of social security, Tugwell believes, consolidated a rank-and-file support from labor "that from then on could be counted on. There was nothing labor leaders could do but go along."[33] Thus, even after the Senate committee's favorable report, when Wagner called on Roosevelt, he managed to get only a pledge that the administration would not oppose the bill's coming to the Senate floor. This was enough for the Senator, however, since he was convinced his bill would pass if it came to a vote.[34]

Directing the NAM's campaign against the bill, James A. Emery was also convinced that the bill's prospects were good and that industry's position was desperate. Early in 1934, the NAM's Employment Relations Committee had decided to seek legislation prohibiting "coercion of workers from any source," and Emery decided to attempt to procure such an amendment to the Wagner bill on the Senate floor. "On the Senate side," he wrote privately, "the struggle is yet to divert it, with an effort to secure amendment, if it comes up, that will prohibit coercion or intimidation by 'any person.' We believe, if this amendment is adopted, the labor group would not want the bill, for it would prevent the tactics which they believe essential for their success."[35]

The bill came to the Senate floor for debate on May 14, and two days later the committee amendments were accepted. Senator Tydings of Maryland then offered the NAM–sponsored amendment which guaranteed the right of employees to organize "free from coercion or intimidation from any source." Wagner immediately attacked the proposal, pointing out that the courts in many instances had interpreted "coercion" to include picketing and peaceful persuasion to join a union. Senator Norris joined Wagner in opposition, saying that "the courts are going to construe this measure, if it shall become law, and when they get through with it, as often happens, we may not know our own child." The Tydings amendment was finally defeated by a vote of 21 to 50, and the opposition was forced to switch to constitutional objections to the bill. Senator Hastings of Delaware submitted a brief citing the *Adair-Coppage-*

---

[33] Rexford G. Tugwell, *The Democratic Roosevelt* (Garden City: Doubleday & Co., Inc., 1957), pp. 336–37.

[34] Bernstein, *op. cit.,* p. 115.

[35] LaFollette Committee, *Hearings,* pt. 17, pp. 14056–202.

*Hitchman* line of cases as proof of the measure's unconstitutionality. "It is more or less a joke around the Senate," he said, "that anybody who talks about the Constitution or raises a constitutional question considers himself a constitutional lawyer. From my point of view, one does not have to be anything more than a law student to reach the conclusion that the proposed act is unconstitutional." The constitutional objections, like the NAM amendment, were brushed aside, however, and on May 16 the bill passed the Senate by a vote of 63 to 12.[36]

This overwhelming vote of approval apparently convinced Roosevelt that the bill was sure to pass the House also, and on May 25, after holding a conference with Wagner, Sidney Hillman, John L. Lewis, and administration officials, the President announced his support of the bill.[37] The measure had already been reported favorably by the House Committee on Labor, which had added only one major amendment making the NLRB a part of the Department of Labor.[38] Two days after the President's endorsement of the bill, however, the Supreme Court invalidated the NIRA in the *Schechter* case and by its narrow reading of the commerce clause cast new doubt on the constitutionality of the Wagner bill. The decision buoyed up the hopes of the employer groups opposing the bill but did not lessen their campaign of protest directed against the President and Congress. On May 28, the president of the NAM telegraphed another industrial leader that he believed the "Court decision clearly destroys foundation of the legislation, but proponents are redoubling efforts for such a bill which makes it necessary to keep up telegrams of industrial protest to President. Status in Congress uncertain but until finally disposed of keep up the effort." Another NAM official advised continuance of "every form of expression on House members, especially members of House Rules Committee. . . . Letters to President should emphasize lack of 'coercion from any source provision.' "[39] Publishers, too, feared the measure would pass despite the *Schechter* decision. An American Newspaper Publishers' Association spokesman advised that "some group representing all daily newspaper publishers be equipped to act in their behalf without delay," and The National Editorial Association suggested that publishers "wire their congressmen to call on House leaders and especially on members of the House Rules Committee to prevent issuance of a rule which would ensure a vote on the Bill."[40]

Although the *Schechter* opinion seemed to confirm the constitutional

---

[36] *79 Cong. Rec.* 7648–81.
[37] Bernstein, *op. cit.,* p. 118.
[38] NLRB, *Legislative History,* Vol. II, p. 2946.
[39] LaFollette Committee, *Hearings,* pt. 17, pp. 14206–07.
[40] *Editor & Publisher,* Vol. 68 (June 1, 1935), pp. 3, 11.

tions employer groups had always voiced against his bill, Wagner
_ered with a public statement arguing that the Court's language left
.ᵤ_ within the commerce clause to sustain the bill. "The Court has
made it clear in a long series of decisions," he said, "that the issue of
whether a practice 'directly' affects interstate commerce, and thus is
subject to federal regulation depends more upon the nature of the
practice than upon the area of activity of the business in which the
practice occurs." "It is clear," he continued, "that the *Schechter* decision
limits federal supervision of wages and hours in situations where federal
efforts to maintain industrial peace, and thus to prevent interference with
the physical flow of goods, would be sustained." While giving this public
show of confidence, Wagner was able to have the bill recommitted to the
House Labor Committee for the purpose of redrafting the declaration of
policy and the definitions of commerce in the light of the Court's
action.[41]

As re-reported on June 10, the bill contained a new "Finding and
Policy," which was more careful and more specific in explaining the act's
basis on the commerce clause. The bill now declared that the denial by
employers of the right to organize led "to strikes and other forms of
industrial strife or unrest, which have the intent or the necessary effect of
burdening or obstructing . . . commerce by (a) impairing the efficiency, safety, or operation of the instrumentalities of commerce;
(b) occurring in the current of commerce; (c) materially affecting, restraining, or controlling the flow of raw materials or manufactured or
processed goods from or into the channels of commerce; or (d) causing
diminution of employment and wages in such volume as substantially to
impair or disrupt the market for goods flowing from or into the channel
of commerce." In the new "Finding and Policy," the purchasing power
theory—that is, that the inequality of bargaining power and the employee's lack of "full freedom of association or actual liberty of contract"
reduced wages and aggravated depressions—followed the more specific
argument on the commerce question. Finally, the "Finding and Policy"
stated the finding of Congress that the protection of the right to organize
and bargain collectively "safeguards commerce from injury, impairment,
or interruption, and promotes the flow of commerce by removing certain
recognized sources of industrial strife and unrest. . . ."[42]

As further clarification, the term "commerce" was redefined as
meaning "trade, traffic, commerce, transportation, or communication
among the several States . . . ,"[43] and the term "affecting commerce"

---

[41] Bernstein, *op. cit.*, p. 121–22.

[42] NLRB, *Legislative History*, Vol. II, pp. 3033–34.

[43] *Ibid.*, p. 3035. The bill as passed by the Senate had defined commerce as
"trade, traffic or commerce, or any transportation or communication relating
thereto. . . ." The new draft therefore narrowed the definition somewhat.

was also redefined as meaning "in commerce, or burdening or obstructing commerce or the free flow of commerce, or having led to or tending to lead to a labor dispute burdening or obstructing commerce or the free flow of commerce."[44]

After these changes had been made, the bill was re-reported and given a rule by the Rules Committee on June 18. The Committee's rule allowed consideration of the bill in the Committee of the Whole with debate limited to three hours and with amendments subject to the five-minute rule.[45] Despite the care with which the measure had been redrafted to reinforce its constitutional basis, the opposition's major attack was along constitutional lines. "We have," an opposition member declared, "the remarkable situation of the legislative and executive branches deliberately and willfully engaged in enacting legislation to vest powers in the administrative branch which powers they know the Constitution says are not within the jurisdiction of the Federal Government." Representative Cox of Georgia believed that the "purpose of the measure, as all honest minds must confess, is to circumvent the effect of the recent ruling of the Supreme Court in the *Schechter* case," and another Representative asked, "Is there a good lawyer in this House who for one moment believes that such a law would be upheld by the Supreme Court? Certainly it will not stand. Passing this bill is a futile thing. It is a mere gesture."[46]

The opposition's constitutional arguments were answered principally by Representative Truax of Ohio. The opposition, he said, "talk about the Constitution. If I felt the way some of the constitutional lawyers feel about the Constitution and about the decisions of the Supreme Court, I would be in favor of abolishing the Congress and letting the Supreme Court do the legislating for the people of this country. Mr. Chairman, do you know if you gave the people of this country a vote on some of these decisions of the Supreme Court, the people would sweep the Supreme Court into oblivion by a vote of 100 to 1?" The Court, Truax charged, had failed to think in terms of humanity and thought instead in terms of property rights. Closing his defense of the bill, he castigated the opposition for their interminable constitutional objections and asked, "What are you going to do with this sacred old Constitution? You cannot eat it, you cannot wear it, and you cannot sleep in it."[47]

When the bill was read for amendment, the NAM–sponsored "coer-

---

[44] *Ibid.* The Senate version had read "in commerce, or burdening or affecting commerce, or obstructing the free flow of commerce, or having led or tending to lead to a labor dispute that might burden or affect commerce or obstruct the free flow of commerce."

[45] *79 Cong. Rec.* 9668.

[46] *Ibid.,* 9678–9701.

[47] *79 Cong. Rec.* 9714–15.

cion from any source" amendment was again offered several times but was voted down on each occasion. The committee's amendment placing the NLRB in the Department of Labor was rejected, however, and the provision in the bill describing the units appropriate for collective bargaining as being "the employer unit, craft unit, plant unit, or other unit" was amended to limit the appropriate unit to the employees of one employer.[48] The success of this amendment was probably due to the uneasiness expressed by A.F. of L. leaders on the appropriate unit question. The issue of industrial unionism was growing more serious as the federation's convention, scheduled for October, approached, and Wagner had been forced, in early June, to reassure some of the adamant craft union leaders on the lodging of this crucial power in the Board.[49]

Pressure from publishers was also in evidence when an amendment was introduced by Representative Connery, the sponsor of the bill in the House, which provided that nothing in the act "would abridge freedom of speech or the press as guaranteed by the First Amendment." The publishers had convinced Wagner of the genuineness of their fears that unless such a provision were added to the bill it would imperil a free press. "I suggested it to Chairman Connery for inclusion in the House," Wagner later said of the provision, "although I believed at the time, and still believe, it is not necessary and that the fears are unfounded."[50] With both Wagner's and Connery's sponsorship, the amendment was easily adopted in the House.

Following the "free press" amendment, the House quickly passed the bill by an unrecorded vote. The Senate refused to accept the House amendments and a conference committee was agreed to.[51] The committee, which reported on June 26, accepted the House's rejection of the Board as a part of the Department of Labor and rewrote the provision relating to appropriate bargaining units so that it read "employer unit, craft unit, plant unit, or subdivision thereof," thus narrowing the NLRB's discretion on the issue.[52] The conference committee also spurned efforts by industry, acting through the Secretary of Commerce, to procure adoption of the "coercion from any source" amendment, and agreed to the elimination of the "free press" amendment under pressure from the American Newspaper Guild.[53] "There is no reason," the conference

[48] 79 *Cong. Rec.* 9718–28.

[49] Bernstein, *op. cit.,* p. 126.

[50] *Editor & Publisher*, Vol. 68 (June 29, 1935), p. 3. Here I disagree with Bernstein's excellent analysis, since he states that the pressure for this amendment came from the White House. See Bernstein, *op. cit.,* p. 126.

[51] 79 *Cong. Rec.* 9730–31; 9778; 9864.

[52] National Labor Relations Board, Report No. 1371, House of Representatives, 74th Cong., 1st sess. (June 26, 1935), pp. 2–4.

[53] Bernstein, *op. cit.,* p. 127.

committee report stated, "why the Congress should single out this provision of the Constitution for special affirmation. The amendment could not possibly have had any legal effect, because it was merely a restatement of the first amendment of the Constitution, which remains the law of the land irrespective of congressional declaration."[54]

The report of the conference committee was accepted by both houses on June 27, and the congressional battle was over.[55] Roosevelt signed the bill on July 5, issuing a statement drafted by the Department of Labor and approved by Wagner which again confronted the constitutional issues involved with caution. The Wagner Act, the President said, "does not cover all industry and labor, but is applicable only when violation of the legal right of independent self-organization would burden or obstruct interstate commerce. Accepted by management, labor, and the public with a sense of sober responsibility and of willing cooperation, however, it should serve as an important step toward the achievement of justice and peaceful relations in industry."[56] With Roosevelt's signature affixed to the bill, Wagner's long fight in behalf of labor had come to an end. He had maneuvered the National Labor Relations Act through Congress despite indifference and hostility from the executive branch and a campaign of opposition which was called "the greatest ever conducted by industry regarding any Congressional measure."[57]

Under the terms of the act, employers were now prohibited from interfering with the exercise of their employees' right to organize, from dominating or financing a company union, and from discharging or discriminating in regard to conditions of employment for the purpose of discouraging membership in a union. The act also provided that employers who refused to bargain collectively with their employees were guilty of an unfair labor practice. A majority of employees in any given bargaining unit, on the other hand, could determine the collective bargaining representatives of all the employees in such a unit after an NLRB-supervised election. The greatest test for the Wagner Act, that of its constitutionality, remained to be met, however, and despite the care with which its drafters had handled the issue, those who held the negative position could speak with much assurance in the spring of 1935. The act was essentially a bet on the broad conception of interstate commerce which the Supreme Court had embraced in the *Stafford* and *Olsen* cases and the conception of due process to which the Court had adhered in the *Texas and New Orleans* case. But as the act passed Congress, the Court

[54] National Labor Relations Board, Report No. 1371, p. 6.
[55] 79 *Cong. Rec.* 10259; 10300.
[56] Bernstein, *op. cit.*, p. 127. For the text of Roosevelt's statement, see NLRB, *Legislative History*, Vol. II, p. 3269.
[57] *Ibid.*, p. 110.

appeared to be reading the commerce clause with increasing narrowness. In addition to the doctrine of the *Schechter* case, the Court had also adopted a narrow reading of the commerce power in *Railroad Retirement Board* v. *Alton,* where it invalidated a railroad pension scheme adopted by Congress in 1934.[58]

The act had provided that employee and employer contributions be paid into the federal treasury and that the fund thus established would be used for the pensioning of superannuated railway employees. Coverage was extended to persons in the employ of carriers one year prior to the passage of the act, if they re-entered the service at some future date. In an opinion by Justice Roberts, the Court held that treating the contributions of all railroads as one retirement fund and the extension of coverage to employees who had left the service were denials of due process of law. The act, Roberts said, "is not only retroactive in that it resurrects for new burdens transactions long since past and closed; but as to some of the railroad companies it constitutes a naked appropriation of private property upon the basis of transactions with which the owners of the property were never connected. Thus the Act denies due process of law by taking the property of one and bestowing it upon another."[59]

Having found the act unconstitutional on due process grounds, the Court proceeded to hold it invalid also on commerce grounds. The act's purpose was stated as being "the satisfactory retirement of aged employees," the creation of possibilities for "greater employment opportunity and more rapid advancement," and the "greatest practicable amount of relief from unemployment and the greatest possible use of resources available for said purpose and for the payment of annuities for the relief of superannuated employees."[60] The Court held, however, that the purpose of the act was simply to foster "a contented mind" on the part of railroad employees, and that if such a reason could be allowed for the exercise of the commerce power, "obviously there is no limit to the field of so-called regulation."[61] The act, the Court said, was "an attempt for social ends to impose by sheer fiat non-contractual incidents upon the relation of employer and employee, not as a rule or regulation of commerce and transportation between the States, but as a means of assuring a particular class of employees against old age dependency. This is neither a necessary nor an appropriate rule or regulation affecting the due fulfillment of the railroads' duty to serve the public in interstate transportation."[62]

[58] 295 U.S. 330 (1935).
[59] 295 U.S. at 349–50.
[60] *Ibid*. at 362–63.
[61] 295 U.S. at 368.
[62] *Ibid*. at 374.

The majority in the case was composed of Justices Roberts, McReynolds, Sutherland, Butler, and Van Devanter. Chief Justice Hughes was followed by Justices Stone, Brandeis, and Cardozo in dissent on the grounds that the Court should have sustained the act as an exercise of the commerce power, since the provisions objectionable on due process grounds were separable. "It could not be denied," the Chief Justice wrote, "that the sovereign power to govern interstate carriers extends to the regulation of their relations with their employees who likewise are engaged in interstate commerce. The scope of this sort of regulation has been extensive. There has been not only the paramount consideration of safety, but also the recognition of the fact that fair treatment in other respects aids in conserving the peace and good order which are essential to the maintenance of the service without disastrous interruptions, and in promoting the efficiency which inevitably suffers from a failure to meet reasonable demands of justice."[63] Unfortunately for the proponents of the Wagner Act, these comments were the views of only a minority of the Court. The exercise of regulatory power in relation to the railroads had been one of the most extensive uses of the commerce clause by Congress and one of the uses of the commerce power most readily accepted by the Court. The majority's failure to accept a relation between a pension for railroad employees and the promotion of interstate transportation under the commerce power did not bode well for judicial validation of the Wagner Act's declaration of a broad conception of commerce.

Among the opponents of the Wagner Act, the *Alton* and *Schechter* cases bolstered belief in the act's unconstitutionality and encouraged resistance to its enforcement.[64] In Richmond, Virginia, for example, organizers for the Amalgamated Clothing Workers held a unionization meeting for employees of the Friedman–Harry Marks Clothing Company on June 27. The meeting was held in the Trinity Methodist Church and was addressed by Jacob S. Potofsky, vice president of the ACW, but only eight employees attended. Harry Marks, co-owner of the company, and Irving November, a company superintendent, however, observed the meeting through a window, and the following day four of the eight employees attending the meeting were fired.[65] On July 6, one day after the Wagner Act became effective, an ACW organizer charged that the company officials were of the opinion "that they can not only intimidate

[63] 295 U.S. at 376–77.

[64] Milton Derber and Edwin Young (eds.), *Labor and the New Deal* (Madison: University of Wisconsin Press, 1957), p. 290.

[65] NA–Case No. C-40, Friedman–Harry Marks Clothing Co., Folder No. 1, Memorandum from Gerhard Van Arkel to Charles Fahy, Sept. 19, 1935; Miscellaneous Correspondence Folder, Letter from Charles C. Webber to Bennet Schauffler, June 29, 1935.

their workers and fire them unjustly, but that they can also violate the
Wagner labor disputes bill and the social pronouncements of Jewish,
Catholic and Protestant religious leaders, all of which declare that the
workers have the right to organize and bargain collectively."[66] ACW
officials were soon pressing the NLRB for action as the company
continued its anti-union campaign. In Detroit, this pattern of employer
resistance was the same, as the Fruehauf Trailer Company continued the
firing of union members among its employees. About forty employees
had been discharged before the effective date of the act, but others were
to follow, and many resigned from the union because of threats from
company officials.[67]

The resistance of employers such as the Fruehauf and Friedman–
Harry Marks companies to recognition of the rights guaranteed by the
Wagner Act was complemented by broader attacks by employer groups
on the constitutionality of the act as well as resistance to any action by
the NLRB. Having decided upon the issue of the Constitution as a
defensive tactic, the Liberty League and other hostile groups soon issued
public and private briefs holding the act invalid and encouraging a legal
attack which sought to stymie the Board at every turn. Thus, employer
groups which had effectively resisted enforcement of the right to organize
during the NRA period, but had lost the crucial congressional battle over
the passage of the Wagner Act, were now forced to pursue their aims in
the area of legal and constitutional adjudication.

[66] Richmond *Times Dispatch* (July 6, 1935), p. 1.
[67] NA–Case No. C-2, Fruehauf Trailer Co., Folder No. 1, Memorandum from
G. L. Patterson to NLRB, Sept. 24, 1935.

# 5

# ORDEAL BY LITIGATION

□ □ □ □ □ □ □ □ □ □ □ □ □ □ □ □ □ □ □ □ □ □ □ □ □ □ □ □ □ □ □ □ □ □ □ □ □ □ □ □ □ □ □ □

THE MOST IMMEDIATE PROBLEM AFTER THE PASSAGE OF THE Wagner Act was the creation of adequate and effective machinery for its enforcement in a hostile legal and constitutional environment. The President did not appoint the members of the National Labor Relations Board until late August, 1935. As Chairman, Roosevelt selected J. Warren Madden, a professor of law at the University of Pittsburgh. The other two members of the Board were John M. Carmody, a member of the National Mediation Board, and Edwin S. Smith, a former member of the Public Resolution No. 44 NLRB. The infant agency was fortunate in that there was left over from the old NLRB an experienced staff which alleviated many of the problems that would have been serious had the agency been forced to build from the ground up. Because of the dominance of the legal problem, however, it was necessary to create a competent legal staff and integrate it with the older administrative organization.[1]

Charles Fahy, former chairman of the Petroleum Labor Board and Assistant Solicitor of the Department of Interior, was recruited by the Board as General Counsel, and a conference of the regional staff was soon called for the purpose of organizing for the legal battle ahead. The staff was principally composed of specialists in labor problems and included few lawyers. It was decided, therefore, despite some expression of mistrust of lawyers by staff members, to appoint in each regional office a regional attorney who would work with the regional director of his region but would be under the immediate supervision of the General Counsel in Washington to insure that the early crucial work of the Board would be performed with legal competence.[2]

[1] National Labor Relations Board, *First Annual Report* (June 30, 1936), p. 14. (Hereinafter cited as NLRB, *First Annual Report*.)
[2] Louis G. Silverberg (ed.), *The Wagner Act: After Ten Years* (Washington: The Bureau of National Affairs, 1945), J. Warren Madden, "The Birth of the Board," pp. 36–37.

The Board thus organized for a battle of approximately two years during which the constitutional basis of the statute it was attempting to enforce would be in doubt. The overwhelming opposition of employer groups forced the new agency to operate in a constant glare of usually unfavorable publicity throughout this period. As Malcolm Ross, the Board's Director of Information, wrote later, the NLRB during this period, "in three words, caught unmitigated hell."[3] The creation of the LaFollette Committee in June, 1936, however, had the effect of counter-acting some of this discrediting publicity. The Committee was authorized to investigate denials of the civil rights of labor and turned out a volume of startling material on the labor espionage, strike-breaking, and indus-trial munitions industries which many large corporations had been sup-porting.[4] The Board clearly recognized the importance of the counter-acting publicity supplied by the Committee and during the period 1936–37 loaned a total of thirty-four investigators at the cost of $25,481 to the Committee.[5]

In addition to the flood of adverse publicity, the Board was further handicapped when its clientele group, organized labor, split into two warring camps in the fall of 1935 and reduced the support which a unified labor movement would otherwise have supplied it. The issues of industrial versus craft unionism and the organization of the mass pro-duction industries had seriously threatened the cohesion of the A.F. of L. since the beginning of the New Deal, and John L. Lewis, president of the United Mine Workers, had become the acknowledged leader of those elements within the federation which advocated a vigorous drive using the industrial form of organization in the mass production indus-tries.[6] Lewis was particularly concerned with the steel industry, since as long as it remained unorganized, he believed the mine workers' position to be threatened. In addition, the steel industry was the acknowledged leader of anti-unionism in the country, and the leaders of the industrial union faction within the federation knew that an organizing drive must be effective in steel to be successful elsewhere.[7]

In the 1934 A.F. of L. convention, the report of president Tighe of the Amalgamated Association of Iron, Steel and Tin Workers that only 5,300 recruits of the 1933–34 NIRA-inspired drive in the steel industry remained in the union spurred Lewis to propose that the organization of

---

[3] Silverberg, *op. cit.*, Malcolm Ross, "The G—— D—— Labor Board," p. 68.
[4] *Ibid.*
[5] Hearings before the Special Committee to Investigate the NLRB, House of Representatives, 76th Cong., 3rd sess., p. 5790.
[6] Herbert Harris, *Labor's Civil War* (New York: Alfred A. Knopf, 1940), p. 33.
[7] Walter Galenson, "The Unionization of the American Steel Industry," *International Review of Social History*, Vol. I, pt. 1 (1956), p. 9.

the industry be taken out of Tighe's hands.[8] The convention concurred and resolved to issue charters for the organization of the mass production industries and at "the earliest possible date inaugurate, manage, promote and conduct a campaign of organization in the steel industry." The problem of the division of the workers thus organized among the various trades which claimed jurisdiction over them was to be determined by the A.F. of L. executive council.[9] The experience under this compromise was disappointing in autos and rubber,[10] and by January, 1935, Tighe was writing Lewis that he was "firmly convinced by the experience of the past 18 months that to make any headway, plants must be organized industrially."[11]

The issue was still unresolved when the federation held its convention at Atlantic City in October, 1935, three months after the passage of the Wagner Act. The majority of the resolutions committee, however, again adopted a proposal similar to the 1934 convention resolution, but a minority report urged that in the "great mass production industries and those in which the workers are composite mechanics, specialized and engaged upon classes of work which do not qualify them for craft-union membership, industrial organization is the only solution. . . . "[12] With the issue clearly drawn, the A.F. of L. now faced a clear-cut decision on the question which would finally split the labor movement. Lewis, eloquent as always, spoke for the adoption of the minority report, asking the delegates to heed "this cry from Macedonia that comes from the hearts of men. Organize the unorganized and in doing this make the A.F. of L. the greatest instrument that has ever been forged to befriend the cause of humanity and champion human rights."[13] Again the steel industry was pointed to as an example of the failure of craft unionism in mass production industries. Phillip Murray, a vice president of the UMW, told the convention that 8,000 employees at the Jones & Laughlin Aliquippa plant had organized themselves into an independent industrial union and had refused to accept craft union charters from the A.F. of L.

The craft unionists would not be swayed by the oratory of the industrial unionists, however, and the majority report was adopted by a vote of 18,204 to 10,933.[14] The following day, the industrial union faction,

[8] Edward Levinson, *Labor on the March* (New York: Harper & Brothers, 1938), p. 71.

[9] *Ibid.*, p. 113.

[10] *Ibid.*, pp. 88–96.

[11] Galenson, *op. cit.*, p. 8.

[12] Levinson, *op. cit.*, pp. 108–09.

[13] *Ibid.*, p. 113.

[14] *Ibid.*, p. 114. See also Galenson, *op. cit.*, p. 10.

led by Lewis, Sidney Hillman of the Amalgamated Clothing Workers, and David Dubinsky of the International Ladies' Garment Workers Union, met and planned the Committee for Industrial Organization. In January, 1936, the A.F. of L. executive council condemned the CIO and later expelled the participating unions from the federation. The unity of the American labor movement was at an end.[15]

The first goal of the CIO was the organization of the steel industry. Through a protracted series of negotiations, the CIO persuaded president Tighe of the Amalgamated Association to confer his union's jurisdiction over the industry on the CIO-sponsored Steel Workers Organizing Committee. Supported by a loan of $500,000 from the UMW, the SWOC was soon spending $45,000 per week and using over a hundred full-time organizers in a drive to organize steel.[16] Similar campaigns were soon undertaken by the CIO in autos, rubber, and other mass production industries.

The effect of this split in the labor movement on the NLRB was soon felt, especially on the question of determining the appropriate bargaining unit where the choice was all too often a choice between the craft and industrial forms of unionism. Thus, by November, 1937, the A.F. of L. was denouncing the NLRB as having "disrupted tried and tested principles of collective bargaining" and having "brought turmoil and havoc into industrial relations, usurped the prerogatives of the courts essential to our democratic form of government, and jeopardized industrial freedom and initiative."[17] The most severe attacks on the Board growing out of labor's disunity came after the crucial period of doubt as to the Wagner Act's constitutionality, however, and the Board was able to gain from labor leaders in this early period agreement not to press it for action in cases which might have been embarrassing from a legal or constitutional standpoint.[18] Probably the most serious consequence of labor's civil war during this period, therefore, was the dissipation of considerable effort and attention in inter-union rivalry which would have been better spent in support of the Board.

A disunited labor movement and the LaFollette Committee could aid the NLRB but very little in its most immediate task of answering the constitutional objections being raised by employer groups against the Wagner Act, because settlement of the issue of the constitutionality of the act could be accomplished only by a decision in the courts. The

[15] Levinson, *op. cit.*, pp. 117–20.
[16] Galenson, *op. cit.*, pp. 15–16.
[17] Levinson, *op. cit.*, p. 234.
[18] Silverberg, *op. cit.*, p. 39.

earliest and most publicized attack came with the publication in September, 1935, of the Liberty League's report demonstrating the Act's complete invalidity.[19] The report was drafted by a committee of eight lawyers under the chairmanship of Earl F. Reed, a prominent attorney known widely as a counsel for steel corporations,[20] but it was issued under the signatures of fifty-eight corporation lawyers, among them being James M. Beck, former United States Solicitor General, and John W. Davis, the Democratic presidential candidate in 1924. The purpose of the report was apparently to make an impression, on both the public and the courts, which, as one writer said, "could not be made by separate law review articles written by the few who actually drafted the report for the fifty-eight."[21] In addition, the practical effect of the report was to present to the Board's potential legal adversaries a canned brief demonstrating the Act's unconstitutionality.

The report opened with a discussion of the *Schechter* case and a defense of the Court's emphasis on the distinction between "direct" and "indirect" effects on interstate commerce in that case. Purely local affairs might affect commerce indirectly, the report said, but this "is no excuse for attacking the Court for distinguishing between commerce and that which is not commerce, a distinction which the Constitution required it to obey."[22] The report emphasized that the Court, in interpreting the commerce clause and other provisions of the Constitution, was only carrying out the mandate which the people had imposed upon themselves. "We have, ourselves," it said, "deliberately created limitations on our powers as a people, not merely to restrain our governors, but also to restrain our own temporary beliefs and enthusiasms. Settled opinions of the people, in the long run, will and do make use of the machinery which the Constitution itself provides for its amendment, but in brief periods of temporary frenzy, the Constitution and the Supreme Court justly hold us to the limits that we, ourselves, have established."[23]

On the commerce question, the Liberty League report argued that the *Texas and New Orleans* case had not overruled the *Adair* case and thus that even in the field of interstate transportation, where the rationale and

[19] National Lawyers Committee of the American Liberty League, *Report on the Constitutionality of the National Labor Relations Act* (Sept., 1935). (Hereinafter cited as *Report.*)

[20] Carroll R. Daugherty, Melvin G. DeChazeau, and Samuel S. Stratton, *The Economics of the Iron and Steel Industry* (New York: McGraw-Hill Book Co., 1937), Vol. II, p. 1065, note 1.

[21] Thomas Reed Powell, "Fifty-eight Lawyers Report," *New Republic,* Vol. 85 (Dec. 11, 1935), pp. 120–21.

[22] *Report,* p. 7.

[23] *Ibid.,* p. 108.

precedent for the validity of congressional regulation were the strongest, the Wagner Act was invalid.[24] It was further argued that the *Stafford* and *Olsen* cases were highly isolated applications of the commerce clause to local activities and could not be interpreted as sustaining the regulation of employer-employee relations contemplated by the Wagner Act.[25] The report concluded, therefore, that "relations between employers and employees, whether peaceful or hostile, may have some bearing upon interstate commerce, but the bearing is too remote to permit of regulation. A succession of speculative possibilities cannot substitute for the direct relation the cases discussed require."[26]

The second basic objection of the fifty-eight lawyers to the act was its alleged violation of the liberty of contract as guaranteed by the fifth amendment. The lawyers felt that the provisions of the act regarding unfair labor practices represented an unconstitutional attempt to "force a novel economic policy" into the employer-employee relationship. First, it was believed that the provision by which a majority of employees could determine the exclusive bargaining agent for a given group of employees violated the right of individuals or minority groups to make their own contracts. Secondly, the Act's provisions prohibiting employers from discharging or discriminating against union members were held to be violations of the employers' right to contract and to select their own employees as protected by the doctrine of the *Adair* and *Coppage* cases.

According to the report, these clearly unconstitutional provisions could not be excised and leave a workable piece of legislation. The separability provision, therefore, could not save the Act from being considered unconstitutional as a whole.[27] "We have examined the Act," the committee said, "with a view to expressing our opinion as to its constitutionality and whether or not it represents a departure from our established system of government. . . . Considering the Act in the light of our history, the established form of government, and the decisions of our highest Court, we have no hesitancy in concluding that it is unconstitutional and that it constitutes a complete departure from our constitutional and traditional theories of government."[28]

Financed chiefly by the Du Pont family and the General Motors group, the Liberty League as a "nonpartisan organization founded to defend the Constitution" attained a membership of about 150,000 at its peak and spent about a million dollars denouncing New Deal measures

[24] *Ibid.,* pp. 58–62.
[25] *Ibid.,* p. 91.
[26] *Ibid.,* p. 101.
[27] *Ibid.,* pp. 113–26.
[28] *Ibid.,* pp. x–xi.

in constitutional terms. Although its founders had originally planned to include divisions of farmers, laborers, investors, etc., in the League's organization, the National Lawyers Committee was to remain the only subsidiary. Because of its obvious advocacy of the aims of the upper economic stratum of the country, the League's political potentiality was quite limited, and Republican Party leaders considered it too much of a liability to have it as an ally in the 1936 presidential campaign.[29] Its report on the Wagner Act, however, since it presented to employers a constitutional rationale for their desire to escape the consequences of unionization, must be counted as a major factor in the severity of the legal attack on the NLRB and the Act during 1935–37.

Like the Liberty League's National Lawyers Committee, the NAM's Law Department was quick to assure NAM members that the Wagner Act was invalid. In July, 1935, the NAM distributed twelve thousand copies of a legal opinion advising industralists on the constitutional issues raised by the Act.[30] The NAM's brief was more cautious on the commerce question than the Liberty League had been. The brief advised only that the Act "does not apply to employment relations between a manufacturer and his employees engaged in ordinary manufacturing operations. The Act is based upon the power of Congress to regulate interstate and foreign commerce. Manufacturing is not commerce at all. Commerce does not begin until manufacturing has ended. The employment relations at issue arise *in production* and not intercourse. This rule has been uniformly adhered to by the Supreme Court of the United States."[31]

The Act, however, was entirely invalid, according to the brief, under the fifth amendment. "By denying to an individual employee his fundamental right to bargain or contract with his employer," the brief said, "without associating with a group, we believe the majority rule principle is invalid for reasons expressed by the Supreme Court of the United States in *Adair* v. *U.S.* . . . and *Coppage* v. *Kansas*. . . . " The NAM advised employers that should a complaint be issued against them by the NLRB, they should be careful to make a full and complete response to the charge and clearly state their reservations as to the jurisdiction of the Board. "It will be well to consider," the brief said, "even in cases where it is believed the Board has no jurisdiction, whether appearance should be made, directly or through counsel, for the purpose of seeing that the

---

[29] Frederick Rudolph, "The American Liberty League, 1934–1940," *American Historical Review*, Vol. 55, No. 1 (Oct., 1950), pp. 19–31. See also George Wolfskill, *The Revolt of the Conservatives, A History of the American Liberty League 1934–1940* (Boston: Houghton Mifflin Co., 1962).

[30] LaFollette Committee, *Hearings*, pt. 17, p. 7440.

[31] *Ibid.*, p. 7589.

*record* is accurate and complete. It must be remembered that on appeal the courts will review the record made before the Board, and in some cases the nature of the record may determine the character of the court's decision."

In addition to these instructions on the constitutional issues and procedural questions raised by the Act, the NAM also distributed posters to its membership for the purpose of informing employees of the nature of the Act. The posters advised employees (1) that the Act did not apply to all industry; (2) that an employer was not required to sign an agreement; (3) that the Act did not require employees to join a union; (4) that an employee could not be discharged for failing to join a union under a non-closed shop contract; (5) that company unions, organized by employees, were legal; (6) that the act did not give the federal government the power to set working conditions; and (7) that the act did not impair the employer's right to discharge for incompetence or promote for aptitude. By posting this material, the NAM said, the employer might not only escape "unjustified labor disputes by fostering some intelligent self-thinking by employees, but serve notice on outside agitators that the employer will not, through ignorance, be coerced into agreement with unwarranted demands backed by unenforceable threats."[32]

The NAM also formed in 1935 the National Industrial Information Committee as a result of polls it had conducted which revealed that the prestige of American business was extremely low with the general public.[33] Under the chairmanship of Ernest T. Weir of the Weirton Steel Company, the Committee solicited contributions from industrialists with the warning that the "hazard facing industrialists is the newly realized power of the masses. Unless their thinking is directed toward sane and established measures we are definitely headed for adversity." The "information program" thus instituted by the NAM concentrated primarily on popularizing classical economics, attacking the expansion of governmental power, and defending laissez-faire constitutionalism.[34]

The NAM and the Liberty League were the leaders in the campaign of constitutionalism against the Wagner Act, but more specialized employer groups soon followed. Elisha Hanson, general counsel of the American Newspaper Publishers Association, had characterized the act soon after its passage as "unconstitutional beyond question or doubt,"[35] but the ANPA withheld a legal brief on the act until the fall of 1936, when the NLRB had begun to assume jurisdiction over

[32] *Ibid.*, pp. 7596–97.

[33] *Ibid.*, pp. 7458, 7687–92.

[34] *Ibid.*, pp. 7693–95. See also Richard W. Gable, "NAM: Influential Lobby or Kiss of Death?", *Journal of Politics*, Vol. 15 (May, 1953), p. 254.

[35] *Editor & Publisher*, Vol. 68 (June 29, 1935), p. 3.

cases in the newspaper industry. Then, in an opinion printed and distributed to publishers, editors, and managing editors throughout the country, Hanson advised that publishers "should flatly refuse to have anything to do with the National Labor Relations Board, other than to notify it it is without power under the Constitution to interfere with their business." "There is," Hanson said, "in so far as the business of the press is affected by its terms, the question as to whether Congress has the power to vest an agency of the government with authority to dictate to publishers whom they shall or shall not employ. If the law is valid, that authority has been conferred on a Board, and without limitation. Such a power is now being exercised by the Hitler government in Germany." Hanson assured publishers, therefore, that "no order of the Board directed to a publisher requiring him to comply with a decision thereof will, if contested, be upheld by the courts."[36]

In addition to circulating Hanson's brief, the ANPA, through its Standing Committee on Labor, informed publishers that the act was invalid and advised them to "tell any National Labor Relations Board representative coming into contact with them that the Board is without jurisdiction and to refuse to deal with such representative."[37] Publishers were also requested by the ANPA to refuse to sign contracts with editorial employees which contained closed shop provisions, provisions which meant the "regimentation of his news or editorial employees in favor of any political party or other pressure group," or provisions establishing conditions "designed to embarrass a competitor."[38]

While the ANPA's reaction to the Wagner Act thus closely followed those of the Liberty League and the NAM, the Iron and Steel Institute adopted a different tactic in dealing with the threat of unionization. Facing the Steel Workers Organizing Committee drive in the industry, the Institute selected as its line of defense the maintenance of the industry's company unions. Steel companies had uniformly adopted the company union (employee representation plan) with the inauguration of NRA and had discovered it useful not only as a means of warding off "outside" unions but also as a managerial technique.[39] Thus, in June, 1936, the Institute spent about a half million dollars for advertisements in 375 newspapers defending the company unions before the public and warning against the consequences of the SWOC campaign.[40] The SWOC's object, the advertisements asserted, was "the 'closed shop,'

[36] *Editor & Publisher,* Vol. 69 (Oct. 10, 1936), pp. 7, 49.

[37] *Ibid.* (Oct. 17, 1936), p. 9.

[38] *Ibid.,* (Dec. 12, 1936), p. 12.

[39] Robert R. R. Brooks, *As Steel Goes . . . Unionism in a Basic Industry* (New Haven: Yale University Press, 1940), pp. 78–79.

[40] Levinson, *op. cit.,* p. 190.

which prohibits the employment of anyone not a union member. The Steel Industry will oppose any attempt to compel its employees to join a union or pay tribute for the right to work." The employees in the steel industry, the Institute said, had elected representatives under their employee representation plans, which had proven themselves effective as devices for peaceful employer-employee relations. "The Steel Industry," the advertisements said in closing, "will use its resources to the best of its ability to protect its employees and their families from intimidation, coercion and violence and to aid them in maintaining collective bargaining free from interference from any source."[41]

This publicity campaign by the Institute was probably a strategic blunder, since its effect was to put the industry in the position of publicly refusing to abide by the Wagner Act and to focus attention on the SWOC drive.[42] It also resulted in a division within the Institute on the question of the desirability of the publicity campaign, a division which was later reflected in the industry on the question of granting recognition to the SWOC.[43]

Another threat to the NLRB was the use by other employer groups of legal briefs demonstrating the Wagner Act's unconstitutionality. As soon as the Board began to accept complaints in October, 1935, it was faced with a flood of injunction suits encouraged by these briefs. The Board's newly recruited legal staff was put under a heavy strain in opposing these suits in federal district courts in most of the major industrial centers of the country. The first suit for an injunction against the Board was filed in November, and the ordeal by litigation began. "The process was like a rolling snowball," the Board reported later. "The allegations in a pleading filed by an employer in Georgia, for example, would show up in precisely the same wording in a pleading filed in Seattle. There came a very rapid and widespread exchange of pleadings all over the country until all had exhausted their ingenuity in conjuring up the many and gross injuries which it was alleged a hearing before the Board would entail."[44]

The NLRB's contention was that the Act provided the procedure for judicial review of its proceedings and that there was afforded adequate opportunity for aggrieved parties to challenge its actions on legal and constitutional grounds when the circuit courts were petitioned to enforce an order.[45] Counsel for employers were nevertheless able to convince many district court judges that their clients would suffer irreparable in-

[41] "It Happened in Steel," *Fortune*, Vol. 15 (May, 1937), pp. 91–94.
[42] Levinson, *op. cit.*, p. 191.
[43] "It Happened in Steel," *op. cit.*, p. 94.
[44] NLRB, *First Annual Report*, p. 48.
[45] *Ibid.*, p. 47.

jury even from a Board hearing. Thus, a federal district judge in Missouri enjoined an NLRB hearing on a complaint against an employer for failure to bargain collectively and ruled the entire act unconstitutional. "The individual employee," he said, "is dealt with by the act as an incompetent. The government must protect him even from himself. He is the ward of the United States to be cared for by his guardian even as if he were a member of an uncivilized tribe of Indians or a recently emancipated slave." Further, the judge said, the act was not a valid regulation of commerce. "Manufacturing is not commerce. Nothing is more firmly established in constitutional law than that." He did not believe that any individual "could be found who seriously will maintain that interstate commerce *directly* is affected by the manner in which an employer bargains with his employees." Since it was unconstitutional on due process and commerce grounds, the judge held that the Act as a whole, including the procedure for judicial review of Board orders, was invalid, and an injunction should be issued.[46]

The major danger of this type of litigation was that, if a substantial number of courts could be persuaded to issue injunctions against the Board's proceedings, the selection of test cases through the careful choosing of businesses against which to issue complaints and compile adequate hearing records would be greatly handicapped. The Board was faced with about one hundred such suits from the fall of 1935 to the spring of 1937, with the threat of paralysis by injunction being considerably heightened during 1936 when the Supreme Court announced decisions which cast even graver doubts on the Wagner Act's validity.[47] With these decisions, the constitutional thesis embodied in the briefs of the Liberty League, the NAM, and other employer groups seemed to be almost completely confirmed by the Court.

In January, the Court renewed its slaughter of New Deal legislation by invalidating the Agricultural Adjustment Act in *United States* v. *Butler*.[48] The AAA had laid a tax on the processors of agricultural products, the proceeds of which were used to support commodity prices and induce farmers to reduce production of surplus products. Over scathing dissents by Justices Stone, Cardozo, and Brandeis, the majority of the Court held that the act could not be considered a taxing measure but was instead an attempt to regulate agricultural production, an activity not within the power of the federal government. The principal blow to the chances of the Wagner Act came, however, when in May the Court invalidated the Bituminous Coal Conservation Act of 1935 (Guffey

---

[46] *Stout* v. *Pratt,* 12 F. Supp. 864, at 867–71 (W.D. Mo., 1935).
[47] *First Annual Report,* p. 48; for a list of injunction suits see pp. 56–59.
[48] 297 U.S. 1 (1936).

Act).[49] This act was essentially an attempt to salvage from the NIRA system adequate regulation of the badly depressed soft coal industry. The statute provided that the mining areas of the country were to be divided into districts and that codes prescribing minimum prices be drafted for each district. To insure adherence to these codes the measure provided for a fifteen per cent tax on all coal mined, ninety per cent of which would be refunded to operators observing the code regulations. The act also guaranteed the right of employees to organize and provided that a majority vote by the employees in each district would determine the exclusive collective bargaining agent for all employees in a given district. When producers of two-thirds of the tonnage mined within a district had agreed to wage standards through collective bargaining, the act provided that these wage standards would be accepted by all code members within the district. A Bituminous Coal Labor Board was also established for the purpose of enforcing the right to organize as guaranteed by the act.

The Guffey Act was subjected to condemnation in a Liberty League report utilizing much the same constitutional arguments which had been directed against the Wagner Act.[50] Challenged before the Court in *Carter* v. *Carter Coal Company,*[51] the counsel for the company also argued that the collective bargaining provisions of the Guffey Act were "a regulation of production and not a regulation of interstate commerce, and are even more remotely connected with interstate commerce and more indirect in their effect thereon than the attempted regulation of wages and hours of miners." Appearing for the government, Assistant Attorney General John Dickinson argued to the contrary that "labor relations in this industry . . . are not merely connected with competition in interstate commerce; and that their relationship to this aspect of the industry is far more important and significant than their relation to the mere physical removal of the coal from the ground."[52]

The Court, in a majority opinion by Justice Sutherland, reiterated the doctrine that coal mining and manufacturing did not constitute commerce and found the entire act unconstitutional. "The employment of men, the fixing of their wages, hours of labor and working conditions, the bargaining in respect of these things," Sutherland wrote, "whether carried on separately or collectively—each and all constitute intercourse for the purposes of production not of trade. The latter is a thing apart from the relation of employer and employee, which in all producing occu-

[49] 49 Stat. 991.
[50] National Lawyers Committee of the American Liberty League, *Report on the Constitutionality of the Bituminous Coal Conservation Act of 1935* (Dec., 1935).
[51] 298 U.S. 238 (1936).
[52] *Ibid.* at 247, 267.

pations is purely local in character." The labor provisions of the act, the Court held, "including those in respect of minimum wages, wage agreements, collective bargaining and the Labor Board and its powers, primarily fall upon production and not commerce; and confirms the further resulting conclusion that production is a purely local activity. It follows that none of these essential antecedents of production constitutes a transaction in or forms any part of interstate commerce. . . . Everything which moves in interstate commerce has had a local origin. Without local production somewhere, interstate commerce, as now carried on, would practically disappear. Nevertheless, the local character of mining, of manufacturing and of crop growing is a fact, and remains a fact, whatever may be done with the products."[53]

The Court rejected the government's arguments, which relied on the anti-trust cases and the *Swift, Stafford,* and *Olsen* flow of commerce cases as a basis for sustaining the act. The anti-trust cases, it said, concededly dealt with local activities, but they involved conspiracies which had an intent to restrain commerce. Only "superficially considered" did they lend constitutional support to the Guffey Act. Nor were the flow cases in point either. "If the court had held that the raising of cattle, which were involved in the Swift & Co. case," Sutherland wrote, "including the wages paid to and working conditions of the herders and others employed in the business, could be regulated by Congress, that decision and decisions holding similarly would be in point: for it is that situation, and not the one with which the court actually dealt, which here concerns us."[54] Again, the Court emphasized that wages, hours, working conditions, and the employer-employee relationship, no matter how disruptive strikes relating to these questions might be, were essentially local relations and could affect commerce only indirectly. "The relation of employer and employee," Sutherland said, "is a local relation. At common law, it is one of the domestic relations. . . . Working conditions are obviously local conditions. The employees are not engaged in or about commerce, but exclusively in producing a commodity. And the controversies and evils, which it is the object of the act to regulate and minimize, are local controversies and evils affecting local work undertaken to accomplish that local result. Such effect as they may have upon commerce, however extensive it may be, is secondary and indirect. An increase in the greatness of the effect adds to its importance. It does not alter its character."[55]

Because the labor provisions were an inseparable part of the Guffey

[53] *Ibid.* at 303–304.
[54] *Ibid.* at 304–306.
[55] *Ibid.* at 308–309.

Act's regulatory scheme, the Court held, their invalidity rendered the act as a whole void in spite of the separability clause. Chief Justice Hughes concurred in part with the majority, believing the labor provisions to be invalid, but he believed them to be separable from the price-fixing and production control features of the act.[56] Justice Cardozo, joined by Stone and Brandeis in dissent, rejected the majority's adherence to the direct-indirect effects formula and argued for an approach to commerce questions which would allow a more realistic consideration of the facts in individual cases in determining if local practices affected commerce. A great principle of constitutional law, Cardozo said, "is not susceptible of comprehensive statement in an adjective. The underlying thought is merely this, that 'the law is not indifferent to considerations of degree.' "[57] The minority's appeal for a more flexible basis for decision-making by the Court could not, however, obscure the fact that six of the Justices apparently felt that labor relations in manufacturing and mining enterprises was completely outside the scope of federal power and that under the doctrine of the *Carter* case the Wagner Act could not be applied to such enterprises.[58]

With the *Carter* case thus casting doubt upon any but a very limited application of its provisions under the commerce clause, the Wagner Act suffered another blow to its constitutional basis when the Court reaffirmed the liberty of contract doctrine of the *Adkins* case in *Morehead v. New York*.[59] In holding unconstitutional New York's minimum wage law for women, the Court in a five-four decision held that in "making contracts of employment, generally speaking, the parties have the equal right to obtain from each other the best terms they can by private bargaining. Legislative abridgement of that freedom can only be justified by the existence of exceptional circumstances. Freedom of contract is the general rule and restraint the exception."[60] The Chief Justice dissented on the ground that the statute could be distinguished from the one involved in the *Adkins* case, while Justice Cardozo, again joined by Stone and Brandeis, attacked the majority in a sharp dissent. But from the *Morehead* case it appeared that the majority of the Court was still insistent upon adhering to a rigid doctrine of liberty of contract which, unlike the *Carter* decision, threatened the Wagner Act's validity in its entirety.

[56] *Ibid.* at 317–21.

[57] *Ibid.* at 327.

[58] Lloyd K. Garrison, "The Constitution and the Future," *New Republic*, Vol. 85 (Dec. 29, 1936), p. 328. For a business reaction, see Lawrence Stafford, "The Ghost of Section 7(a)," *Nation's Business*, Vol. 24 (July, 1936), p. 28.

[59] 298 U.S. 587 (1936).

[60] *Ibid.* at 610–11.

As a result of these disappointing decisions and the widespread injunctive attack on its jurisdiction, the NLRB began in the spring of 1936 to consider the necessity of reducing its operations in the manufacturing and production industries on the grounds that a continuance of such activities would only result in giving false hopes to workers in these industries.[61] The seriousness of the Board's position is suggested by the proposal of one staff member that the Board continue hearings in doubtful industries as an aid to unionization drives, even though decisions based on these hearings would ultimately be voided. "NLRB at present sits on its triple throne," he said, "a bit like the church shorn of its right to prosecute and hang. Despite the loss of temporal power, NLRB can still thunder from the pulpit and excommunicate from the congregation of the righteous. That comforts the flock, disconcerts the heathen,—and marks down the latter against the day of wrath to come. Relegate metaphysics to the Supreme Tribunal, and get on with good works?" Another alternative that was suggested was that the Board present its cases before the LaFollette Committee when it found itself enjoined from proceeding. "It ought not to take more than one or two such hearings," the proposal said, "to make companies hesitant about rushing to courts for injunctions, at least as far as hearings go."[62]

In spite of these possible alternatives, the Board issued in May, 1936, an order requiring its regional staffs to reduce hearings in doubtful industries and instructing them to subject new cases "to more careful scrutiny than they have been in the past." The regional staffs were also instructed that the case which "should get first preference in preparation and hearing, is that involving interstate transportation and communication. . . ." It was anticipated that because of this reduction in activities the confidence of labor in the Board might be shaken, but the regional staffs were urged to cooperate fully in the effort to retain it.[63]

Although these were the darkest days for the NLRB, there were some bright spots in an otherwise gloomy legal and constitutional picture. First, the uniformity of the pleadings in the injunction suits against the Board which had permitted the rapid resort to this tactic in widely scattered areas also aided the Board's legal staff in meeting the suits. Because of this uniformity of pleadings, the legal staff could, after a time, "prepare the appropriate pleadings in detail as soon as it got wind of the filing of a suit."[64] The NLRB was thus able to win almost three-fourths of the in-

[61] Hearings before a Special Committee to Investigate the NLRB, House of Representatives, 76th Cong., 3rd sess., pp. 4256–58.

[62] *Ibid.*, p. 4317.

[63] *Ibid.*, pp. 5542–44.

[64] Silverberg, *op. cit.*, p. 44.

junction cases on the district court level, and, during this early period, all but one of these cases on the circuit court level.[65] Also, an employer's petition for a writ of certiorari to review a denial of an injunction by the lower federal courts was denied by the Supreme Court in October, 1936.[66]

On the broader front of testing the Act's constitutionality, the Board was given what would become a major tactical advantage when in July, 1935, a federal district court in Virginia upheld the 1934 amendments to the Railway Labor Act in *System Federation* v. *Virginian Railroad Company*.[67] The 1934 amendments had outlawed company unions on the railroads and empowered the National Mediation Board to hold elections to determine the exclusive bargaining agent for any given class of railroad employees.[68] The Virginian Railroad had formed a company union among its mechanical employees in 1922, but in 1934 an A.F. of L. union demanded recognition as the bargaining agent of these employees. Pursuant to the 1934 amendments, the National Mediation Board held an election and certified the A.F. of L. union as the legitimate bargaining agent, but the railroad refused to bargain with the union, forcing the latter to procure an injunction from the federal district court. The injunction ordered the railroad to refrain from interfering with its employees' right to organize and to refrain from negotiating with any other organization.[69]

The employees involved in the *Virginian Railroad* case were so-called "back shop" employees who were engaged in the repair of equipment temporarily out of service in interstate commerce. Thus the litigation presented questions on the validity of the application of the Railway Labor Act's provisions guaranteeing the right to organize and providing for majority rule to employees not directly engaged in work on the railroads. This litigation paralleled the cases testing the constitutionality of the Wagner Act, and the Board was able to cite the *Virginian Railroad* case at strategic moments in its own litigation.[70] The case would also be

[65] NLRB, *First Annual Report,* p. 49; the circuit court case was *Pratt* v. *Stout,* 85 F.2d 172 (CCA 8th, Aug. 5, 1935). A total of 95 injunction suits were filed against the Board during this period. The federal district courts refused to issue injunctions in 73 of the 95 suits, and of the 31 appeals from such rulings, the circuit courts sustained the lower court's denial of an injunction in 30 cases and reversed the lower court's ruling in only one. See NLRB, *Second Annual Report* (1937), p. 31.

[66] *Bradley Lumber Co.* v. *NLRB,* 299 U.S. 559 (Oct. 12, 1936).

[67] 11 F. Supp. 621 (DC, E.D. Va., 1935).

[68] Irving Bernstein, *The New Deal Collective Bargaining Policy* (Berkeley: University of California Press, 1950), p. 50.

[69] 300 U.S. at 539–41.

[70] The 1934 amendments were upheld on the circuit court level in *Virginian Railroad Co.* v. *System Federation,* 84 F.2d 641 (CCA 4th, June 18, 1936).

argued before the Supreme Court at the same time as the Wagner Act cases and again probably had the effect of bolstering the Board's assertion of jurisdiction over unfair labor practices in clearly interstate enterprises.

This, then, was the broader environment of conflict in which the Board set out to test the validity of its statute and the limits of its power. The attacks of the Liberty League, the NAM, and other employer groups on the Wagner Act had encouraged a massive injunction attack on the Board, but because of its success in meeting these suits and because of the refusal of the lower federal courts generally to sustain such suits, the Board was able to maintain the procedure provided by the act as the method by which it would finally be tested. This meant the retention by the NLRB of the power to select the cases upon which appeal to the courts would be made—an important, perhaps crucial, advantage. As the Wagner Act cases approached the Supreme Court, however, it remained to be seen whether the briefs of the employer groups had been more effective in the broader sense of influencing the courts than they had been in restraining the NLRB by injunction.

# 6

# THE WAGNER ACT CASES

□ □ □ □ □ □ □ □ □ □ □ □ □ □ □ □ □ □ □ □ □ □ □ □ □ □ □ □ □ □ □ □ □ □ □ □ □ □ □

UNLIKE THE GOVERNMENT AGENCIES INVOLVED IN THE CASE OF NIRA, the National Labor Relations Board was prepared to proceed with a test of the Wagner Act's constitutionality as rapidly as circumstances permitted, but, having learned from the government's experience in the *Schechter* case, the Board was cognizant of the need to present to the Supreme Court cases which would picture the constitutional issues in the best possible light. "We were aware," Warren Madden wrote later, "that the Supreme Court case in which the NIRA had been held invalid had become popularly known as the 'sick chicken case.' We did not intend to allow ourselves to be maneuvered into a litigation in which we would be asserting that it was necessary to draw upon the vast arsenal of the national power in order to bring under control a situation which could, in fact, be quieted with a pop-gun."[1]

Since the fifth amendment liberty of contract objections to the act would, if sustained, result in its invalidation as a whole, the Board was initially determined to select a strong interstate commerce case upon which to gain a quick constitutional test on the issue. If the act were sustained under the fifth amendment, there would at least be assurance that it could be applied to obviously interstate businesses, such as bus companies; and its applicability to more doubtful areas, such as manufacturing enterprises, could be tested later.[2] The first case over which the NLRB asserted jurisdiction involved, therefore, a complaint against the Pennsylvania Greyhound Lines, Inc., charging the company with discharging union members and dominating a company union. The Board held hearings on the case in late October, and in December it issued a decision finding the company guilty of unfair labor practices and ordering it to

[1] Louis G. Silverberg (ed.), *The Wagner Act: After Ten Years* (Washington: The Bureau of National Affairs, 1945), J. Warren Madden, "The Birth of the Board," p. 39.
[2] *Ibid.*, pp. 39–40.

106

cease and desist from engaging in such practices and to reinstate the discharged employees. "Operated as an integrated system through traffic agreements, interline tariffs, connecting schedules and joint advertising," the Board said, "the Greyhound Lines presents striking similarities to our national railroad systems."[3] Thus the case was as close as practicable to the railroad situation involved in the *Texas and New Orleans* decision. The Board petitioned the Third Circuit Court of Appeals for an enforcement order on December 10, 1935, believing it had a very good interstate commerce case upon which to test the fifth amendment objections to the Act.[4]

## THE FRUEHAUF CASE

Almost simultaneously with the *Greyhound* case, the Board had taken jurisdiction of its first manufacturing case, which involved a charge of unfair labor practices against the Fruehauf Trailer Company in Detroit. The case had come to the attention of the Board as early as September, when the company, continuing its efforts to rid itself of employees belonging to the A.F. of L. auto workers union, had discharged seven employees after the effective date of the Act. On September 24, an organizer for the A.F. of L. auto workers union had notified G. L. Patterson, the Board's regional attorney in Detroit, of the company's antiunion policies. Patterson was soon enthusiastic about the case as one in which to test the NLRB's jurisdiction over manufacturing enterprises. "The investigation thus far made," he reported to the Board, "seems to indicate that proof of a flagrant discrimination is clear. Apparently the employer assumed a brazen attitude in the assertion of its reason for discharging the Union men instead of attempting to conceal the reason by some other excuse. For a manufacturing case, it appears that this one has some very favorable possibilities."[5] In addition, Patterson discovered that the Fruehauf company was being prosecuted under the Interstate Commerce Act on twenty-five charges of falsifying billings in interstate commerce. He urged the Board not to take action immediately, since the federal district attorney believed the company planned to plead guilty. "Obviously," Patterson said, "this Company is not going to be in a good position to resist the Board's jurisdiction after having entered a plea of guilty to an indictment charging a violation of the interstate commerce act. With the background of strong facts already received establishing

---

[3] In the Matter of Pennsylvania Greyhound Lines, Inc., 1 NLRB 1, at 3.

[4] NLRB, *First Annual Report*, p. 50. See also Silverberg, *op. cit.*, pp. 39–40.

[5] NA–Case No. C-2, Fruehauf Trailer Co., Folder No. 1, Memorandum from Patterson to NLRB, Sept. 24, 1935.

unfair labor practices and these facts regarding interstate commerce, I am very enthusiastic about the case."[6]

During the next few days, Patterson interviewed at the regional office the employees discharged by the Fruehauf company. J. N. Martin, the company's spy in the union, also appeared at the Board's office and volunteered to testify at any hearing that might be held.[7] A union member who had not yet been discharged by the company was seen by Martin at the office and the following week was also discharged. Martin, however, had by this time been spotted by the union members, and within a few weeks after the NLRB's investigation began, the company made a point of discharging him in the presence of other employees. He then disappeared, but not without the union's treasury of thirty dollars.[8] After hearing the testimony of the discharged men, Patterson reported to the Board that he was convinced that "this case should be one of the first the Board handles. If the company opposes our jurisdiction upon the ground that interstate commerce is not affected, we will certainly have more facts and be in a position to make a better argument than we will be in many other manufacturing cases."[9] The men who had been discharged, Patterson reported, "are sound, straight forward, truthful, and apparently hard-working men. As witnesses, they can be placed in the category of good witnesses. All of them appear to be men who give full value for the wages which they receive."[10]

The Board was apparently convinced, and on October 23 a complaint charging the Fruehauf Trailer Company with unfair labor practices was issued. The regional office gave the issuance of the complaint immediate publicity because the employees at the company were in an angry mood, and it was hoped the Board's action would head off a strike, "which in this case would have indicated that the Union believed that they would have to resort to direct action and did not have much confidence in the ability of the Board to punish."[11] The regional director, Frank H. Bowen, announced to the press that the case was the first manufacturing case over which the Board had asserted jurisdiction. "Consequently," he said, "the case is suited for a test on the constitutionality of the Wagner bill before the United States Supreme Court."[12] The Fruehauf company's

<hr>

[6] Memorandum from Patterson to NLRB, Sept. 26, 1935.

[7] Letter from Patterson to Warren Madden, April 22, 1936.

[8] Official Report of the Proceedings before the NLRB, In the Matter of Fruehauf Trailer Co., pp. 355, 619, 761-74. (Hereinafter cited as Off. Rep. of Proceedings before NLRB–Fruehauf.)

[9] Memorandum from Patterson to Charles Fahy, Oct. 2, 1935.

[10] Memorandum from Patterson to NLRB, Oct. 4, 1935.

[11] Memorandum from Patterson to Benedict Wolf (Secretary of NLRB), Oct. 23, 1935.

[12] Detroit Times, Oct. 24, 1935, p. 1.

counsel, Victor W. Klein, stated that "the employees were involved solely in the manufacturing operation and had nothing to do with transportation. The Supreme Court decision outlawing the NRA stated that manufacturing is strictly a local affair. On this basis we feel that this Act is entirely unconstitutional." "Further," Klein added, "we deny that the employees were discharged because of union activities. We don't care whether they belong to any union. However, we do claim the right to get rid of a worker who does not properly do his work."[13]

After the filing of the charge, preparations were begun immediately for the hearing. In the garnering of evidence of the interstate commerce implications of the company's operations, the Board was confronted with the possibility that if it sought to subpena company officers in order to gain such information, the company's counsel might seek an injunction against the enforcement of the subpena, causing a delay in the proceedings and perhaps forcing a defense of the act's constitutionality in such a suit. This was to be a continuing problem in many of the Board's early cases, and as a result it usually sought to build its interstate commerce evidence from sources other than testimony or materials from the companies involved. Added to this problem in the *Fruehauf* case was the alleged antagonism of local judges in Detroit toward the Board. "Inquiry has been made regarding the tendencies of the local Judges," Patterson reported, "and I have found that they are inherently antagonistic to New Deal legislation." He suggested, therefore, that resort to compulsory process would be avoided if possible.[14]

The importance which was attached to the *Fruehauf* case was indicated when the members of the Board announced that they would come to Detroit to hear the case. Patterson received careful instructions from Washington on the manner in which the evidence on interstate commerce, espionage, and the discharges should be built. It was suggested that he put in the interstate commerce evidence first and then call his best witness among the discharged employees, because "if cross-examination of the first witness is not particularly fruitful, the opposition oftentimes will neglect to cross-examine a witness appearing later who might be less able to withstand cross-examination."[15] Patterson himself continued to be enthusiastic about the case, reporting to the Board that "Fruehauf obviously contemplates contesting the case on the merits, which is decidedly pleasing to me. . . . Undoubtedly the officers of this Company will be present at the hearing. If they are, I contemplate calling them for cross-examination because I feel reasonably cer-

---

[13] Detroit *News,* Oct. 24, 1935, p. 1.
[14] Memorandum from Patterson to Charles Fahy, Oct. 21, 1935.
[15] Memorandum from Robert Watts to Patterson, Oct. 30, 1935.

tain that their own testimony will convict them."[16] The company's counsel, Victor Klein, was also confident, however, that if the Board found his client guilty of unfair labor practices on the basis of the hearing, the circuit court would not sustain the Board's order. He was convinced, therefore, that the best procedure was not to file an injunction suit but to allow the case to proceed as rapidly as possible into court.[17]

With the Michigan Manufacturers' Association appearing as an intervener in behalf of the Fruehauf company, the hearings were held on November 6 through 8. Klein allowed Earl L. Vosler, vice president of the company, to testify on the nature of the company's operations, and, although Patterson was not allowed to introduce the company's plea of guilty to the indictment under the Interstate Commerce Act, he presented further evidence on the company's operations as they affected interstate commerce. This evidence demonstrated that the Fruehauf Trailer Company was the largest truck trailer manufacturer in the United States, maintaining thirty-one branch offices in twelve states and grossing over three million dollars in sales in 1934. More than 50 per cent of the materials used by the company in manufacturing trailers came from outside Michigan, and more than 80 per cent of its products were shipped out of the state. The company also had a registered trade-mark which it had declared in its application was used in interstate commerce.[18]

Following the introduction of this evidence, Klein argued his motion to dismiss on the grounds that the Wagner Act was unconstitutional, using a brief later described by Patterson as appearing "to be a series of blank pages to which were pasted clippings." "I have a suspicion," he said, "that said clippings came out of the brief of the National Liberty League."[19] Chairman Madden continually interrupted Klein's points of law, finally warning him that he was arguing a grave constitutional question and that "the best we can expect of you is that you will deal frankly with the precedents and that you talk to the Board about those precedents as the courts actually talked in them."[20] Klein, however, persisted in his argument that under the decisions of the Supreme Court an employer had complete liberty to discharge any em-

[16] Memorandum From Patterson to Charles Fahy, Oct. 31, 1935.
[17] Letter from Patterson to Robert Watts, Feb. 13, 1936.
[18] Off. Rep. of Proceedings before NLRB–Fruehauf, pp. 20–200; this evidence is summarized in In the Matter of Fruehauf Trailer Co., 1 NLRB 68, at 69–72. The use of respondent's declarations on trade-mark applications or in registrations of stock with the SEC was a favorite device used by the NLRB to bolster its interstate commerce evidence.
[19] Memorandum from Patterson to Charles Fahy, Nov. 12, 1935.
[20] Off. Rep. of Proceedings before NLRB–Fruehauf, p. 200.

ployee for any reason. "As long as we have a Supreme Court and Constitution," he said, "I think the due process clause is fixed, and the employer and employee relationship is fixed."[21]

Klein's motion to dismiss was overruled by the Board, and Patterson re-called Earl Vosler to the stand to question him on the spy the company had planted in the union. Klein objected to the questioning, but the counsel of the Michigan Manufacturers' Association disagreed. "We know no reason," he said, "why any employer desiring to know the facts in his plant, should not have the right to hire a detective."[22] Following this statement of the Association's position, Patterson was able to extract from Vosler a full account of the spy's operations since he had been hired in 1934.[23] The account obviously shocked the Board, and it brought an angry outburst from member John Carmody.

> Mr. Carmody: We heard a good deal yesterday about fundamental Americanism and constitutionalism and a good deal about the danger that the workmen all over the country are in if such an act as the Wagner Act were declared constitutional, and we heard a good deal about due process and about the right to take a man's life and liberty and property away from him without due process of law. Would you say if a man was discharged because he was mentioned in one of these secret reports, that that could be due process?
>
> Mr. Vosler: I don't know.
>
> Mr. Carmody: I don't know either and I ask your counsel if a man would be given the benefit of due process if he lost his job by reason of one of these secret reports?
>
> Mr. Klein: Yes. An employer is not required to have any one in the plant that he does not care to have.[24]

Because of Vosler's testimony, the regional director felt that the Board had "won the case on the Company's testimony before we have put one of our witnesses on the stand."[25] After Vosler's testimony, the discharged men were called and testified with regard to their dismissals by company officials, who openly admitted union membership as the cause.[26]

On December 12, the Board concluded from the record that the Fruehauf Trailer Company had engaged in interference with its employees' right to organize, and it ordered the company to cease and

---

[21] *Ibid.,* p. 241.
[22] *Ibid.,* p. 277.
[23] *Ibid.,* pp. 288–311.
[24] *Ibid.,* p. 317.
[25] Memorandum from Frank H. Bowen to Benedict Wolf, Nov. 7, 1935.
[26] Off. Rep. of Proceedings before NLRB–Fruehauf, pp. 255–776.

desist from discrimination against union members and to reinstate the seven discharged employees with back pay for time lost.[27] The company filed a petition with the Sixth Circuit Court of Appeals to have the Board's order set aside, while the Board filed a petition of enforcement almost simultaneously. In a letter to the clerk of the court, the Board urged that the court hear the case as soon as possible, pointing out that the case "was fully tried and raises almost every constitutional objection to the National Labor Relations Act which has been publicly advanced. Not only have lawyers' committees and manufacturers' associations made public statements that in their opinion this Act is wholly unconstitutional, but various applications have been made to District Courts throughout the United States for injunctions against the the Board's proceedings, which applications are usually predicated upon the alleged invalidity of the law. . . . We therefore believe that the most grave reasons of public policy justify us in asking of the Court the very earliest hearing possible. This would permit us to obtain not only a ruling of the Circuit Court on these issues, but also would permit the submission of those constitutional issues by an aggrieved party to the Supreme Court at its Spring session."[28] In addition to entering this request for speed, the NLRB attorneys were making sure the court clerk was favorably disposed toward the Board. One suggested that the Washington office send the clerk "a letter with a little baloney in it, for he is quite fond of the aforementioned article"; he had also discovered that the clerk did not possess a Washington phonebook and requested that one be sent, so that it could be presented to him "on behalf of the Board."[29]

From the letter to the court expressing the hope that the case could be decided in time to be before the Supreme Court in the spring term, it is clear that the Board desired that the *Fruehauf* case either accompany or immediately follow the *Greyhound* case to the Court. Indeed, the letter to the circuit court had pointed out that district courts were "enjoining the Board from proceeding until the constitutionality of the Act may be determined, while on the other hand we have only the Fruehauf case and one case in the Third Circuit in which it will be possible to obtain from the appellate courts a determination of these constitutional issues."[30] The Board was encouraged when the circuit court sustained a lower court's denial of an injunction against it; one attorney remarked that having won one case, "I think we had better

[27] 1 NLRB 68, at 80.

[28] Letter from Robert Watts to Clerk of CCA 6th, Jan. 3, 1936.

[29] Memorandum from Philip G. Phillips to Robert Watts, Jan. 13, 1936.

[30] Letter from Robert Watts to the Clerk of CCA 6th, Jan. 3, 1936; the case referred to in the Third Circuit was the *Greyhound* case.

leave the old buzzards alone."[31] The court refused to rush the case, however, and it was not argued until June 2. The importance attached to the case was again demonstrated when the Solicitor General, Stanley Reed, intervened in behalf of the government and argued the case before the circuit court. The Board's hopes in the case were buoyed up not only by Reed's participation but by the validation by the Fourth Circuit Court of Appeals of the 1934 amendments to the Railway Labor Act in the *Virginian Railroad* case[32] on June 18. Noting that the opinion was "very helpful both on commerce and due process," Charles Fahy rushed it to a regional attorney with instructions to "place copies of the opinion in the hands of the judges who have the *Fruehauf* case under consideration just as soon as possible."[33]

Reed's effort and the *Virginian Railroad* case were not enough to convince the court, however, and on June 30 it denied the Board's petition for enforcement in a brief *per curiam* opinion. "Since the order is directed to the control and regulation of the relations between the trailer company and its employees in respect to their activities in the manufacture and production of trailers," the court said, "and does not directly affect any phase of interstate commerce in which the trailer company may be engaged, and since under the ruling of *Carter* v. *Carter Coal Co.* . . . the Congress had no authority or power to regulate or control such relations between the trailer company and its employees, the National Labor Relations Board was without authority to issue the order."[34]

The Board had thus lost the first court test of its jurisdiction over manufacturing enterprises. The defeat in the circuit court in the *Fruehauf* case and the defeats which were to follow in other manufacturing cases, however, meant that the Board retained control over these crucial cases as far as an appeal to the Supreme Court was concerned, since a petition for a writ of certiorari would have to come from the NLRB. Thus the Board could not be forced to defend its manufacturing jurisdiction before the Court in weak cases not of its own choice. Meanwhile the *Greyhound* case had not been decided in the Third Circuit, giving the NLRB more time in which to select other cases to use in testing its jurisdiction over manufacturing enterprises. The Board was thus soon moving against the Jones & Laughlin Steel Corporation.

[31] Memorandum from Philip G. Phillips to Robert Watts, Feb. 7, 1936; the case referred to was *NLRB* v. *Bemis Brothers Bag Co.*, (Unreported case, federal district court, E.D., Tenn.; CCA 6th).

[32] *Virginian Railroad Co.* v. *System Federation*, 84 F.2d 641 (CCA 4th, June 18, 1936).

[33] Memorandum from Fahy to Philip G. Phillips, Jan. 25, 1936.

[34] *NLRB* v. *Fruehauf Trailer Co.*, 85 F.2d 391 (CCA 6th, June 30, 1936).

## THE JONES & LAUGHLIN CASE

In June, 1935, Jones & Laughlin held elections for representatives under its employee representation plan, while Harry Phillips, the president of the Amalgamated Association local in Aliquippa, and other union leaders urged a boycott of the election by the employees. The company countered by exerting great pressure on its employees to turn out for the election. Clinton S. Golden, who had served under the old NLRB and long kept an eye on developments at Aliquippa, noted reports that "the Company went to considerable effort to get the employees to vote, that Company police were sent to the homes of the workers and there threatened them with discharge unless they did participate in the election, and that in fact some twenty odd employees were dismissed for refusing to participate." It seemed to Golden that "there is a very real possibility of trouble developing."[35]

Trouble did develop the following month when the company began to discharge the leaders of the union, giving as the reason rather negligible infractions of company rules. The first to go was Martin Dunn, a charter member of the union and a crane operator, who was discharged on July 9 for leaving the key to his crane on a bench in violation of company rules. Next came Harry Phillips, the president of the union, who was discharged for failure to answer a whistle while he was in the restroom, and a few days later, Angelo Volpe, the union's vice president, was discharged for operating his crane on the basis of head signals from his helper, rather than the required hand signals. Seven more of the union's leaders were discharged over the months from July through January: Domenic Brandy, the leader of Aliquippa's Italian community; George Royal Boyer, a leader of the Negro workers; Martin Gerstner, financial secretary and charter member of the union; Ronald Cox, a charter member; Angelo Razzano, who had signed up fifteen hundred members for the union; and Eli Bozich, a leader of the Croatian workers and a charter union member.[36]

In answer to complaints by the union, the company said that the "cases have all been fairly investigated and the men were discharged for cause."[37] Accordingly a charge of unfair labor practices was filed

[35] NA–Case No. C-57, Jones & Laughlin Steel Corp., Folder No. 1, Memorandum from Golden to old NLRB, June 28, 1935.

[36] Official Report of the Proceedings before the National Labor Relations Board, In the Matter of Jones & Laughlin Steel Corp., pp. 118–381. (Hereinafter cited as Off. Rep. of Proceedings before NLRB—Jones & Laughlin.) For a summary of the testimony see 1 NLRB 503, at 511–16.

[37] *Ibid.*, p. 381.

by the local with the NLRB on January 28, 1935. Jones & Laughlin immediately secured as its counsel Earl F. Reed, who had been chairman of the committee which had drafted the Liberty League report condemning the Wagner Act. Clinton Golden, who had been retained as regional director by the Board, began to worry about the prospective hearing on the discharges. "I am sure you realize," he wrote the Board, "that Jones & Laughlin is one of the major units in the steel industry, that Earl Reed is their attorney, and that the case is bound to be fought vigorously by the Company. While our Regional Attorney is a bright and intelligent chap, he has been out of college only a little over a year. I am inclined to believe that this case may be one of the most important ones coming before the Board, and I would personally feel a lot safer if he had some assistance on handling same."[38] He also requested that the Board not use M. W. Acheson, who had heard an earlier case for the Board, as the trial examiner in the Jones & Laughlin hearing, because Acheson was already overburdened with work and because "Earl Reed, counsel for Jones & Laughlin Steel Corp., is an ex-partner and deadly enemy of Mr. Acheson."[39] In addition, Golden suggested that expert testimony be introduced by the Board in the hearing, again warning that "Mr. Earl Reed is their attorney, and I am inclined to believe this case will be of major importance."[40]

Reed was busy elsewhere at the time the Board's complaint was issued and requested a postponement of the hearing, which was scheduled for February. Reed's request was granted, but the Board was able to extract a *quid pro quo.* Thanking the Board for the postponement, Reed assured it that he had "asked them at the plant to be particularly careful that nothing occurs to change the situation during the month of adjournment, and it is also understood that we will not ask for any injunction against the holding of the hearing, although our appearance may be a special appearance."[41] On February 20, Reed again requested that the hearing be postponed, but this time his request was refused, and a week later the Board announced that it would come from Washington to Pittsburgh to hear the case.[42]

At the hearing, the Board's attorney introduced evidence purporting to show the interstate nature of the company's operations, but Reed objected to any evidence on the merits of the case before he obtained a determination on the jurisdictional issue. He put on company officials

[38] Letter from Golden to Robert Watts, Jan. 29, 1936.
[39] Memorandum from Golden to NLRB, Jan. 16, 1936.
[40] Memorandum from Golden to Benedict Wolf, Jan. 29, 1936.
[41] Letter from Reed to Warren Madden, Jan. 29, 1936.
[42] Telegrams from Reed to Madden and from Madden to Reed, Feb. 20, 1936.

and attempted to establish that only raw materials entered the plant and that only manufacturing operations took place within the plant.[43] Reed then moved to dismiss on the grounds that the NLRB lacked jurisdiction over manufacturing enterprises:

> Mr. Reed: That is all the evidence that respondent has on the question of the interstate commerce feature of the case, and we move to dismiss, on the ground that the evidence adduced by the Board and also that adduced by respondent, shows conclusively, within the decisions of the courts, that the business of the respondent is not interstate commerce, and any labor controversy, therefore, would not be within the jurisdiction of the Board. Further, the complaint only complains of matters of hiring or discharging employees, which is a matter that is not interstate commerce, even if it related to any agency in interstate commerce, and it seems clear to us that there is no jurisdiction in this case.
>
> Mr. Madden: It would be very interesting, Mr. Reed, to hear you argue this question, but I suppose you do not care to do it, and I doubt whether we can take the time to do it. We are quite definitely committed to the doctrine that an enterprise such as has been shown, both by the government's evidence and by your own evidence here, is in a situation where its labor relations do affect interstate commerce, within the meaning of the Act, and so your motion to dismiss is denied.
>
> Mr. Reed: With respect to the specific complaints relating to employees, the respondent takes the position that it is the sole judge of the right to hire and fire, and that it is not subject to the Board in that respect, and therefore, declines to offer any testimony on that subject and withdraws from the hearing. We will stand on our legal position that the Board has no jurisdiction in this case.[44]

The evidence introduced by the Board and the company had shown Jones & Laughlin to be the fourth largest steel producer in the United States, with gross assets valued at more than 181 million dollars and with over 22,000 employees, 10,000 of whom were employed at the Aliquippa plant. The company was shown to be a completely integrated steel manufacturer, owning iron ore, coal, and limestone properties in Michigan, Minnesota, Pennsylvania, and West Virginia, and owning railroad and river barge subsidiaries. Approximately seventy-five per cent of its products were shipped out of the state of Pennsylvania to its subsidiaries scattered across the country.[45]

[43] Off. Rep. of Proceedings before NLRB—Jones & Laughlin, pp. 1–102.
[44] *Ibid.*, pp. 101–03.
[45] *Ibid.*, pp. 1–102, 408–54; for a summary of this evidence, see In the Matter of Jones & Laughlin Steel Corp., 1 NLRB 503, at 504–506.

Following Reed's withdrawal, the discharged men were called, and they testified on the history of intimidation in Aliquippa and their own discharges. The hearing ended on March 14 but was reopened in Washington for additional testimony from April 2 through 8. The evidence introduced in the Washington hearing was in the nature of testimony by numerous experts in labor problems which covered the whole gamut of labor relations in the United States. By this testimony and by statistical evidence, the Board sought to demonstrate that (1) a substantial proportion of the strikes in industry were caused by the refusal of employers to recognize the right to organize and bargain collectively; (2) where this right was recognized by employers, labor relations were generally more peaceful, as in the garment and printing industries; (3) there were many precedents historically for federal intervention in labor disputes; (4) the steel industry, since the formation of the large integrated combinations, had denied the right to organize to its employees; (5) strikes in most manufacturing and production industries, and thus the steel industry, drastically affected the flow of goods in interstate commerce. The addition of this evidence to the record in the case was, in short, the use of the Brandeis brief technique on a grand scale and was the Board's answer to the briefs of the Liberty League, the NAM, and other employer associations purporting to demonstrate the Wagner Act's unconstitutionality. The material from this hearing was issued in summarized pamphlet form "for the information and assistance of the courts and others who may desire to have in convenient form some of the learning which has been gathered during the years in the various fields covered by the witnesses."[46]

On April 9, the Board issued its decision finding the company guilty of unfair labor practices and ordering it to cease and desist from such practices and to reinstate the ten discharged employees with back pay for time lost. "The ramifications of the Jones & Laughlin Steel Corporation," the Board said, "are . . . as broadly extended as the nation itself. It is impossible to isolate the operations of the Works in Pittsburgh and Aliquippa or to consider them as detached, separate—'local'— phenomena. These Works might be likened to a heart of a self-contained, highly integrated body. They draw their raw materials from Michigan, Minnesota, West Virginia, and Pennsylvania in part through arteries and by means controlled by respondent; they transform the materials and then pump them out to all parts of the nation through the vast mechanism which the respondent has elaborated."[47]

[46] NLRB, *Governmental Protection of Labor's Right to Organize*, Bulletin No. 1 (August, 1936), p. III.
[47] In the Matter of Jones & Laughlin Steel Corp., 1 NLRB 503, at 517–18.

The Board's legal staff had in the meantime been circuit shopping in an effort to find the most favorable court in which to bring a petition of enforcement. Robert Watts, an experienced trial lawyer recruited by the Board to handle its litigation as Associate General Counsel, telegraphed Charles Fahy from the field suggesting that he "consider seriously petition to enforce in the Fifth Circuit instead of Second or Third. Believe would secure early argument and favorable ruling which would greatly assist general situation."[48] The Wagner Act, however, required that an enterprise against which a petition of enforcement was sought had to be conducting business within the circuit where the petition was filed.[49] Jones & Laughlin owned a structural steel fabricating shop in New Orleans, which was within the Fifth Circuit, and the Board ordered a regional attorney to discover "whether the company does business in Louisiana only through its subsidiary, or whether it does business directly in its own name. Will you make every effort to get us that information, since the Board may desire to bring its court case in the Fifth Circuit. . . . "[50] It was confirmed on March 21 that Jones & Laughlin did business in Louisiana in its own name, and on April 9 the Board filed a petition of enforcement in the Fifth Circuit Court of Appeals in New Orleans.[51]

Arguments were delayed to June 1 on the request of the company's counsel,[52] and at the same time the NLRB asked the court for more time for oral argument. Robert Watts requested a regional attorney to ask for at least two hours for oral arguments because of the case's "importance and because of the somewhat complex constitutional questions raised. . . ." "At the same time," he said, "I am most anxious that we shall not jeopardize our present friendly relations with the Court. With that in mind, use the utmost courtesy and deference in contacting the Court and present our request as largely our own honest feeling. . . ."[53] The request was granted, and Watts argued the case on June 1, reporting to Fahy that it "went very well with the Court appearing friendly . . . ,"[54] but appearances were deceiving since the court denied the Board's petition in a *per curiam* opinion on June 15. Relying on the *Carter Coal Company* case, the court held that the "petition must be denied, because, under the facts found by

[48] Telegram from Watts to Fahy, March 12, 1936.
[49] Section 11(2).
[50] Letter from Benedict Wolf to Charles H. Logan, March 19, 1936.
[51] Memorandum from V. C. Finch to Charles N. Feidelson, March 21, 1936; NLRB memorandum, April 9, 1936.
[52] Telegram from John E. Laughlin to Watts, April 27, 1936.
[53] Letter from Watts to Gerhard Van Arkel, May 8, 1936.
[54] Telegram from Watts to Fahy, June 1, 1936.

the Board and shown by the evidence, the Board has no jurisdiction over a labor dispute between employer and employees touching the discharge of the laborers in a steel plant, who were engaged only in manufacture. The Constitution does not vest in the federal government the power to regulate the relations as such of employer and employee in production or manufacture."[55]

The *Jones & Laughlin* case thus joined the *Fruehauf* case as evidence that the *Carter Coal Company* decision was an apparently impenetrable barrier to the Board's assertion of jurisdiction over manufacturing enterprises. While Jones & Laughlin was meeting success in contesting the Board in the courts, however, it was faced with a new threat in maintaining the status quo in its employee relations when the Steel Workers Organizing Committee sent an organizer into Aliquippa on June 19, just four days after the court had sustained the company's objections to the Board's jurisdiction.[56] The first SWOC organization meeting was attended by only eighteen men, but throughout the summer of 1936 SWOC membership steadily climbed in Aliquippa and elsewhere in the steel industry. The company had apparently escaped the enforcement of the Wagner Act only to fall prey to the CIO.[57]

## THE FRIEDMAN–HARRY MARKS CASE

The Board meanwhile was shepherding yet another test of its jurisdiction over manufacturing enterprises in a case against the Friedman–Harry Marks Clothing Company in Richmond. This company discharged four employees for attending an Amalgamated Clothing Workers organization meeting, and the case had been drawn to the attention of the staff of the old NLRB in June, 1935, even before the Wagner Act was finally passed.[58] The regional director for the old Board, Bennett Schauffler, who would be retained by the new NLRB, kept in touch with the situation throughout the summer of 1935 and attempted to obtain the reinstatement of the four workers through the methods of persuasion which characterized the sanctionless old Board. He wrote to Morton Thalhimer, a local businessman who had served as the business representative on an NRA labor panel in Richmond, and asked him to urge Morton Marks, co-owner of the company, to reinstate the employees. "I honestly believe," Schauffler said, "that

[55] *NLRB* v. *Jones & Laughlin Steel Corp.*, 83 F.2d 998 (CCA 5th, June 15, 1936).

[56] Robert R. R. Brooks, *As Steel Goes . . . Unionism in a Basic Industry* (New Haven: Yale University Press, 1940), p. 115.

[57] *Ibid.*, pp. 116–18.

[58] See above, Chapter IV.

Mr. Marks is achieving nothing constructive, and incurring serious and unnecessary criticism through his failure to see the broader aspect of this problem. . . ."[59] A conference was arranged between Marks and Schauffler on July 12, and Marks admitted that the discharges were for union activity. He insisted that Schauffler visit the factory and was "very solicitous" as to his opinion of the working conditions there. "The company had just moved into a new building; the conditions were substantially good enough to warrant moderate approval." At the end of the conference, Marks agreed to consider reinstatement of the employees.[60]

Thalhimer, however, wrote Schauffler that as far as "the Friedman–Marks Company is concerned and their relationship here in Richmond, it is still my personal and confidential opinion that they are handling and will continue to handle the people employed by them in a very fair way, seeing that they receive proper wages, proper hours, and proper working conditions. It is my opinion that they are unalterably opposed to any union in their plant and, furthermore, that the vast majority, perhaps over 95%, of the employees, themselves, are in no way interested in any type of union. . . . The very nature of the people of Virginia, in my opinion, is such that the benefits that have been secured under union in other sections of the United States are not applicable to the State of Virginia."[61] Despite the company's continued truculence on the reinstatement issue, union members soon were being "singled out for special favor and privileges" by the company,[62] while a Methodist ministers' committee and a local rabbi attempted to have the discharged employees reinstated.[63]

In early August the company began the circulation of a petition ostensibly initiated by its employees declaring that they wanted "our employer, and anyone else interested, to know that we are happy with our working conditions, and what we particularly desire now is that we be allowed to enjoy them peacefully,"[64] and ACW organizers complained to Schauffler that employees were being threatened with dismissal unless they signed.[65] Schauffler again called Thalhimer, explaining

[59] NA–Case No. C-40, Friedman–Harry Marks Clothing Co., Miscellaneous Correspondence Folder, Letter from Schauffler to Morton G. Thalhimer, July 11, 1935.

[60] Confidential Memorandum by Schauffler, July 12, 1935.

[61] Letter from Thalhimer to Schauffler, July 12, 1935.

[62] Memorandum of conference between Schauffler and Charles Webber (ACW organizer), July 29, 1935.

[63] Richmond *News Leader,* July 30, 1935, p. 1.

[64] Folder No. 1, Memorandum from Gerhard Van Arkel to Charles Fahy, Sept. 30, 1935.

[65] Miscellaneous Correspondence Folder, Telegram from Webber to Schauffler, Aug. 2, 1935.

that the Wagner Act was then effective and that he could "do Marks a valuable service by dissuading him from coercion or intimidation of employees."[66] On August 22, he again journeyed to Richmond and attempted to persuade the company to obey the Act,[67] but the company had already begun layoffs, and ACW officials were beginning to bring pressure to bear on the Board in the case. Schauffler had to warn the ACW's vice president, Jacob Potofsky, that the union should stop issuing press releases indicating that the Board would immediately proceed against the company. Schauffler explained that it was important for the union to prevent "this kind of publicity for the time being, since initial cases must be chosen with great care and discrimination."[68]

The company soon resorted to discharges rather than layoffs of union members, however, with two union members being fired in August and twelve more in September, and the union again began to exert pressure on the Board for action. An organizer in Richmond wrote Schauffler that she hoped "you are able to reinstate our people before the American Liberty League declares the Wagner Bill unconstitutional."[69] Schauffler had to assure Potofsky that the NLRB would act if the company failed to reinstate the employees, and Potofsky agreed that the union would be satisfied with reinstatement.[70] When the Board had failed to act by mid-October, however, the union's attorney in Richmond told Schauffler he would ask "President Hillman to get in touch with the National Board and urge upon its members the desirability of prompt action in this case."[71] An NLRB attorney had meanwhile been assigned to the case since early September, and on October 17 recommended "that the Board issue a complaint in this case. . . . They are one of the largest manufacturers of men's clothing. I think a substantial effect towards interstate commerce can be shown. The case seems very clear on its merits."[72] On October 26 the Board issued a formal complaint against the company, and because the company discharged eleven more employees in September and October, bringing the total number of discharged employees to nineteen, another complaint was issued on November 15.

[66] Memorandum of telephone conversation between Schauffler and Thalhimer, Aug. 2, 1935.
[67] Memorandum of conference between Schauffler and company, Aug. 24, 1935.
[68] Memorandum of telephone conversation between Schauffler and Potofsky, Aug. 26, 1935.
[69] Letter from Clemmie Shuck to Schauffler, Sept. 15, 1935.
[70] Memorandum of telephone conversation between Schauffler and Potofsky, Sept. 18, 1935.
[71] Memorandum of telephone conversation between Schauffler and H. Blumberg, Oct. 16, 1935.
[72] Memorandum from Van Arkel to Fahy, Oct. 17, 1935.

The company retained as its counsel Leonard Weinberg of Baltimore, whose habit, a regional attorney reported, "was to fight the case with every possible technicality, but to present no witnesses on his side of the case." Weinberg refused any cooperation with the NLRB as to evidence of the company's operations or their possible effects on interstate commerce.[73] A. L. Wirin was the regional attorney finally assigned the task of preparing the case, a task in which he received full cooperation and assistance from the ACW and employers' associations representing unionized firms in the men's clothing industry, the ACW assigning a member of its research staff to aid Wirin in his work.[74] Affidavits on the relation between unionization and the industry were prepared according to Wirin's suggestions and given to the Board for the hearing record. For example, Wirin suggested that Sidney Hillman cover in his affidavit a brief history of unionism in the clothing industry, with particular emphasis "on the growth of employers' associations prior to or at least accompanying the development of the Amalgamated, so that we may be able to make the argument that workers need organization in order to adequately deal with their employers who are organized. . . ." Wirin also suggested that "very great emphasis" should be placed on strikes in the industry before the Amalgamated was recognized and that as to the causes of such strikes "emphasis should be placed on the effort of the Union to secure recognition to prevent interference with organizational activities by the employer; and particular emphasis with respect to discriminatory discharges on account of union activities, since that is the major case against Friedman–Harry Marks. By all means, additional emphasis should be placed on the obstruction and effect on interstate commerce that such strikes caused."[75] The New York Clothing Manufacturers' Exchange was also asked by Wirin to submit an affidavit on employer associations in the industry "in order that we may be able to make the argument in the courts that organization by the workers is quite necessary since the employers are organized in order for the workers to have equality of bargaining power. This may go a long way to uphold the constitutionality of the Act."[76]

By the date of the hearing, December 5, Wirin felt that the record would be in "much better shape than I dared anticipate," especially since he expected Weinberg to offer no countervailing testimony to

[73] Memorandum from Van Arkel to NLRB, Oct. 2, 1935.
[74] Memorandum from Wirin to Fahy, Nov. 21, 1935.
[75] Letter from Wirin to Sidney Hillman, Nov. 26, 1935.
[76] Letter from Wirin to David Drechler, New York Clothing Manufacturers' Exchange, Nov. 26, 1935.

rebut his affidavits.[77] The record demonstrated that the men's clothing industry was among the twenty most important industries in the United States, utilizing a flow of interstate commerce in fabrics to produce clothing which again re-entered a nationwide flow of commerce. The Amalgamated Clothing Workers was shown to have brought industrial peace to a large portion of the industry through collective agreements and arbitration systems. The Friedman–Harry Marks Clothing Company, according to the record, purchased more than 99 per cent of its fabrics outside the state of Virginia, and more than 80 per cent of the garments produced were purchased by customers outside the state. The company was shown to be one of fifty largest men's clothing manufacturers, grossing $1,750,000 in 1935 and employing 800 persons.[78] The testimony of the discharged employees demonstrated a clear denial of the right to organize as guaranteed by the Act.[79] "On the whole," Wirin said, "I feel that we made a strong case in favor of the constitutionality of the Act. To all intents and purposes, in view of the fact that Weinberg put on no countervailing testimony, we had practically an ex parte hearing. . . . The explanation for it all is that Weinberg is anxious to be in the Supreme Court in a hurry and is apparently willing to make the sacrifice (which he considered minor) in terms of the record in order to get out of his system his speech to the Supreme Court."[80]

Upon receiving the trial examiner's intermediate order to reinstate the discharged employees, Weinberg directed to the Board the first of a long series of objections to its proceeding in the case. "We desire to notify you now," he said, "just as we did on November 4, 1935, that the National Labor Relations Board has no jurisdiction over our client in any respect, that the National Labor Relations Act is unconstitutional and invalid, particularly with respect to our client and its business, and that it will not recognize the authority of the National Labor Relations Board or the National Labor Relations Act, unless and until it is directed to do so by the Courts of the United States." The Supreme Court, he continued, had ruled in a long line of decisions, culminating in the *Schechter* case, that manufacturing was not commerce and had only just rejected in *United States* v. *Butler* "the very theories upon which your Trial Examiner has now had the audacity . . . to hold that out client was engaged in interstate commerce." "In the light of

[77] Memorandum from Wirin to Fahy, Dec. 4, 1935.
[78] 1 NLRB 411, at 413–25.
[79] *Ibid.* at 426–28; 447–50. Since there were two separate charges issued by the Board, there were two hearings in the case, but they were consolidated on appeal to the courts and are treated singly here.
[80] Letter from Wirin to Louis Waldman, Dec. 7, 1935.

all this," Weinberg closed, "we cannot help but conclude . . . that the entire purpose of these proceedings is to harass and embarrass our client in the conduct of a legitimate business, which has always been fairly and decently conducted."[81]

The case was now considerably delayed because of the pressure of other litigation on the Board's legal staff and the Board's desire to "forward more certain 'interstate commerce' cases."[82] The NLRB's decision and order in the case was not announced until March 26, after a delay of more than two months. The Board's legal staff in the meantime had again been circuit shopping in the hope of finding a favorably disposed court in which to bring a petition of enforcement. In February, the Board's regional attorney in New York was instructed to discover whether "the . . . corporation is doing business in New York to an extent that will permit us to file our petition for enforcement in the Second Circuit if we so desire."[83] It was ascertained that Friedman–Harry Marks maintained a New York City sales office and show room, and the attorney reported that "it is obvious from the physical appearance of the operation that the business conducted here is substantial. I would think that the aforementioned is sufficient for your purpose."[84] Two days following the NLRB's decision ordering the discharged employees reinstated, therefore, a petition for enforcement was filed in the Second Circuit Court of Appeals in New York.

The Board barely beat Weinberg to the punch, since he filed an appeal from the decision in the Fourth Circuit Court of Appeals in Richmond on March 31.[85] Weinberg contested the Board's filing in the Second Circuit, on jurisdictional grounds. In the resulting oral arguments, Judge Learned Hand of the Second Circuit Court of Appeals inquired of NLRB attorneys why they had filed in that circuit and why "should you try to play a trick like that?" The newspapers immediately seized on the comment, and there was some embarrassing publicity for the Board as a result. NLRB Chairman Madden fired a telegram to Hand greatly deploring "the false impression which this report will undoubtedly create." "We are not in the habit of playing tricks," he said, "but we are attempting to administer a law. We are advised by our attorneys that paragraph (E) of section ten meant what it seems very plainly to say, namely, that the Board 'shall have the power to petition any Circuit Court of Appeals wherein such person transacts business, for the enforcement of such order.' We do not think it is a

[81] Letter from Weinberg to NLRB, Jan. 14, 1936.
[82] Letter from Wirin to Waldman, Feb. 25, 1936.
[83] Letter from Nathan Witt to David Moscowitz, Feb. 19, 1936.
[84] Memorandum from Moscowitz to Witt, Feb. 24, 1936.
[85] Letter from Weinberg to NLRB, April 2, 1936.

trick to apply the law as it is written and we think that it is unfair for anyone to so designate it. Since your reported statement from the bench has been given publicity, I shall give copies of this telegram to the press."[86] Despite Madden's public lecture on the law, Judge Hand and the other judges of the court decided in May that the case could be brought in the Second Circuit, and the case was set down for arguments on June 2.[87]

The decision of the Supreme Court in the *Carter Coal Company* case, however, encouraged Weinberg to attempt again to obtain dismissal of the case by the NLRB. He wrote the Board that he had as clients several businesses against which it had filed complaints and "in all of these cases we have raised issues with respect to the National Labor Relations Act which were decided by the Supreme Court of the United States the day before yesterday in holding the Guffey Coal Act to be invalid." "It now must be obvious to you that labor conditions in the manufacturing industries are not subject to regulation by the Federal Government under the commerce clause and due process amendment to the Constitution, and that under this decision the National Labor Relations Act is unconstitutional. . . ." His clients were therefore entitled, Weinberg concluded, "to now have you say that they have not been acting in violation of any valid law. We, therefore, request, in view of the great publicity given by you to these charges when you instituted them and again when you found these companies guilty, that you now publicly dismiss these cases."[88]

The Board's emphatic reply was that it intended "to proceed with the cases to which you refer as it has in the past." "You undoubtedly realize," the Board said, "that the Guffey coal decision affected the Guffey Coal Act, and had no legal effect on the Act under which the Board operates. We are sure that you also realize that the recent decision of the Supreme Court was based on the facts before it, and not on anything involved in cases before the Board, nor on the Statute under which the Board operates."[89] In line with this resoluteness in the face of the *Carter* case's apparent death knell for its manufacturing jurisdiction, the Board's attorneys argued the Friedman–Harry Marks case before the Second Circuit Court of Appeals on June 16, but the court's *per curiam* opinion delivered on July 13 fully supported Weinberg's arguments. "The relations between the employer and its employees in this manufacturing industry," it said, "were merely incidents

[86] Telegram from Madden to Judge Learned Hand, April 21, 1936.
[87] Telegram from Lester Lenin to NLRB, May 7, 1936.
[88] Letter from Weinberg to NLRB, May 19, 1936.
[89] Letter from Benedict Wolf to Weinberg, May 23, 1936.

of production. In its manufacturing, respondent was in no way engaged in interstate commerce, nor did its labor practices so directly affect interstate commerce as to come within the federal commerce power."[90]

Thus in the first three important tests of its manufacturing jurisdiction the Board was unable to surmount the constitutional barriers imposed by the *Schechter* and *Carter Coal Company* cases, despite careful preparation of hearing records and selection of circuit courts in which petitions for enforcement were brought. In interstate commerce cases, too, the Board's progress was not encouraging. The *Greyhound Bus* case remained undecided in the Third Circuit Court of Appeals, and by February of 1936 it was apparent that the Board's initial strategy of gaining a quick test of the Act in that case would fail. Accordingly, the decision was made to move on to other cases which appeared strong on interstate commerce grounds. A proceeding against a radio and telegraph company was thus filed in the Ninth Circuit and argued on April 16, while two other interstate commerce cases were also being prepared for the courts, one involving the Washington, Virginia and Maryland Coach Company and the other involving a charge of unfair labor practices against the Associated Press in New York.[91]

## THE ASSOCIATED PRESS CASE

In October, 1935, the Associated Press announced that it was preparing to restore the six-day week which it had abandoned when first approached by its American Newspaper Guild–affiliated employees with a request for collective bargaining in 1934. The Guild immediately objected to the move and formed a committee to meet with the AP management on the question. This committee included Morris Watson, who had been elected a vice president of the ANG at its June convention.[92] Watson had sponsored a resolution adopted by the AP Guild members proposing a renewal of their demand for collective bargaining, and on October 17, Heywood Broun wrote the AP management requesting a bargaining conference. The following afternoon Watson was dismissed by the AP.[93] A memorandum prepared by J. M. Hendrick, AP's executive news editor, listed five reasons for his dismissal,

[90] *NLRB* v. *Friedman–Harry Marks Clothing Co.*, 85 F.2d 1, at 2 (CCA 2d, July 13, 1936).
[91] NLRB, *First Annual Report*, p. 51. The radio and telegraph company case was In the Matter of MacKay Radio & Telegraph Co., 1 NLRB 201.
[92] *Editor & Publisher*, Vol. 68 (Oct. 19, 1935), p. 8.
[93] Official Report of the Proceedings before the National Labor Relations Board,

one of them being because he "is an agitator and disturbs the morale of the staff at a time when we need especially their loyalty and best performance." The executive editor, however, noted on the memorandum that the dismissal was *"solely* on grounds of his work not being on a basis for which he has shown capability."[94]

The ANG executive committee immediately adopted a resolution pledging "the full resources of the American Newspaper Guild to gaining reinstatement for Vice President Watson and recovery of the livelihood of himself and family, and seek the support of other employee organizations to the same end." The resolution also pledged the Guild to "by all means at its disposal acquaint the reading public with the anti-labor policies of the Associated Press."[95] J. M. Hendrick, however, declared publicly that any assertion that Watson had been discharged for his Guild activities was "ridiculous." "It is a well known fact," he said, "that he has been very active in the guild for two years without repression by his employer. The sole concern was that he do the work of which he is capable. Until the last few months he had done so. He had to be removed from an early day assignment because of unsatisfactory work. He was given another assignment as a reporter on the day city staff and was told an improvement in his work was expected. The improvement hoped for did not result and he was therefore released. Had he continued to do the work of which he is capable he could still have been an employee of the Associated Press service."[96]

On November 7, the Guild filed a complaint against the AP in the Watson case with the NLRB regional office in New York, and the following day the regional director, Elinore Herrick, met with AP officials to discuss the case.[97] The AP adopted a cooperative attitude toward the Board's investigation of the case and readily permitted an examination of Watson's personnel file. Herrick wrote AP officials expressing appreciation for their "frank and cooperative attitude," adding that she was "very hopeful that we can solve this problem without much fuss."[98] After examining Watson's file, however, the regional office was convinced that it was probable that he had been dismissed because of his Guild activities and recommended that a charge of unfair labor prac-

---

In the Matter of the Associated Press, pp. 293–301. (Hereinafter cited as Off. Rep. of Proceedings before NLRB—AP.)

[94] Off. Rep. of Proceedings before NLRB—AP, p. 326.

[95] *Editor & Publisher,* Vol. 68 (Oct. 26, 1935), p. 24.

[96] *Ibid.*

[97] NA–Case No. C-84, Associated Press, Folder No. 1, Memorandum from 2nd Region to NLRB, Nov. 7, 1935.

[98] Letter from Elinore Herrick to Lloyd Stratton, Nov. 9, 1935.

tices be filed against the AP.[99] The charge was duly issued on December 7 and a hearing scheduled for January 8, 1936.[100]

The decision to issue the complaint was undoubtedly a carefully considered one on the part of the Board. On one hand, the AP was the largest distributor of domestic news in the United States, and proceedings against it would have to be handled with great care.[101] In addition, the American Newspaper Publishers' Association was strongly attacking the Wagner Act, particularly as a violation of freedom of the press, and could be expected to back the AP on the issue. On the other hand, the American Newspaper Guild was possibly the most vociferous and volatile group in the labor movement in the 1930's, and this was particularly true of the New York Guild which furnished the leadership for the entire movement. The Board could expect, therefore, that from the beginning to the end the AP case would be a focal point of considerable publicity and acrimony between two rather uncompromising groups. It was soon clear that the AP intended to fight the case to the end when it retained John W. Davis, of Liberty League fame, as its counsel. The Guild was just as determined as the AP in its attitude toward the case. In fact, the Board almost immediately experienced the danger of the overzealousness of the Guild when its counsel, Morris Ernst, informed Davis that the NLRB hearing in the case would involve the subpena of many of the AP's key personnel to testify. Whatever Davis' strategy may have been before this Guild blunder, on January 3 he sought an order from a federal district court to enjoin the Board from holding the hearing.[102] "The National Labor Relations Act," the AP's petition said, "is not in truth and in fact a law and cannot be enforced, and said pretended statute is void and unconstitutional in its entirety." The Guild charged that the AP was seeking to prevent exposure of its anti-union policies and pledged that the facts in the Watson case "will be brought out even though the AP challenged the right of Congress to legislate and the right of the United States Government to administer."[103]

The Board's legal staff was now concerned with the temperament of the judge before whom the argument on the injunction proceedings would be heard. It was at first thought that the NLRB should seek a postponement until a more favorable judge was sitting, but it was

[99] Memorandum from 2nd Region to NLRB, Nov. 27, 1935.

[100] *Editor & Publisher,* Vol. 68 (Dec. 7, 1935), p. 4.

[101] Letter from Herrick to Warren Madden, Nov. 27, 1935.

[102] The Board was informed later that Davis only sought the injunction because Ernst's statement indicated great disruption of the AP's operation; Memorandum from Moscowitz to Fahy, Jan. 9, 1936.

[103] *Editor & Publisher,* Vol. 69 (Jan. 11, 1936), p. 11.

discovered that the judge assigned to sit after Judge William Bondy, who ultimately heard the case, was "just as unpredictable," while Bondy, "though slow, irritable, etc., is a good lawyer."[104] The case was thus argued before Judge Bondy on January 17, with John W. Davis appearing for the AP, David Moscowitz representing the NLRB, and Morris Ernst representing the Guild. Davis argued that the Wagner Act was "null and void in toto." "These are the two cardinal objections to this law," he said, "that the employer-employee relationship is not interstate commerce and that the law is an invasion of contract." Moscowitz argued that there was no question of the law's constitutionality and that the Board was convinced "that men like Morris Watson are entitled to protection under the Constitution just as well as corporate interests like the Associated Press." Ernst added that since the AP had not dealt in good faith with its employees, the court should not issue the injunction, since an employer who "comes into court must come with clean hands." The Guild again injected itself dramatically into the case when Ernst requested that Heywood Broun be permitted to make a statement to the court following the formal arguments. The court denied the request, but in the interchange Broun told the court that "John W. Davis is asking you for permission for the Associated Press to run a yellow-dog shop." Davis, however, had the statement stricken.[105]

There now ensued a two-month delay while Judge Bondy weighed the merits of the case and both Davis and the Board bombarded him with the latest decisions by federal courts in injunction cases involving the enforcement of the Act.[106] As the delay lengthened into the second month, the Board's legal staff became impatient, with even Charles Fahy wondering "why in the world Judge Bondy does not disclose his intentions. It begins to look as if his views will remain an unfathomable secret."[107] While the legal staff wondered thus among themselves, the waiting was just too much for Heywood Broun. On February 27 he wrote the judge, pointing out that the Wagner Act "until invalidated is the law of the land and the delay deprives us of its potential benefits." "You did not grant an injunction," Broun continued, "but you have presented the Associated Press with an easement, a kind of legal laxative which works while you sleep. In the event of an adverse decision, we can appeal, but as things stand the Labor Board is not free to proceed, Morris Watson has not got his job and the Associated

[104] Memorandum from Moscowitz to Fahy, Jan. 14, 1936.
[105] *Editor & Publisher,* Vol. 69 (Jan. 25, 1936), p. IV.
[106] For example, Letter from John W. Davis to Judge Bondy, Feb. 7, 1936; Letter from Fahy to Judge Bondy, Feb. 7, 1936.
[107] Memorandum from Fahy to Moscowitz, March 11, 1936.

Press sits just as prettily as if you had already decided in its favor. We think we have a right to protest against this situation. We do protest. We think your Honor should make up your mind."[108]

The harassed Judge finally refused to issue the injunction or to declare the act unconstitutional on March 17, basing his decision on the *Texas and New Orleans* case.[109] The Board was now free to proceed with the case to the hearing stage. Dean Charles E. Clark of the Yale Law School accepted appointment as hearing examiner in the case, and the NLRB staff turned toward preparations for building a strong record. As in many other early cases, it was decided that the Board's subpena power would not be used for the purpose of obtaining testimony from AP officials, since it appeared that Davis would force another court test on the validity of the subpena, causing further delay.[110] As the hearing date approached, Charles Fahy cautioned Moscowitz, the regional attorney, that because of the attention focused on the case, the hearing should be handled with great care. "In the conduct of this case," he said, "perhaps more than any other case which you have handled for the Board, care must be taken orderly to present it, and we must prove in fact as well as in law that, as Judge Bondy has decided, our hearings do not wreck anybody's business or unnecessarily expose them to unnamed and horrible injuries. You may find yourself under pressure to make a field day, but remember this is just another case being diligently and vigorously handled by a government agency."[111]

The hearing was held on April 7 and 8, and counsel for the Associated Press moved immediately for dismissal on the grounds that the act was unconstitutional under the fifth and first amendments and was an invalid exercise of the commerce power as applied to the Associated Press. Dean Clark denied the motion, reserving a ruling on the interstate commerce question until evidence on the nature of AP's operation was introduced.[112] An AP official was then permitted by counsel to testify on the nature of the business. This testimony, along with Board evidence, demonstrated that the AP was a nonprofit corporation whose membership was composed of newspapers belonging to the AP system. In 1935 there were 1350 such members, which included 1200 of the 2000 daily newspapers in the United States and newspapers in twenty foreign countries. The AP was linked with

---

[108] Letter from Heywood Broun to Judge Bondy, Feb. 27, 1936.
[109] *Editor & Publisher,* Vol. 69 (March 21, 1936), p. 8.
[110] Memorandum from Moscowitz to Fahy, March 27, 1936.
[111] Memorandum from Fahy to Moscowitz, March 18, 1936.
[112] Off. Rep. of Proceedings before NLRB—AP, pp. 4–10.

affiliates in Britain, France, and Germany, while AP news in the United States was communicated via leased wires from the Western Union Telegraph, the American Telephone & Telegraph, and the Pacific Telephone and Telegraph companies. The news transmitted over these wires to member newspapers was edited and rewritten in several regional centers, the New York office being the eastern regional center in the system. In 1935, the AP was shown to have grossed over nine million dollars in income and to have employed over 1700 employees.[113]

Following this testimony, Dean Clark denied the AP's motion to dismiss on interstate commerce grounds and ruled that there was evidence that the AP was engaged in interstate commerce, whereupon counsel for AP withdrew from the hearing.[114] Morris Watson then testified about the coercion to which the AP management had subjected him since the NRA days. He testified that he had been refused a foreign assignment because of his Guild activities; that he had been given less desirable work which had resulted in a nervous breakdown; that when he returned to work in the summer of 1935 he had been assigned to the twelve to eight A.M. shift, a job recognized by newspapermen as punishment; and that upon the renewal of the Guild's demand for collective bargaining with the AP, he had been fired.[115] Elinore Herrick testified that she had discovered evidence in Watson's personnel file indicating a long-standing dissatisfaction with Watson by the AP because of his Guild activities, while there was much praise of his work as a reporter.[116]

On the basis of this record, Dean Clark filed his report on April 24, finding the AP guilty of committing unfair labor practices affecting commerce by interfering with the exercise of Watson's right to join a union and by discriminatorily discharging him because of his Guild activities and membership. The AP was ordered, therefore, to reinstate Watson with back pay for time lost.[117] Upon being advised of the report, Watson said that Dean Clark's opinion "may well become an imperishable bill of rights for editorial workers." "The text for next year's meeting of the AP and ANPA," he said, "should be the sixteenth paragraph of Dean Clark's findings of fact:—'and freedom of the press would be facilitated by a freedom of organization granted

---

[113] Off. Rep. of Proceedings before NLRB—AP, pp. 10–218; the evidence is summarized in 1 NLRB 788, at 790–92.

[114] *Ibid.,* p. 216.

[115] Off. Rep. of Proceedings before NLRB—AP, pp. 217–303.

[116] *Ibid.,* pp. 319–26.

[117] Dean Clark also found the AP guilty of failure to bargain collectively, but this charge was later dropped by the NLRB.

to its highest skilled equally with its other employees.' "[118] The voice of the ANPA, *Editor & Publisher,* was less impressed with Dean Clark's report and expressed the editorial view that the Wagner Act would be interpreted by the courts to the effect that "newspaper organizations cannot be held to compulsory employment of men disqualified by any reason for the special work of writing the nation's news." Morris Watson, it said, "set out to achieve martyrdom, to be discharged by the AP for Guild activity, and to become the Dred Scott of the newspaper craft."[119] The case was also a major topic of discussion at the Guild convention which met in June and re-elected Morris Watson as a vice president. In addition, the convention voted to affiliate with the A.F. of L. and passed a resolution condemning the Supreme Court for making the Constitution into a "strait-jacket so binding that now it is imperative for the people to amend the Constitution specifically authorizing legislation to establish adequate protection of labor's rights, civil liberties, collective bargaining and majority rule in collective bargaining."[120]

David Moscowitz reported that he believed "our enthusiastic work in this case is more than warranted because I think it looks awfully good," and when the AP failed to comply with Dean Clark's order the case was referred to the NLRB for action on May 8.[121] The Board reviewed the record, sustaining Clark's findings and concluding that AP's dismissal of Watson would "tend to lead to labor disputes burdening and obstructing commerce and the free flow of commerce." "Watson and the other editorial employees of respondent at its New York office in the activities hereinbefore described were directly engaged in interstate and foreign commerce by facilitating and making possible the flow of news from place to place throughout this country and other countries; and any interference with or cessation of such activities would hamper, impede, and interfere with such commerce." On May 21, therefore, the NLRB again ordered the AP to reinstate Watson,[122] but again it failed to do so, and a petition for enforcement was filed in the Second Circuit Court of Appeals on May 30.[123] The Guild immediately requested and received permission from the Board to file a brief of *amicus curiae* with the court.[124] The Board's position on the interstate commerce question was

---

[118] *Editor & Publisher,* Vol. 69 (May 2, 1936), p. 18.
[119] *Ibid.*
[120] *Ibid.* (June 6, 1936), p. 7.
[121] Memorandum from Moscowitz to Fahy, May 27, 1936; Memorandum from Elinore Herrick to NLRB, May 8, 1936.
[122] In the Matter of the Associated Press, 1 NLRB 788, at 800, 802.
[123] *Editor & Publisher,* Vol. 69 (May 30, 1936), p. 13.
[124] Letter from Fahy to Ernst, May 29, 1936.

good, since the Supreme Court had held that commerce included the transmission of telegraph signals,[125] radio signals,[126] and intelligence across state lines.[127] These precedents, therefore, plus the hearing evidence on the interstate nature of AP's operations, made it an especially strong commerce case upon which to test the act's vulnerability to the liberty of contract objections based on the fifth amendment.

The court heard arguments in the case on June 16, and almost a month later on July 13 it handed down a decision sustaining the NLRB's order and the Wagner Act as applied to the Associated Press. It pointed out that while manufacturing and production were not interstate commerce, under several Supreme Court decisions "the federal power to regulate interstate communication which constitutes interstate commerce has been established as far as the instrumentalities of interstate communication are concerned, as in the regulation of telegraph companies or broadcasting companies." "The business of respondent," the court decided, "which merely is a special form or instance of interstate communication is included in the concept of interstate commerce."[128] On the question of liberty of contract, the court accepted the *Texas and New Orleans* case as controlling and held that the act did not unduly interfere with the AP's right to select its employees. "This act," it said, "does not hamper the legitimate right of the employer, who may discharge his employees for inefficiency or any other cause agreeable to him, provided he does not use the power of discharge as a weapon for interfering with the right of employees to organize and bargain collectively."[129]

Thus the Board had won on every major point, and for the first time the Wagner Act's application to a business enterprise had been upheld. The Board at last had its interstate commerce case, but victory at the circuit court level meant that it lost control over the case insofar as an appeal to the Supreme Court was concerned, since a petition for a writ of certiorari would now have to be initiated by John W. Davis and the Associated Press. Given Davis' views on the constitutionality of the Wagner Act, it could be expected that an appeal to the Court would be made as a matter of course, but the decision was not with the Board. It had under way by this time, however, another interstate commerce case which would be the fifth and last case upon which the act's constitutionality would be decided.

[125] *Pensacola Telegraph Co.* v. *Western Union Telegraph Co.*, 96 U.S. 1 (1878).
[126] *Federal Radio Commission* v. *Nelson Brothers*, 289 U.S. 266 (1933).
[127] *International Textbook Co.* v. *Pigg*, 217 U.S. 91 (1910).
[128] *NLRB* v. *Associated Press*, 85 F.2d 56, at 59 (CCA 2d, July 13, 1936).
[129] 85 F.2d, at 60–61.

## THE WASHINGTON, VIRGINIA AND
## MARYLAND COACH COMPANY CASE

The other interstate commerce case arose almost in the Board's lap when the Washington, Virginia and Maryland Coach Company, which operated about forty-eight buses between points in Virginia and Washington, D.C., discharged eighteen of its approximately eighty employees in March, 1936.[130] An organizer for the Amalgamated Association of Street, Electric Railway and Motor Coach Employees of America had been hired by the company in September, 1935, and succeeded in planting the seeds of a union among its employees.[131] The owner of the company had become aware of the unionization of his employees by February and had placed an advertisement in a Washington paper toward the end of that month advertising for new employees.[132] The union held meetings in late February and early March, and the son of the owner appeared at the March meeting wearing a bus driver's cap and reading the names on the local's charter.[133] On March 3, the union sent a letter to the company requesting a collective bargaining conference,[134] and on March 4, 5, and 6, eighteen of the union members were discharged, the owner having told one member that he wasn't going to recognize the union "and you can put that in your God damn pipe and smoke it."[135]

On March 6, the union filed a charge against the company with the NLRB, and six days later the Board issued a formal complaint.[136] Hearings were held in March and early May, with the company's counsel cross-examining most of the discharged men as they testified and attempting to establish that they had been discharged for cause. The company, though small, was clearly operating in interstate commerce. The Board determined that the act applied to the company and that the evidence supported the charge of interference with the right to organize, whereupon it ordered the company to cease and desist engaging in unfair labor practices and to reinstate the eighteen discharged men with back pay.[137]

[130] Official Report of the Proceedings before the National Labor Relations Board, In the Matter of Washington, Virginia and Maryland Coach Co., p. 10.

[131] Ibid., p. 14.

[132] Ibid., pp. 17, 80.

[133] Ibid., pp. 236–47.

[134] Ibid., p. 53.

[135] Ibid., p. 166.

[136] NA–Case No. C-63, Washington, Virginia and Maryland Coach Co., Folder No. 1, Memorandum of NLRB, 5th region, March 12, 1936.

[137] In the Matter of the Washington, Virginia and Maryland Coach Co., 1 NLRB 769.

The A.F. of L. had interested itself in the case, and its counsel, Charlton Ogburn, had appeared along with the local's attorney at the hearing.[138] The company approached the Board's representatives proposing a settlement soon after the issuance of the formal order on May 21, and appointments were arranged between the company and the union attorneys.[139] On June 3, however, Ogburn informed the NLRB that the company had not complied with the order and "failed to keep engagements with us to discuss compliance. I therefore ask the Board to proceed today with a petition to the court for immediate enforcement."[140] The Board responded by instructing its regional attorney that "in view of the repeated failure of the Washington, Virginia and Maryland Coach Company to offer any definite basis for compliance, and of its persistent refusal to confer with representatives of the complainant in regard to any basis for settlement, in spite of several occasions arranged for such meeting . . . , it is recommended that this case be referred to the courts immediately."[141] On June 6 the Fourth Circuit Court of Appeals in Richmond was petitioned for an order of enforcement against the company.[142]

Because of the admitted interstate nature of the bus company's operations, the counsel for the company, Robert E. Lynch, argued before the court that the act was invalid because it was intended to apply to all industry and as such was beyond the scope of the commerce power. In addition, Lynch argued that the act was totally invalid due to its interference with the right of liberty of contract. The Board answered that the Act was not intended to apply to all industry but extended only to the limits set by the commerce clause, and when the *Associated Press* and *Friedman–Harry Marks* cases were decided in the Second Circuit, copies of the opinions were sent to the court to demonstrate this point. Charles Fahy pointed out to the court "the fact that the Court upheld the validity of the Act in the *Associated Press* case, and the validity of its application to the Associated Press, while it held in the *Friedman–Harry Marks Clothing Company* case that the order could not be enforced because it related to employers engaged in manufacture or production is a complete answer to the contention made by the respondent in the *Washington, Virginia and Maryland Coach Company* case that the Act is unconstitutional *in toto,* that it applies to 'all industry,' and may not in

[138] Official Report of the Proceedings before the National Labor Relations Board, In the Matter of Washington, Virginia and Maryland Coach Co., p. 1.
[139] Telegram from Bennett Schauffler to Charles H. Clarke, May 25, 1936.
[140] Telegram from Ogburn to Warren Madden, June 3, 1936.
[141] Memorandum from NLRB to Schauffler, June 3, 1936.
[142] Letter from Malcolm Halliday to Claude M. Dean, Clerk of CCA 4th, June 6, 1936.

the normal administration and court review be validly applied in one case although the Board might err in its attempted application of it to some other circumstances."[143]

As in its other cases, the Board urged the court to deliver an early decision in the case so that it would be ready for the October term of the Supreme Court. In a letter to Chief Judge John J. Parker, the Board said that "such a decision would provide, along with the manufacturing cases in the Fifth and Sixth Circuits already decided, an opportunity for possible determination by the Supreme Court of the general validity and application of the Act. Such a determination at the earliest possible date, we believe to be a matter of great public importance, as well as of great importance to the Board in the administration of the statute. . . ."[144] The Board encountered, however, the usual delay in obtaining a decision in the case, and the court did not announce its opinion until October, 1936. But for the second time the Board was victorious in a test case in the circuit courts as the court sustained the Act and the Board's jurisdiction. On the liberty of contract question, the court accepted the *Texas and New Orleans* case as controlling[145] and rejected the company's contention that the Act was intended by Congress to apply to all industry. By its definitions of the terms "commerce" and "affecting commerce," the court said, "Congress did not intend to regulate intrastate as well as interstate commerce, and there is no ground for the argument that an important and inseparable part of the act having been condemned, the whole should fall."[146]

## THE APPROACH TO THE SUPREME COURT

The five cases with which the Board would approach the Supreme Court were now out of the circuit courts. Although there had been constant contact between the Board and Solicitor General Stanley Reed's office on the status of the Board's litigation, except for Reed's intervention in the *Fruehauf* case at the circuit court level, the Board had controlled the selection of cases in which to file complaints and those in which petitions for enforcement would be filed.[147] As the cases passed the circuit court level, however, the Solicitor General assumed the ultimate power of selection as to cases with which to approach the Court and also as to who should be allowed to join in the cases with briefs

[143] Letter from Fahy to the Judges of CCA 4th, July 14, 1936.

[144] Letter from NLRB to Chief Judge John J. Parker, CCA 4th, July 3, 1936.

[145] *NLRB* v. *Washington, Virginia and Maryland Coach Co.*, 85 F.2d 990, at 993 (CCA 4th, Oct. 6, 1936).

[146] *Ibid.* at 994.

[147] NLRB, *First Annual Report*, p. 55.

*amicus curiae*. Fortunately, under Reed, the Office of Solicitor General had been reorganized since the early New Deal period, and government attorneys from line agencies had been added to the staff, thus strengthening the government's position in this period of joint NLRB–Solicitor General cooperation on the final mile to the Court.[148]

Because the Board's original strategy for a quick test of the act in the *Greyhound Bus* case had gone awry,[149] two of its manufacturing cases, the *Fruehauf* and *Jones & Laughlin* cases, were decided in the circuit courts before an interstate commerce case had reached that stage.[150] Since the constitutionality of the Board's manufacturing jurisdiction was extremely doubtful, the Board was forced to hold these manufacturing cases back until an interstate commerce case which could accompany them to the Supreme Court was brought out of the circuit courts. As was pointed out previously, the Board in losing its manufacturing cases retained the discretion as to whether petitions for writs of certiorari would be filed, but in its interstate commerce cases it was forced to wait upon the decision of respondent's counsel on the question of an appeal to the Court.

Following the Fifth Circuit Court of Appeals decision in the *Jones & Laughlin* case on June 17, therefore, Charles Fahy had written Robert Watts pointing out that they must find out how much time was allowed for filing a petition for a writ of certiorari and "whether we should ask for a rehearing from a tactical standpoint in order to keep the case alive in its present status for a longer period of time until our other Circuit Court situations have cleared up and we will have more decisions to consider as a basis for approaching the Supreme Court."[151] It was decided that a petition for a rehearing should be filed. Similarly, after the *Fruehauf* case was lost in the Sixth Circuit on June 30, Fahy telegraphed the regional attorney that it was "possible we will petition the Supreme Court for a writ of certiorari in the *Freuhauf* case so we desire motion filed for stay of mandate, although it is not desired that motion state that certiorari will be applied for if it is possible to avoid such commitment at this time. . . ."[152] Both the *Fruehauf* and *Jones & Laughlin* cases were thus

---

[148] Arthur M. Schlesinger, Jr., *The Politics of Upheaval* (Boston: Houghton Mifflin Co., 1960), pp. 261–62.

[149] The case had been pending decision in the Third Circuit since April 1, 1936, and on September 9, the court requested a reargument which was held on October 6. The case was too much delayed to constitute another test case.

[150] The *Associated Press* and *Friedman–Harry Marks* cases were decided simultaneously by the Second Circuit Court of Appeals on July 13.

[151] Memorandum from Fahy to Watts, June 18, 1936. The citations following this note are generally from the case files of the case referred to in the text; if they are not, however, the note will refer to the appropriate case file.

[152] Telegram from Fahy to Philip Phillips, June 25, 1936.

kept alive pending the decision of an interstate commerce case in the circuit courts and its appeal to the Supreme Court.

In the *Associated Press* case, John W. Davis approached the Board on July 20 and requested its agreement for a stay of the circuit court's mandate for forty days to allow time for the filing of a petition for a writ of certiorari.[153] The Board was thus assured at last of obtaining review of a strong interstate commerce case before the Supreme Court. "I think the *Associated Press* case is a very good one to go to the Supreme Court," Charles Fahy wrote, "and I am perfectly willing, from the standpoint of the Board, not to object to a stay of the order in exchange for an agreement by the Associated Press that within a definite period of time it will apply for review by the Supreme Court."[154] Fahy met with Solicitor General Reed on July 29 and reported that he was sure that "this is also his position, although I cannot speak positively as to this for the reason that there has been no occasion for him to make a categorical statement."[155] Davis was informed, therefore, that the Board would not object to a stay nor would it oppose a petition for a writ of certiorari, "subject to the approval of the Solicitor General,"[156] and on September 14 the Associated Press filed its petition with the Supreme Court.[157]

With the *Associated Press* case thus pending before the Court, the Board began to move again on its manufacturing cases. In addition to the *Fruehauf* and *Jones & Laughlin* cases, the *Friedman–Harry Marks* case, decided on the same day as the *Associated Press* case, was being considered as a possible test case. On August 1, Fahy informed a regional attorney that "the Department of Justice desires us to print the proceedings in the Second Circuit in the *Friedman–Harry Marks* case to have the matter in condition for filing with the Supreme Court a petition for certiorari."[158] Petitions for writs of certiorari in the three manufacturing cases were drafted by the Board, but no final decision on their filing had been made by August 22. Robert Watts submitted the drafts to the Solicitor General's Office on that date, stating his "understanding that no final action will be taken in filing any of these petitions until the return of Mr. Fahy and further discussion between him and the Solicitor General on the subject."[159] After John W. Davis had filed for a writ in the *Associated Press* case on September 14, however, the decision was

---

[153] Letter from Davis to Fahy, July 29, 1936.
[154] Letter from Fahy to Elinore Herrick, July 22, 1936.
[155] Memorandum from Fahy to Moscowitz, July 29, 1936.
[156] Letter from Fahy to Davis, July 27, 1936.
[157] Telegram from Fahy to Warren Madden, Sept. 15, 1936.
[158] Memorandum from Fahy to Malcolm H. Halliday, August 1, 1936.
[159] Case No. C-40, Friedman–Harry Marks Co., Folder No. 1, Letter from Watts to Wendell Berge, August 22, 1936.

soon made and petitions were filed by the government in the three manufacturing cases on September 30. The *Washington, Virginia and Maryland Coach Company* case was not decided in the circuit court until October 6, after petitions in the four other cases had been filed. Within three days after the decision, however, Fahy was reporting that the "company indicates that it will certainly apply to the Supreme Court for review by that Court of the decision of the Fourth Circuit, so it seems likely this will be one of our test cases in the Supreme Court along with those now pending before that tribunal."[160] On October 17 the company duly filed its petition, and the fifth and final test case was pending before the Court.

Since the rules of the Supreme Court required both parties to a suit to approve the filing of briefs *amicus curiae,* the Board was now requested by several interested groups to approve their participation in the cases. In addition to the American Newspaper Guild, the American Newspaper Publishers' Association and the Commercial Telegraphers Union requested permission to file in the *Associated Press* case. Fahy reported to Stanley Reed that he felt the Telegraphers' brief should be approved "provided we could pass on it to be sure that it does not take any position inconsistent with ours . . . ,"[161] and the request was granted. On the ANPA request, however, Fahy reported to Reed that "no doubt this brief would be in opposition to affirmance of the Second Circuit Court decision and would probably emphasize the contention that the National Labor Relations Act abridges freedom of the press. I shall not take any position without your approval." Reed replied only, "We should agree."[162] The American Federation of Labor requested and received permission to file briefs in the *Fruehauf* and *Washington, Virginia and Maryland Coach Company* cases, in the latter case in association with the Amalgamated Association of Street, Electric Railway and Motor Coach Employees' union. The Pennsylvania Greyhound Lines also requested permission to file a brief in the bus case, since "the Circuit Court of Appeals at Philadelphia has not yet handed down its decision in the *Greyhound* case. . . ."[163] This request was also granted,[164] and thus, including the briefs of the government and respondents, a total of sixteen briefs were filed in the cases.

On October 26, the Supreme Court granted the petitions for certiorari in the *Associated Press* and *Washington, Virginia and Maryland Coach*

[160] Letter from Fahy to Schauffler, Oct. 9, 1936.
[161] Letter from Fahy to Reed, Sept. 28, 1936.
[162] Letter from Fahy to Reed, Oct. 2, 1936; Reed's answer was handwritten on the margin.
[163] Letter from Ivan Bowen to Fahy, Nov. 4, 1936.
[164] Letter from Fahy to Bowen, Nov. 16, 1936.

*Company* cases, and on November 9 it granted the government's petitions in the *Fruehauf, Jones & Laughlin,* and *Friedman–Harry Marks* cases. Charles Fahy still hoped that the two interstate commerce cases would be argued first, separately from the manufacturing cases,[165] but this hope, along with the Board's desire to have the cases decided during the December, 1936, term of the Court,[166] was frustrated when the cases were set down to be argued together during the spring term in 1937. The *Jones & Laughlin* and *Associated Press* cases, involving the largest enterprises of the manufacturing and interstate commerce cases, were selected as the ones in which the government's major briefs would be filed, and drafts were soon being circulated.

This last winter of delay in the determination of the constitutionality of the Wagner Act, however, saw the beginning of events which would soon overshadow the careful work then proceeding in the offices of the NLRB and the Justice Department on the five cases. Franklin Roosevelt had been re-elected in November, 1936, carrying every state but Maine and Vermont and receiving the largest popular vote in history, but in his first term he had seen almost every major part of his domestic program fall before the constitutional strictures of the Supreme Court. Thus at the first cabinet meeting following the election, Roosevelt raised the issue of what to do about the Court and was soon setting in motion plans which when announced would precipitate the greatest executive-judicial conflict since the Civil War and make the decision of the Wagner Act cases a crucial turning point in this broader conflict.[167]

[165] Case No. C-63, Washington, Virginia and Maryland Coach Co., Folder No. 1, Letter from Fahy to Reed, Nov. 6, 1936.

[166] NLRB, *First Annual Report,* p. 54.

[167] James MacGregor Burns, *Roosevelt: The Lion and the Fox* (New York: Harcourt Brace and Co., 1956), p. 296.

# 7

## COURT IN CRISIS

□ □ □ □ □ □ □ □ □ □ □ □ □ □ □ □ □ □ □ □ □ □ □ □ □ □ □ □ □ □ □ □ □ □ □ □ □ □ □ □ □ □

THE COALITION WHICH ELECTED FRANKLIN ROOSEVELT TO THE PRESidency in 1932 contained, as all successful American political coalitions must, elements which diverged on most major policy issues. One of these elements, including those who believed in a balanced budget and fiscal soundness as the greatest bulwarks against the destruction of civilization, was particularly strong during the early days of the New Deal and had as its most important representative in the administration the Director of the Bureau of the Budget, Lewis Douglas. Roosevelt had promised during the campaign to reduce governmental costs by twenty-five per cent, and Douglas was convinced such a reduction would be the most important step toward economic stabilization. On March 15, 1933, the President, following Douglas' advice, pushed through Congress the Economy Act[1] which reduced all federal salaries and pensions.[2] Whatever may have been the merits of such a reduction in federal expenditures during a period of acute depression, the act was to have serious repercussions in an unexpected quarter. Justice Holmes had retired in 1932 under the terms of an act of 1869 which provided that "any judge of any court of the United States, who, having held his commission as such at least ten years, shall, after having attained the age of seventy years, resign his office, shall thereafter, during the residue of his natural life, receive the same salary which was by law payable to him at the time of his resignation."[3] The effect of the Economy Act, however, was to reduce substantially Holmes' pension, with the result that there was a hesitancy on the part of some Justices to retire during the 1930's because of their distrust of Congress and their unhappiness over the treatment of

[1] 48 Stat. 8.
[2] Arthur M. Schlesinger, Jr., *The Coming of the New Deal* (Boston: Houghton Mifflin Co., 1959), pp. 8–11.
[3] 16 Stat. 45 (1869).

Holmes.[4] The New Deal's fiscal policies would change before 1937, but the impact of the Economy Act on the Justices' attitude toward retirement was an important contributing factor in the constitutional crisis of that year, since Franklin Roosevelt failed to have the opportunity to appoint a single Justice to the Supreme Court from 1933 to 1937.

By the spring of 1937, the Supreme Court appeared to New Dealers not only to have challenged the New Deal policies but also, as Robert H. Jackson noted, to have "erected judicial barriers to the reasonable exercise of legislative powers, both state and national, to meet the urgent needs of a twentieth-century community."[5] To Justices McReynolds, Butler, Van Devanter, and Sutherland, the members of the conservative bloc on the Court, however, these barriers seemed necessary to the preservation of essential constitutional rights from encroachment by a too-powerful government.

As death approached Chief Justice Taft in 1929, he had written Butler that he feared for the preservation of conservative constitutionalism and that they must hope for "continued life of enough of the present membership . . . to prevent disastrous reversals of our present attitude. With Van and Mac and Sutherland and you and Sanford, there will be five to steady the boat . . . we must not all give up at once."[6] Taft and Sanford had died in 1930, but Van Devanter, Sutherland, Butler, and McReynolds were still "steadying the boat," maintaining the custom, begun by Taft, of meeting together often. With the aid of Justice Roberts, these men succeeded in controlling the decision of cases testing the most important policies of the New Deal. The conservative four were convinced, as they indicated in the *Carter,*[7] *Alton,*[8] and *Butler*[9] cases, that the federal government's power under the commerce clause could not be extended to manufacturing, mining, and agricultural enterprises and that the "direct-indirect" effects formula was fundamental to the preservation of state power and to the restriction of federal power within its proper limits. They had, in addition, composed four of the majority of

[4] Both Justice Van Devanter and Justice Sutherland apparently would have retired earlier had not the Holmes affair occurred. See Alpheus T. Mason, *Harlan Fiske Stone: Pillar of the Law* (New York: The Viking Press, 1956), pp. 454–55, and Merlo J. Pusey, *Charles Evans Hughes* (New York: The Macmillan Co., 1951), Vol. II, p. 760.

[5] Robert H. Jackson, *The Struggle for Judicial Supremacy* (New York: Alfred A. Knopf, 1941), p. 175.

[6] Henry F. Pringle, *The Life and Times of William Howard Taft* (New York: Farrar & Rinehart, Inc., 1939), Vol. II, p. 1044.

[7] *Carter v. Carter Coal Co.,* 298 U.S. 238 (1936).

[8] *Railroad Retirement Board v. Alton,* 295 U.S. 330 (1935).

[9] *United States v. Butler,* 297 U.S. 1 (1936).

five on the Court which had revived the doctrine of liberty of contract in the *Adkins* case[10] in 1923, and, with the aid of Justice Roberts, continued its vitality by invalidating New York's minimum wage statute in *Morehead* v. *New York* in 1936.[11] The combination of their views on commerce and due process, separated from the context of constitutional doctrine, amounted essentially to a determination to preserve as much as possible of a laissez-faire economic order. Having reached maturity during the period when the courts had begun to accept as their proper function the prevention of legislative abridgments of property rights as defined by classical economic theory, the Four Horsemen, as they were called, unhesitatingly accepted this use of judicial power as the proper function of the courts and continued with substantial success in the 1930's to make their views those of the Supreme Court itself.[12]

Ranged against the conservative bloc on the Court were Justices Brandeis, Stone, and Cardozo. Louis Brandeis, the famed "people's attorney" appointed by Wilson in 1916, was in 1937, at the age of eighty-one, the overshadowing symbol of liberalism on the Court, but Stone and Cardozo registered the liberal's basic objections to the conservative trend of the Court's decisions during the 1930's. After a majority of the Court had declared the Agricultural Adjustment Act invalid as an invasion of the reserved powers of the states, Stone exploded in a dissent so vehement that Roberts, the author of the majority opinion, complained to Chief Justice Hughes, but the dissent, even after some softening, was a scathing indictment of the majority opinion of the Court.[13] Stone admitted that the taxing power—upon which the AAA had been based—might be abused, but so might judicial power. "A tortured construction of the Constitution is not to be justified," he said, "by recourse to extreme examples of reckless congressional spending which might occur if courts could not prevent it. . . . Such suppositions are addressed to the mind accustomed to believe that it is the business of courts to sit in judgment on the wisdom of legislative action. Courts are not the only agency of government that must be assumed to have capacity to govern. Congress and the courts both unhappily may falter or be mistaken in the performance of their

[10] *Adkins* v. *Children's Hospital,* 261 U.S. 525 (1923).

[11] 298 U.S. 587 (1936).

[12] On the conservative bloc see Joel Francis Paschal, *Mr. Justice Sutherland: A Man Against the State* (Princeton: Princeton University Press, 1951); Ronald F. Howell, "Conservative Influence on Constitutional Development, 1923–1937: The Constitutional Theory of Justices Van Devanter, McReynolds, Sutherland and Butler" (Baltimore: Unpublished Ph.D. Dissertation, The Johns Hopkins University, 1952); and Doris Arlene Blaisdell, "The Constitutional Law of Mr. Justice McReynolds" (Madison: Unpublished Ph.D. Dissertation, University of Wisconsin, 1952).

[13] Mason, *Harlan Fiske Stone,* p. 408.

constitutional duty. But interpretation of our great charter of government which proceeds on any assumption that the responsibility for the preservation of our institutions is the exclusive concern of any one of the three branches of government, or that it alone can save them from destruction, is far more likely, in the long run, 'to obliterate the constituent members' of 'an indestructible union of indestructible states' than the frank recognition that language, even of a constitution, may mean what it says. . . ."[14]

Stone's dissent, in which he was joined by Justices Brandeis and Cardozo, was, in addition to being a classic argument for judicial self-restraint, a source of encouragement to New Dealers who sought broader constitutional power as an instrument of reform. "For the first time," Edward S. Corwin wrote, "a powerful segment of the Court, embracing three of its most highly regarded members, extended a sympathetic gesture toward the New Deal, assuring its sponsors that their reading of the Constitution was not utterly untenable. . . ."[15] Stone also was the spokesman for the liberal bloc in its dissent from the majority's opinion in the *Morehead* case.[16] "There is grim irony," he said, "in speaking of the freedom of contract of those who, because of their economic necessities, give their services for less than is needful to keep body and soul together." Time, he said, had proved the inadequacy of the rule of the *Adkins* case as a doctrine of constitutional law. Since it was decided, Stone declared, "we have had opportunity to learn that a wage is not always the resultant of free bargaining between employers and employees; that it may be one forced upon employees by their economic necessities and upon employers by the most ruthless of their competitors. We have had opportunity to perceive more clearly that a wage insufficient to support the worker does not visit its consequences upon him alone; that it may affect profoundly the entire economic structure of society and, in any case, that it casts on every tax payer, and on government itself, the burden of solving problems of poverty, subsistence, health, and morals of large numbers in the community. Because of their nature and extent these are public problems. A generation ago they were for the individual to solve; today they are the burden of the nation."[17] Despite Stone's excellent showing in his *Morehead* dissent, however, he was much discouraged by the trend of the Court's decisions in the 1936 term. "We finished the term of Court yesterday," he wrote privately. "I think in many ways one of the most disastrous in its history. At any rate it seems

[14] 297 U.S. at 87–88.
[15] Edward S. Corwin, *Constitutional Revolution Ltd.* (Claremont, Calif.: Claremont College, 1941), p. 63.
[16] *Morehead* v. *New York,* 298 U.S. 587 (1936).
[17] 298 U.S. at 632–35.

to me that the Court has been needlessly narrow and obscurantic in its outlook." The Court, it seemed to Stone, had "tied Uncle Sam up in a hard knot."[18]

The third member of the liberal bloc, Justice Cardozo, agreed with Stone's estimate of the 1936 term. "We did indeed have a hard year in the court," he wrote Stone. "Next year may be bad, but certainly can't be worse. . . ."[19] Cardozo, too, had struck out against the trend of the Court's decisions. In 1924, Cardozo had written that in judging it was "vain to seek a sovereign talisman; that the treasure box does not spring open at the magic of a whispered word; that there is no one method of judging, supreme over its competitors, but only a choice of methods changing with the problem."[20] And it was in this spirit that he attacked the Court majority's rigid use of the "direct-indirect" effects formula in deciding the extent of Congress's power to regulate interstate commerce. While concurring in the Court's opinion in the *Schechter* case, he did not accept Chief Justice Hughes' emphasis on the use of the "direct-indirect" effects formula but emphasized that upon the facts of the case, NRA's regulation of wages and hours in the live poultry industry could not stand as a valid regulation of commerce.[21]

In the *Carter* case, however, Cardozo dissented from the majority's use of the formula to classify manufacturing and mining enterprises as "local" in nature and argued that upon the facts of the case, the regulation of wages and hours in the bituminous coal industry could be upheld as a valid exercise of the commerce power. "At times . . . ," he said, "the waves of causation will have radiated so far that their undulatory motion, if discernible at all, will be too faint or obscure, too broken by cross-currents, to be heeded by the law. In such circumstances the holding is not directed at prices and wages considered in the abstract, but at prices and wages in particular conditions. The relation may be tenuous or the opposite according to the facts."[22] The Guffey Act's regulation of prices and wages in the bituminous coal industry, Cardozo thought, could be shown to be a valid exercise of the commerce power, since these matters had often resulted in "strikes, at times nation-wide in extent, at other times spreading over broad areas and many mines, with the accompaniment of violence and bloodshed and misery and bitter feeling." "Congress," he said, "was not condemned to inaction in the face of price wars and wage wars so pregnant with disaster. Commerce had

[18] Mason, *Harlan Fiske Stone*, pp. 425–26.
[19] George S. Hellman, *Benjamin N. Cardozo: American Judge* (New York: McGraw-Hill Book Co., 1940), p. 231.
[20] Hellman, *op. cit.*, p. 127.
[21] 295 U.S. 495, at 551.
[22] 298 U.S. 238, at 327–28.

been choked and burdened; its normal flow had been diverted from one state to another; there had been bankruptcy and waste and ruin alike for capital and labor."[23]

Middlemen between the liberal and conservative blocs on the Court were Chief Justice Hughes and Justice Owen J. Roberts.[24] In 1930, at the time when the Senate rejected President Hoover's nomination of Judge John J. Parker to the Supreme Court, Roberts was nationally known as the special prosecutor of the Teapot Dome scandal. After the Senate's rejection of Parker, Hoover turned to Roberts, a life-long Republican, to fill the Court post, and the Senate quickly confirmed the nomination.

"He is a hard worker, has a good mind, and has had a wide range of experience," Justice Stone wrote in appraisal of Roberts. "I should expect him to deal in the liberal way with important constitutional problems, because he has the type of mind that would take in all aspects of the problem."[25] The new Justice seemed to be bearing out Stone's prediction during the 1934 term of the Court, when he joined the Chief Justice and Stone, Brandeis, and Cardozo to sustain a Minnesota statute conferring on the courts power to postpone mortgage foreclosures,[26] and in *Nebbia* v. *New York*[27] he voted to sustain a New York statute fixing the price of milk. Roberts' uncertainty began to tell when the *Nebbia* case was under consideration by the Court, however, and he paced the floor of his Washington home most of the night before deciding how his vote should be cast.[28]

Finally, in the 1935 term of the Court, Roberts swung to the conservative side and wrote the majority opinion in the *Alton* case,[29] holding that a pension plan for railroad employees was an invalid exercise of the commerce power and a denial of due process of law. During 1936, Roberts was again on the side of the conservatives and now the Chief Justice, in *United States* v. *Butler,* the case in which the AAA was invalidated, and he also joined the majority opinions in the *Carter* and *Morehead* cases, which denied the power to regulate wages to both the federal and state governments, thus creating a "no-man's-land" in which neither sphere of government could act.

It was not until years later that Roberts explained that he joined the

[23] *Ibid.* at 330–31.
[24] See C. Herman Pritchett, *The Roosevelt Court: A Study in Judicial Politics and Values, 1937–1947* (New York: The Macmillan Co., 1948), and Glendon A. Schubert, *Quantitative Analysis of Judicial Behavior* (Glencoe: The Free Press and the Michigan State University Bureau of Social and Political Research, 1959).
[25] Mason, *Harlan Fiske Stone*, p. 300.
[26] *Home Building and Loan Association* v. *Blaisdell,* 290 U.S. 398 (1934).
[27] 291 U.S. 502 (1934).
[28] Corwin, *op. cit.,* pp. 75–76.
[29] *Railroad Retirement Board* v. *Alton,* 295 U.S. 330 (1935).

majority in the *Morehead* case only on the grounds that the New York minimum wage statute involved in the case could not be distinguished from the statute invalidated in the *Adkins* case. The counsel for New York had not asked the Court to overrule the *Adkins* case but had instead argued that the New York act was distinguishable from the act involved in the *Adkins* case. Roberts thought this argument was "disingenuous and born of timidity" and voted with the conservatives to invalidate the New York statute. Because of Stone's rigorous attack on the majority opinion, Justice Butler, who had been assigned the task of writing the majority opinion, added material to his opinion which made the decision rest upon a reaffirmation of the *Adkins* case rather than on the narrow basis to which Roberts had agreed. "My proper course," Roberts wrote later, "would have been to concur specially on the narrow ground I had taken. I did not do so. But at the conference in the Court I said that I did not propose to review and re-examine the *Adkins* case until a case would come to the Court requiring that this should be done."[30]

To the country at large, however, it appeared that a majority of five still believed that the doctrine of liberty of contract prohibited state regulation of minimum wages, so that by not stating his position, Roberts had contributed to the growing crisis. The equivocal role of Roberts in the *Morehead* case was matched, however, by the behavior of Chief Justice Hughes himself in the period prior to Franklin Roosevelt's attack on the Court.[31] As an Associate Justice, Hughes had demonstrated a liberal inclination on constitutional issues. He wrote the Court's opinion in the famous *Shreveport Case*,[32] which extended the federal commerce power to include the regulation of rates charged by an interstate railroad for operations totally within one state. Hughes had also dissented, along with Justices Holmes and Day, in *Coppage* v. *Kansas*,[33] where a majority of the Court had invalidated a statute outlawing the yellow dog contract. Hughes' record as Chief Justice, however, was rather equivocal in several areas. He wrote the unanimous opinion of the Court in the *Texas and New Orleans* case[34] sustaining the Railway Labor Act of 1926 and creating a precedent for the broader use of the commerce power, but in the *Schechter* case, he argued that the distinction "between direct and

[30] See Felix Frankfurter, "Mr. Justice Roberts," 104 *University of Pennsylvania Law Review* 311, 315 (1955).

[31] Hughes' responsibility for constitutional ambiguity during this period has been clearly demonstrated by Alpheus T. Mason in his *Harlan Fiske Stone: Pillar of the Law* and his *Supreme Court from Taft to Warren*. The analysis of Hughes herein owes much to Mason's analysis.

[32] *Houston E. & W.T. Ry. Co.* v. *United States*, 234 U.S. 342 (1914).

[33] 236 U.S. 1 (1915).

[34] *Texas and New Orleans Ry. Co.* v. *Brotherhood*, 281 U.S. 548 (1930).

indirect effects of intrastate transactions upon interstate commerce must be recognized as a fundamental one, essential to the maintenance of our constitutional system."[35]

Then, in the *Alton* case, he joined Stone, Brandeis, and Cardozo in dissenting from the majority's denial that a railroad pension plan was a valid exercise of the commerce power, writing that he could not agree that the government's power should be "conceived to be limited to a requirement that the railroads dismiss their superannuated employees, throwing them out helpless, without any reasonable provision for their protection."[36] But the Chief Justice again joined Roberts and the conservatives in the *Butler* case, and in the *Morehead* case he dissented only on the narrow ground that the New York minimum wage statute could be distinguished from the statute involved in the *Adkins* case.[37] In the *Carter* case he concurred with the majority's opinion holding that mining and manufacturing enterprises and the employer-employee relations incidental to such enterprises could not be regulated under the commerce power, dissenting only on the grounds that the price fixing provisions of the Guffey Act were valid and separable from the labor provisions. He agreed, he wrote, that "production—in this case mining—which precedes commerce, is not itself commerce; and that the power to regulate commerce among the several States is not a power to regulate industry within a state." Congress could not use its protective authority under the commerce clause, he continued, "as a pretext for the exertion of power to regulate activities and relations within the States which affect interstate commerce only indirectly. Otherwise, in view of the multitude of indirect effects, Congress in its discretion could assume control of virtually all the activities of the people to the subversion of the fundamental principle of the Constitution. If the people desire to give Congress the power to regulate industries within the States, and the relations of employers and employees in those industries, they are at liberty to declare their will in the appropriate manner, but it is not for the Court to amend the Constitution by judicial decision."[38]

Hughes seemed to be arguing that the "fundamental" distinction between direct and indirect effects on interstate commerce consigned the effects of labor relations in production industries to the category of "indirect effects" and that such relations could therefore not be regulated by Congress unless the people were to adopt a constitutional amendment conferring such power on Congress. The Chief Justice, as his biographer

[35] 295 U.S. at 548.
[36] 295 U.S. at 381.
[37] 298 U.S. at 618–23.
[38] 298 U.S. at 317–18.

asserts, may well have been going "straight down the line of judicial duty, giving sanction to Acts that squared with the Constitution, as he understood it, and setting aside those that did not,"[39] but his position in several important cases, and particularly in the *Carter* case, must have contributed to the impression both in the administration and in the country at large that the Court would remain adamant in denying the power to govern.

Events outside the Court emphasized the critical nature of the constitutional deadlock when sit-down strikes began to paralyze the country in 1935. Such strikes, by which employees occupied the plants of their employers while refusing to work, were used extensively by workers demanding union recognition and better working conditions during the fall of 1936 and the winter of 1937. From September, 1936, to May, 1937, 484,711 workers engaged in sit-downs which closed plants employing over one million workers. The peak came in March, 1937, when 192,642 workers sat down in their plants, the most spectacular strike being by the CIO United Automobile Workers against General Motors at Flint, Michigan. John L. Lewis publicly pointed out to President Roosevelt that for "six months during the Presidential campaign the economic royalists represented by General Motors and the Du Ponts contributed their money and used their energy to drive this Administration from power. The Administration asked labor for help to repel this attack and labor gave it. The same economic royalists now have their fangs in labor." "The workers of this country," Lewis warned, "expect this Administration to help the strikers in every reasonable way." The striking workers in Flint sent out word that any attempt to dislodge them from the plants would result in "a bloody massacre of the workers." Roosevelt finally persuaded General Motors officials to meet with the union on February 11, 1937, and the strike ended when the corporation agreed to recognize the union. The success of the General Motors sit-down, however, encouraged the use of the tactic in other industries.[40]

It was with this background of industrial crisis that the President finally decided to launch an attack on the Supreme Court. As early as 1935, Roosevelt remarked to Frances Perkins that he had been in office "for two years and haven't had an appointment for the Supreme Court. That is most unusual, I am told. What that Court needs is some Roosevelt appointments. Then we might get a good decision out of them."[41] He had failed to meet the issue of the Court during the 1936

[39] Pusey, *op. cit.*, Vol. II, p. 747.

[40] Edward Levinson, *Labor on the March* (New York: University Books, 1956), pp. 158–69.

[41] Frances Perkins, *The Roosevelt I Knew* (New York: The Viking Press, 1946), p. 249.

campaign, however, and the Democratic platform had only promised, somewhat vaguely, a "clarifying amendment" to meet the Court's restriction of the power of government.[42] Roosevelt rejected the idea of a constitutional amendment, confiding to Secretary of Interior Harold Ickes that the Liberty League had collected a large sum of money in New York to finance a campaign to defeat any proposed amendment. "Give me ten million dollars," he said, "and I can prevent any amendment to the Constitution from being ratified by the necessary number of states."[43] Shortly after the election, the President put the issue of the Court to his cabinet, joking that Justice McReynolds would probably still be on the Court at the age of one hundred and five,[44] and by December, he had instructed Attorney General Homer Cummings to begin drafting alternative proposals for dealing with the Court.[45]

By the end of December, Roosevelt confided to Sidney Hillman that he intended to propose the appointment of additional Justices to the Court,[46] but apparently only a handful of others knew of the imminence of the attack on the Court before the President himself revealed it. He gave a veiled hint of the impending proposal in his State of the Union message in early January, 1937, when he said that with "a better understanding of our purposes, and a more intelligent recognition of our needs as a nation, it is not to be assumed that there will be prolonged failure to bring legislative and judicial action into closer harmony." "Means must be found," he continued, "to adapt our legal forms and our judicial interpretation to the actual present national needs of the largest progressive democracy in the modern world. . . . We do not ask the courts to call nonexistent powers into being, but we have a right to expect that conceded powers or those legitimately implied shall be made effective instruments for the common good."[47] Congressman Hatton W. Sumners, Chairman of the House Judiciary Committee, was encouraged by these words to propose anew a more liberal retirement plan for Supreme Court Justices, since he had learned that Justices Van Devanter and Sutherland would resign if they felt they were protected from a cut in pension such as Holmes received under the Economy Act.[48]

On February 5, however, Roosevelt suddenly announced his plan for

[42] James MacGregor Burns, *Roosevelt: The Lion and the Fox* (New York: Harcourt, Brace and Co., 1956), p. 296.

[43] Harold L. Ickes, *The Secret Diary of Harold L. Ickes: The Inside Struggle, 1936–1939* (New York: Simon and Schuster, 1954), Vol. II, p. 65–66.

[44] Burns, *op. cit.*, p. 296.

[45] Joseph Alsop and Turner Catledge, *The 168 Days* (Garden City: Doubleday, Doran & Co., 1938), p. 33.

[46] Matthew Josephson, *Sidney Hillman: Statesman of American Labor* (Garden City: Doubleday & Co., 1952), p. 404.

[47] Quoted in Mason, *Harlan Fiske Stone*, p. 441.

[48] Alsop and Catledge, *op. cit.*, pp. 40–41.

the Court. Justice McReynolds, when he was Attorney General under Wilson, had proposed that when any federal judge, except Supreme Court Justices, failed to retire upon reaching retirement age, the President should be allowed to appoint a new judge to the court, and Roosevelt had adopted this as the basis of his plan.[49] It proposed that the President be allowed to appoint to any federal court, including the Supreme Court, an additional judge for each judge who failed to retire within six months after reaching retirement age. The number of such additional judges was limited to six on the Supreme Court and to fifty for the lower federal courts.[50] In his message to Congress accompanying the proposed legislation, Roosevelt justified the bill on the grounds that the federal judiciary needed the addition of younger men to keep the law abreast of the times and on the assertion that the Supreme Court was behind in its work and needed additional members to catch up. "Can it be said," Roosevelt declared, "that full justice is achieved when a court is forced by the sheer necessity of keeping up with its business to decline, without explanation, to hear 87 per cent of the cases presented to it by private litigants?"[51]

It was soon pointed out to the President that it was a basic strategic error in his justification of the Court plan to use devious arguments concerning old age and inefficiency rather than to base the issue squarely on the Court's denial to the federal government of power to deal with a depression-struck industrial society. "Nobody knows what you are getting at and nobody knows what your grievance is," Assistant Attorney General Robert Jackson told Roosevelt. "You sound off on old age, and here Brandeis is the best friend on the Supreme Court. This thing has got to be put in different terms or you're going to lose the country." "Well, all right," Roosevelt replied. "I'll make a speech. I've got to protect my flank. After all, I've committed myself to this principle. You'll have to help get up a speech."[52] Thus on March 4, in his speech before the Democratic victory dinner and on March 8, in a fireside chat, Roosevelt attempted to shift his ground and justify his attack on the Court with the argument that it was blocking programs needed and approved by the people since 1933. The effect of these speeches was demonstrated when the Gallup polls, which had indicated an even split in public opinion when the plan was announced, indicated during March that forty-five per cent favored the President's plan while the percentage of those opposing it dropped from forty-five to forty-one.[53]

[49] *Ibid.*, p. 33.
[50] See Hearings on S. 1392, Senate Judiciary Committee, 75th Cong., 1st sess., pp. 1–3.
[51] *The Public Papers and Addresses of Franklin D. Roosevelt* (New York: The Macmillan Co., 1941), 1937 Vol., p. 53.
[52] Gerhart, *op. cit.*, p. 107.
[53] Frank V. Cantwell, "Public Opinion and the Legislative Process," *American Political Science Review*, Vol. 40 (Oct., 1946), pp. 924, 927–28.

Roosevelt in the meantime met with Jim Farley, who also had not been advised of the plan before its introduction,[54] and told him that the bill was "something that affects the heart of my program. I'll keep them (Congress) here all year to pass it, if necessary." Farley was instructed to hold up all patronage appointments for congressmen who opposed the bill and to pass them promptly for those who were favorable.[55] On March 9, Attorney General Homer Cummings opened the administration's case before the Senate Judiciary Committee, pronouncing the court bill "direct, coherent, and well considered." "The more it is studied, the more freely it is debated," he said, "the more clearly will its merits appear."[56] Robert H. Jackson stated to the Committee that "the whole program approved by the people in 1932, 1934, and 1936 is in danger of being lost in a maze of constitutional metaphors." "That the conflict between the Court and the elective branches of the Government is entering a new phase," Jackson said, "is apparent from the extensive assertion of the right to disregard acts of Congress, which is subtly transferring the process of judicial review into a veto power over legislation." He was confident, he said, that the Court had no wish to assume such a veto power, but "powerful interests, by carrying all causes lost in Congress to the Supreme Court, and by resisting lawful authority, meanwhile, are forcing that consequence upon the Court with its effective, if unconscious, consent."[57] Edward S. Corwin, testifying in behalf of the administration, told the Senators that he believed "the realities of the situation are these: In the first place, the doctrines of constitutional law of the majority of the Court involve the entire program of the administration in a fog of doubt as to constitutionality; and second, that cloud or doubt can be dispelled within a reasonable time only by reestablishing that mode of reading the Constitution which adapts it to present needs in harmony with its intent as announced by its earliest expounders, that it should 'endure for ages to come, and consequently be adapted to various crises in human affairs.' "[58]

Despite the President's speeches and the administration presentation before the Judiciary Committee, the bill appeared to be heading for trouble when the farm organizations, despite the Court's invalidation of the AAA in the *Butler* case, failed to support the President.[59] A private poll during February had also indicated that in the Senate, where the

---

[54] James A. Farley, *Jim Farley's Story: The Roosevelt Years* (New York: McGraw-Hill Book Co., 1948), p. 72.

[55] *Ibid.*, pp. 73–74.

[56] Hearings on S. 1392, Senate Judiciary Committee, 75th Cong., 1st sess., p. 11.

[57] *Ibid.*, pp. 44–45.

[58] *Ibid.*, pp. 167–68.

[59] Alsop and Catledge, *op. cit.*, pp. 116–18.

administration determined upon making its major effort, thirty-two members were favorable, twenty-eight were opposed, and thirty-five were uncommitted.[60] Both the administration and the opposition to the bill concentrated on winning over the uncommitted Senators. Senator Burton K. Wheeler, a long-time progressive Democrat from Montana, had assumed the leadership of the opposition forces and persuaded conservatives in his party to allow the liberals to take the lead in the fight. Republicans also decided to remain silent and allow the fight over the bill to be an intra-Democratic party fight.[61]

Wheeler now hoped to devise a plan by which the prestige of the Supreme Court could be thrown in the scales against the bill, with all the effect this would have on public opinion and the undecided Senators. He went to the only Justice he knew personally, Justice Brandeis, and Brandeis immediately suggested that he talk with Chief Justice Hughes.[62] The Chief Justice, whatever may have been his hesitancy on constitutional issues during the 1930's, was now willing to protect the Court even by testifying personally before the Senate Judiciary Committee, but his offer was vetoed by Brandeis. Hughes then agreed to give Wheeler a letter to be introduced before the committee.[63] Thus on March 22, Wheeler appeared before the committee and dramatically produced the letter from the Chief Justice which completely demolished the President's assertion that the Court was behind in its work. "There is no congestion of cases upon our calendar," Hughes wrote. "This gratifying condition has obtained for several years." The addition of new Justices to the Court, Hughes said, "apart from any question of policy, which I do not discuss, would not promote the efficiency of the Court. It is believed that it would impair that efficiency so long as the Court acts as a unit. There would be more judges to hear, more judges to confer, more judges to discuss, more judges to be convinced and to decide. The present number of justices is thought to be large enough so far as the prompt, adequate, and efficient conduct of the work of the Court is concerned." To the suggestion that with more Justices the Court might hear cases in divisions, the Chief Justice pointed out that the "Constitution does not appear to authorize two or more Supreme Courts or two or more parts of a supreme court functioning in effect as separate courts."

Hughes admitted that "on account of the shortness of time" he had been unable to consult all the members of the Court on his letter, but he assured the committee that he was "confident that it is in accord with the

[60] Cantwell, *op. cit.*, p. 926.
[61] Alsop and Catledge, *op. cit.*, pp. 97–104.
[62] Mason, *Harlan Fiske Stone*, p. 450.
[63] Pusey, *op. cit.*, Vol. II, pp. 754–55.

views of the Justices." "I should say, however," he closed, "that I have been able to consult with Mr. Justice Van Devanter and Mr. Justice Brandeis, and I am at liberty to say that the statement is approved by them."[64] It is now apparent that Hughes could have consulted easily with at least three other Justices but failed to do so possibly because he anticipated some difficulty in drafting a letter which would be unanimously endorsed by all the Justices. Justices Stone and Cardozo, at least, indicated later that they disagreed with the expression of an opinion on the question of whether or not the Constitution authorized the Court to sit in divisions.[65] Hughes, however, had hit the President's proposal on its weakest points and demonstrated a political adroitness which the usually masterfully adept Roosevelt had failed to achieve when the plan was announced.

After reading Hughes' letter, Wheeler warned those of the committee "who call yourselves liberals or progressives, that if you put six new men on the Supreme Court of the United States, you are going to do more to hurt the liberal cause and the labor cause in the United States, in my judgment, than anything else that could possibly happen. You will turn back the wheels of progress. You are going to discredit the liberal movement and the labor movement in this country. You are going to discredit the Democratic Party."[66] The effect of his presentation of the Chief Justice's letter was what Wheeler had hoped it would be, as the Gallup polls indicated an upturn in the percentage of the public opposed to the court bill.[67]

Roosevelt, nevertheless, was determined to win the fight. The administration's thinking was indicated by Secretary of Interior Ickes' belief that the issue was "the most important one since the Civil War and it is realized that unless the President wins on it, we will lose everything that we have gained during the last four years and a good deal besides. We will be set back at least ten years, with the fight to make over again."[68] The President himself continued to feel that public opinion would ultimately be with him on the issue and that soon the opposition would be "beating a path to the White House door."[69] But Hughes' letter was only the first shot the Court would fire during the fight. On March 21, Justice Cardozo entered his apartment to find his secretary performing a somersault for the amusement of a friend. "It might be helpful," Cardozo said, "if you would come down and teach some of my

[64] Hearings on S. 1392, pp. 488–91.
[65] Mason, *Harlan Fiske Stone*, pp. 451–52.
[66] Hearings on S. 1392, p. 499.
[67] Cantwell, *op. cit.*, p. 928.
[68] Ickes, *op. cit.*, Vol. II, p. 89.
[69] Farley, *op. cit.*, p. 79.

colleagues to do that in their judicial decisions."[70] Cardozo's prescription of gymnastics as a solution for the Court's difficulties seemed to have been followed as in late March and early April it continued to undermine the rationale for the President's bill through the more orthodox method of deciding cases.

[70] Hellman, *op. cit.*, p. 253.

# 8

# THE WAGNER ACT BEFORE THE COURT

□ □ □ □ □ □ □ □ □ □ □ □ □ □ □ □ □ □ □ □ □ □ □ □ □ □ □ □ □ □ □ □ □ □ □ □ □ □ □ □ □

On February 9, 1937, four days after Franklin Roosevelt launched his attack on the Supreme Court, oral arguments were begun before the Court in the Wagner Act cases. The government and the National Labor Relations Board selected the *Associated Press* and the *Jones & Laughlin* cases as the ones in which to file major briefs in the effort to sustain the constitutionality of the act, filing only rather summary briefs in the *Fruehauf, Friedman–Harry Marks,* and *Washington, Virginia and Maryland Coach Company* cases. The government and the Board were again favored when the *Virginian Railroad* case[1] was appealed to the Supreme Court at approximately the same time as the Wagner Act cases. The litigation of this case, involving a test of the 1934 amendments to the Railway Labor Act,[2] had paralleled the litigation of the Wagner Act cases since 1935 and was now set down for argument along with them. It involved particularly the testing of the provisions of the 1934 amendments establishing majority rule in employee representation elections and requiring carriers to bargain collectively with the representatives of their employees selected in such elections. Such provisions had also been included in the Wagner Act, but none of the NLRB's five cases tested these particular provisions in the Act, and accordingly the *Virginian* case was a welcome addition not only as a strong interstate commerce case in labor relations but also as a case testing issues crucial to the validity of the Wagner Act as well as the Railway Labor Act.[3]

In its brief in the *Associated Press* case, the government argued, citing previous decisions of the Court,[4] that the transmission of news across state lines was definitely interstate commerce and that the Associated

---

[1] *Virginian Railroad Co.* v. *System Federation,* 84 F.2d 641 (CCA 4th, June 18, 1936).

[2] 48 Stat. 1185.

[3] National Labor Relations Board, *First Annual Report* (June, 1936), p. 54.

[4] *Pensacola Tel.* v. *Western Union,* 96 U.S. 1 (1878); *Federal Radio Commission* v. *Nelson Brothers,* 289 U.S. 266 (1933); *Int. Textbook* v. *Pigg,* 217 U.S. 91 (1910).

Press was an instrumentality of interstate commerce subject to the power of Congress under the commerce clause. Editorial employees of the AP, the government contended, were thus links in the continuous process of the gathering and transmission of news across state lines and labor unrest among such employees would interrupt or burden commerce.[5] The anti-trust cases involving labor unions, it was argued, demonstrated that Congress could regulate local relations which affected commerce and that "on the very subject matter here involved, although it be said that the right to join a labor organization is, standing alone, a local matter, that right may be protected by Congress where its protection will assist in maintaining the orderly conduct of interstate commerce, and furthering the peaceful settlement of disputes which threaten it."[6]

Given the fact that the AP was directly engaged in interstate commerce, the government contended that the question of the validity of the Wagner Act's application to its employees was "conclusively answered in the affirmative by *Texas & New Orleans R. Co. v. Brotherhood of Railway Clerks,* 281 U.S. 548. There is no essential difference between the employer there and the employer here."[7] "If any distinction is possible," the government argued, "between these employees and the members of the Brotherhood of Railway Clerks, we submit that the former are closer to, and more directly connected with, the interstate operations of their employer than the latter. . . . The work of these employees in rewriting and filing news dispatches is an important and integral part of the functions of petitioner's world-wide communication enterprise."[8]

On the fifth amendment liberty of contract objections to the act, the government argued that the effect of the *Texas and New Orleans* case was to overrule the *Adair*[9] and *Coppage*[10] cases. The decree of the district court in that case, the brief said, "was cast in terms substantially identical with the statute. Since the discriminatory discharges were held violations of the injunction, as petitioner admits, they were interferences prohibited by the statute." The *Adair* and *Coppage* cases, the argument continued, were vigorously urged by the carrier in the *Texas and New Orleans* case, and "the facts of the latter case are so similar to those of the case at bar that the earlier cases, if inapplicable there, cannot be applicable here."[11] In addition, the government contended that the Board's procedures did not violate due process nor did the order for restoration of

[5] Brief of the National Labor Relations Board, *Associated Press* v. *NLRB*, pp. 25–39. (Hereinafter cited as NLRB Brief, *AP* v. *NLRB*.)

[6] *Ibid.,* pp. 43–44.

[7] *Ibid.,* pp. 69–70.

[8] *Ibid.,* p. 71.

[9] *Adair* v. *United States,* 208 U.S. 161 (1908).

[10] *Coppage* v. *Kansas,* 236 U.S. 1 (1915).

[11] NLRB Brief, *AP* v. *NLRB*, pp. 85–86.

back pay violate the seventh amendment's requirement of a jury trial. Such an order, the brief said, was "a mere incident in the equitable remedy—included in order to effectuate the policy of the Act and to bring about as complete a restoration of the *status quo* as possible."

To the Associated Press' contention that the application of the act to it would violate the first amendment's guarantee of the freedom of the press, the government pointed out that newspaper publishers and news media did not have "a special immunity from the application of general legislation nor a special privilege to destroy the recognized rights and liberties of others." It was pointed out that such enterprises were subject to the general application of libel laws, the contempt powers of courts, anti-trust laws, and general tax laws. "Since neither the Act nor the order in any way abridges petitioner's privilege to discharge an employee for actual bias," the brief said, "petitioner's contention that the First Amendment has been violated comes to this: that employees who belong to labor organizations must be conclusively presumed to be biased in their work, and that any legislation protecting the right of organization of editorial employees of a newspaper is a necessary violation of the guarantee of the freedom of the press. The proposition is obviously unsound."[12]

In his brief for the Associated Press, John W. Davis argued that the AP was not an instrumentality of commerce nor engaged in interstate commerce. Its operations, he contended, were conducted on a non-profit basis and its news transmitted only to its members, the owners of newspapers.[13] The "Findings" of Congress included in the act, it was argued, demonstrated that the act was aimed at the regulation of employer-employee relations in all industry, since only by such regulation could the general purchasing power of the country be raised to the extent necessary to affect commerce.[14] "That the regulation of the employer-employee relationship in all industry," the brief continued, "is not in any sense a regulation of interstate or foreign commerce should require little if any elaboration. There appear to be few propositions in the realm of Constitutional law which are more fundamental or more clearly settled." Here the AP brief relied on the Supreme Court's decisions in the *Schechter*[15] and the *Carter Coal Company*[16] cases.[17]

The cause and effect reasoning by which the Board had connected a labor dispute involving the AP's editorial employees and an interruption

[12] NLRB Brief, *AP* v. *NLRB*, pp. 102–107.
[13] Brief for the Associated Press, *Associated Press* v. *NLRB*, pp. 9–10. (Hereinafter cited as AP Brief.)
[14] *Ibid.*, p. 22.
[15] *Schechter Poultry Corp.* v. *United States*, 295 U.S. 495 (1935).
[16] *Carter* v. *Carter Coal Co.*, 298 U.S. 238 (1936).
[17] AP Brief, pp. 34–35.

of interstate commerce was not sufficient, according to the brief, to demonstrate that direct burden on commerce which was required to be shown before such a dispute could be reached by the federal government under the commerce clause. "According to the philosophers," it said, "the chain of cause and effect has never been broken since Time began, but it is not by such speculations that the Constitution is to be interpreted and statutes sustained. It is direct causes operating directly upon interstate commerce with which Congress is empowered to deal."[18] According to Davis' argument the Associated Press was not engaged in commerce, and its editorial employees were engaged in the gathering and formulation of news, not its transmission, and thus in "this sense the analogy is exact between these employees and the employees of a manufacturing plant engaged in transforming the raw materials into the completed article."[19] It was argued also that even in enterprises where there was an admitted engagement in interstate commerce, such as railroads, the activities regulated by Congress must have a direct effect on commerce according to the Supreme Court's decisions in the *Adair* and *Alton*[20] cases.[21]

Apart from asserting that the Wagner Act was an invalid exercise of the commerce power, the AP's brief contended also that the act violated liberty of contract as guaranteed by the fifth amendment by requiring the reinstatement of discharged employees. "There are rights which have no material or numerical measure," the brief said, citing the *Adair, Coppage, Hitchman,*[22] *Adkins,*[23] and *Morehead*[24] cases. "Such rights, perhaps the most notable of all being freedom of contract, are generally immune, in a free country, from any governmental interference, limitation, or disturbance." It was argued that the *Texas and New Orleans* case had not overruled this right of contract but had only affirmed the lower court's order protecting the status quo in a particular labor dispute.[25] In addition to pronouncing the Wagner Act a violation of liberty of contract, the AP's brief contended also that the act violated due process generally by conferring on the Board an "intrusive and arbitrary power" and that it violated the seventh amendment by authorizing the Board to require back pay for discriminatorily discharged employees without a jury trial.[26]

[18] *Ibid.,* p. 39.
[19] *Ibid.,* p. 45.
[20] *Railroad Retirement Board* v. *Alton,* 295 U.S. 330 (1935).
[21] AP Brief, pp. 50–62.
[22] *Hitchman Coal Co.* v. *Mitchell,* 245 U.S. 225 (1917).
[23] *Adkins* v. *Children's Hospital,* 261 U.S. 525 (1923).
[24] *Morehead* v. *New York,* 298 U.S. 587 (1936).
[25] AP Brief, pp. 64–78.
[26] *Ibid.,* pp. 89–93.

Finally, citing *Near* v. *Minnesota*,[27] the AP contended that the Wagner Act's application to its operations violated the guarantee of freedom of the press. "Can freedom and independence of the press be maintained," the AP brief asked, "if a Federal bureau may dictate to the American newspapers the persons they employ to prepare their news reports? How can impartiality and independence of reporting be maintained under such a system of administrative supervision? How can accuracy, independence and impartiality survive a deliberate attempt by the Government to impose upon the Associated Press a requirement that its news editors be union men?" Newspapers, it was argued, were the interpreters between the government and the people, and the power to name who should write the news "is no different either in principle or in result from naming what shall be written or published. Here the author and the product are one and inseparable. If one is to be free, so must the other."[28]

The American Newspaper Publishers' Association, in its brief as *amicus curiae,* bolstered the AP and John W. Davis in the contention that the act violated freedom of the press. Elisha Hanson, the ANPA counsel, contended that the affiliation "of newspaper reporters or editorial writers with an organization which can demand or command adherence to and support of any particular program affecting broad public interest or assistance to one party or another in a controversy cannot be contenanced by a publisher who desires to preserve the integrity of his news columns."[29] When a publisher believed that a reporter became unsuited for employment because of such affiliations, the ANPA contended, "no agency of the government either has the power or can be endowed with the power by Congress to interfere with the exercise of that judgment, whatever the nature of the employee's affiliations or activities may be."[30]

The briefs filed by the Commercial Telegraphers' Union[31] and the American Newspaper Guild as *amici curiae,* however, supported the government's argument that the act was constitutional under the commerce and due process clauses and especially attacked the contention that the act violated the freedom of the press. Instead of being an orthodox legal brief, the ANG's brief was essentially an essay in support of the act. "The United States is in the throes of a second Civil War," the

[27] 283 U.S. 697 (1931).

[28] AP Brief, pp. 99–102.

[29] Brief for the American Newspaper Publishers' Association as *Amicus Curiae, Associated Press* v. *NLRB*, pp. 8–9.

[30] *Ibid.,* p. 12.

[31] Brief on behalf of the Commercial Telegraphers' Union as *Amicus Curiae.* The Associated Press had long been an enemy of this union insofar as its organizing activities touched the operations of the AP. See "AP," *Fortune,* Vol. 15 (Feb., 1937), pp. 89, 148.

brief said. "Armed strife continues to rock the nation, leaving in its wake lives lost and property devastated. The conclusion that means must be found to resolve the increasing conflicts between employers and employees leaps from the contents of statistical tables."[32] To demonstrate its contention that there was overwhelming public approval of the Wagner Act as the remedy for this condition, the ANG brief utilized the device of dividing the number of Senators into the population of the country and arrived at the interesting conclusion that over ninety million people favored the act and only eight million were opposed, while twenty-two million persons were listed as "not voting."[33] On the free press issue, the ANG argued that the AP's argument "confused freedom of the press with integrity of the news. The Constitution does not guarantee the objectivity of the press," the brief said, "nor is objectivity obtainable in a subjective world. The question really raised by petitioner is not whether news shall be unprejudiced but rather whose prejudices shall color the news. And it should be noted that petitioner, under the Act, as before, remains the complete master of its business. Its prejudices are still supreme."[34]

While in the *Associated Press* case the government's interstate commerce arguments seemed to be confirmed by prior decisions of the Supreme Court, in the *Jones & Laughlin* case, and also in the *Fruehauf* and *Friedman–Harry Marks* cases, the government was confronted with making an argument on interstate commerce which was at best tenuous under the decisions of the Court. The government lawyers first argued, relying again on the *Texas and New Orleans* case, that the power of Congress under the commerce clause extended to the protection of commerce from the burden and injury caused by labor disputes, and they attempted to demonstrate by a recitation of strike statistics and the history of labor relations in the steel industry as well as in the country at large that labor strife in production enterprises had a substantial effect on commerce.[35] It was then argued that Congress had a choice, under the commerce clause, of using its "control power" or its "preventive power" to alleviate such burdens on commerce. An example given for the "control power" was the anti-trust laws, which were aimed at each particular obstruction to commerce as it arose, whereas the use of the "preventive power," such as in the Packers and Stockyards Act,[36] was

[32] Brief on behalf of the American Newspaper Guild as *Amicus Curiae*, p. 5.
[33] *Ibid.*, p. 21.
[34] *Ibid.*, p. 25.
[35] Brief for the National Labor Relations Board, *NLRB* v. *Jones & Laughlin Steel Corp.*, pp. 21–31. (Hereinafter cited as NLRB Brief, *NLRB* v. *Jones & Laughlin.*) The brief also included at page 60 a map showing the nation-wide implications of Jones & Laughlin's operations.
[36] 42 Stat. 159 (1921).

aimed at the *causes* of such burdens on commerce, and the Wagner Act was an example of the exercise of the "preventive power."[37] Given the recognition of the existence of this power, it was argued that the act could not be considered as totally invalid, but only its application to particular cases could be challenged as extensions beyond the commerce power. "Since the language of this statute does not go beyond the ambit of this power, whatever it may be determined to be," the government argued, "the statute is clearly constitutional on its face. The only issue is whether it has been constitutionally applied."[38]

It was then argued that, under the anti-trust cases involving labor,[39] it was settled that Congress had the power to control labor disputes involving an intent to restrain commerce and that therefore where a situation developed in a particular enterprise which presented the likelihood that if a labor dispute occurred, it would involve an intent to restrain commerce, the act could be validly applied to that situation.[40] In addition, the government pointed to the language in the first and second *Coronado* cases implying that the power of Congress extended to labor disputes which lacked an intent to restrain commerce but had the "necessary effect" of substantially burdening commerce, and argued that the act could also be validly applied to such disputes.[41] Finally, it was argued that, if disputes having the "necessary effect" of burdening commerce were defined as disputes involving enterprises in the stream or flow of commerce or as disputes resulting in the substantial reduction of interstate commerce in a particular commodity, then, under the *Stafford*[42] and *Olsen*[43] cases, the act had been validly applied to Jones & Laughlin, since the corporation had been shown to be in such a stream or flow of commerce on the evidence in the record.[44]

The government further argued that Congress had the power under the commerce clause to prevent recurrent local evils, such as industrial strife, from burdening commerce. Here again, the *Olsen, Stafford,* and *Texas and New Orleans* cases were relied upon as precedents for such a use of the commerce power.[45] "We submit, therefore," the brief said, "that industrial strife in respondent's enterprise is of a character which, by its

[37] NLRB Brief, *NLRB* v. *Jones & Laughlin,* pp. 31–33.
[38] *Ibid.,* p. 38.
[39] *Coronado Coal Co.* v. *United Mine Workers,* 268 U.S. 295 (1925); *United Mine Workers* v. *Coronado Coal Co.,* 259 U.S. 344 (1922); *Bedford Cut Stone Co.* v. *Journeymen Stone Cutters,* 274 U.S. 37 (1927); *Duplex Printing Co.* v. *Deering,* 254 U.S. 443 (1921); *Loewe* v. *Lawler,* 208 U.S. 274 (1908).
[40] NLRB Brief, *NLRB* v. *Jones & Laughlin,* p. 40.
[41] *Ibid.,* pp. 44–50.
[42] *Stafford* v. *Wallace,* 258 U.S. 495 (1922).
[43] *Chicago Board of Trade* v. *Olsen,* 262 U.S. 1 (1923).
[44] NLRB Brief, *NLRB* v. *Jones & Laughlin,* pp. 51–71.
[45] *Ibid.,* pp. 72–73.

very recurrence, comes within the control of Congress. Consequently, the Board was justified in holding that the preventive measures of the National Labor Relations Act might be invoked against respondent in order to anticipate industrial strife affecting commerce which would be within the control power of Congress."[46]

Having answered the liberty of contract objections to the act in its Associated Press brief, the government attempted in its Jones & Laughlin brief to distinguish the *Carter* and *Schechter* cases from its three manufacturing cases. It was argued that the *Schechter* case involved the application of statutory regulations of wages, hours, and prices which were said, through an involved argument of causes and effects, to affect commerce. "The contrast is marked," the government submitted, "between that statute and the present Act, which does not depend for its validity upon any such chain of economic causes and effects. The practices to which it applies are brought under regulation in order to prevent the immediate injury to interstate commerce which results from industrial strife."[47] As to the *Carter* case, the government conceded that it could be contended that it was "directly determinative of the present case because the Act there involved contained a provision for collective bargaining which was among the labor provisions held unconstitutional." But despite this, the government argued that the collective bargaining provisions involved in the *Carter* case, "instead of being directly related to avoiding labor disputes interfering with interstate commerce, were subordinated to the main purpose of stabilization of the industry and were in fact the means through which one of the stabilizing factors—the establishment of uniform wages and hours—was to be effected."[48]

In addition, the government contended that the labor provisions in the *Carter* case were applied to every producer of coal in the country and that there was no machinery, as in the Wagner Act, for restricting their application to enterprises in which labor disputes tended to burden or obstruct commerce. Finally, it was argued that in both the *Schechter* and *Carter* cases the facts demonstrated that the flow of commerce had ceased, whereas in the case at bar it had not, and thus the *Olsen* and *Stafford* cases governed the present case where they had not governed the earlier cases. Thus both the *Schechter* and the *Carter* cases were distinguished.[49]

Earl F. Reed's brief for the Jones & Laughlin Steel Corporation was of course an all-out attack on the government's attempt to sustain the act under the commerce clause. As to the Board's evidence and its

[46] *Ibid.*, p. 86.
[47] *Ibid.*, p. 87.
[48] *Ibid.*, pp. 88–89.
[49] *Ibid.*, pp. 89–94.

introduction of expert testimony on labor relations in the record, Reed contended that it was "a defiance of reason and good judgment to argue that guesswork evidence of this character can bridge the distance between the discharge of thirteen [*sic*] employees and the movement of interstate commerce."[50] The question of the validity of the Wagner Act, the brief said, was obscured by "arguments and discussions which have lost the true meaning of the constitutional phrase in an effort to remodel our constitutional system on a basis of expediency, by attributing to the central government powers which might be most conveniently exercised at Washington. And as a result, the plenary powers of the States, like the Charter on which they rest, are cast aside in an endeavor to reach a theoretically convenient goal."[51] The government's argument, Reed charged, was, "in truth, an attack on our Constitutional system rather than a justification of the application of the Labor Act to the present case."[52] Relying on the *Carter, Schechter, Alton,* and *Adair* cases and *Hammer* v. *Dagenhart*[53] to support his contention that the federal commerce power did not extend to production enterprises and that the effect of a local activity on commerce must be direct to be within the federal government's reach, Reed argued that so far as the "effect on interstate commerce is concerned, there is, in reality, no difference between the respondent's Aliquippa plant and a neighborhood grocery store; the cause and effect may be larger, but the causal connection is just as remote."[54]

On the liberty of contract issue, the brief argued as did the AP brief that the *Adair* and *Coppage* cases had not been overruled by the *Texas and New Orleans* decision and that the opinion of the Court in that case "clearly indicates that in ordering the restoration of the union employees, it was merely directing the defendant to purge itself of its contempt of the Court's order."[55] In closing, Reed's brief argued that the government "is asking that the traditions and precedents of a century be cast aside and the Constitution corrupted for the sake of a temporary expediency. To change *the established* meaning of the Constitution now, by judicial decree, without a proper mandate from the people, would make a mockery of constitutional government."[56]

The government's briefs in the *Fruehauf* and *Friedman–Harry Marks* cases were merely recapitulations of its arguments in the *Jones &*

[50] Brief for the Jones & Laughlin Steel Corp., *NLRB* v. *Jones & Laughlin Steel Corp.*, p. 21.
[51] *Ibid.*, p. 44.
[52] *Ibid.*, p. 51.
[53] 247 U.S. 251 (1918).
[54] Brief for the Jones & Laughlin Steel Corp., p. 60.
[55] *Ibid.*, p. 112.
[56] *Ibid.*, p. 129.

*Laughlin* case, while its brief in the *Washington, Virginia and Maryland Coach Company* case was a resumé of the Associated Press brief. In its Fruehauf brief the government pointed out that the automobile industry was particularly "responsible for a constant stream or current of commerce between the States. Factories in Michigan are unable to finish an automobile and fill orders in New York and other States because of inability to procure glass from Pennsylvania or rubber from Ohio, because there are labor disputes at plants in the latter States growing out of the refusal of employers to recognize unions of employees."[57] In its Friedman–Harry Marks brief the government contended that labor disputes at the respondent's plant would disrupt a substantial proportion of interstate commerce, not because of the size of the business, but because "industrial strife in the men's clothing industry . . . may be expected to spread to other enterprises. . . . The strong national unions, and the keen competition between organized and unorganized areas . . . increase the likelihood that strikes will spread to other enterprises and areas, particularly if they have as their basic causes the refusal of employers to allow organization of their employees for collective bargaining and other purposes."[58]

Counsel for the companies in these cases, Victor W. Klein and Leonard Weinberg, also failed to raise any new issues not covered by John W. Davis and Earl F. Reed in their briefs.[59] This was true also of the briefs filed as *amicus curiae* by the American Federation of Labor in the *Fruehauf* case and by the Amalgamated Association of Street, Electric Railway and Motor Coach Employee's Union and the Pennsylvania Greyhound Lines in the *Washington, Virginia and Maryland Coach Company* case.[60] Robert E. Lynch in his brief for the bus company, however, again relied on the argument that, while his client was admittedly operating in interstate commerce, the statute was meant by Congress to apply to intrastate as well as interstate enterprises and was therefore invalid as a whole under the commerce clause. The statute, he contended, "shows on its face a comprehensive scheme to regulate

---

[57] Brief of the National Labor Relations Board, *NLRB* v. *Fruehauf Trailer Co.,* pp. 23–24.

[58] Brief of the National Labor Relations Board, *NLRB* v. *Friedman–Harry Marks Clothing Co.,* pp. 25–26.

[59] Brief of Fruehauf Trailer Co., *NLRB* v. *Fruehauf Trailer Co.;* Brief of Friedman–Harry Marks Clothing Co., *NLRB* v. *Friedman–Harry Marks Clothing Co.*

[60] Brief for the American Federation of Labor as *Amicus Curiae, NLRB* v. *Fruehauf Trailer Co.;* Brief for the American Federation of Labor and Amalgamated Association of Street, Electric Railway and Motor Coach Employees of America, as *Amici Curiae, Washington, Virginia and Maryland Coach Co.* v. *NLRB;* Brief of the Pennsylvania Greyhound Lines as *Amicus Curiae, Washington, Virginia and Maryland Coach Co.* v. *NLRB.*

intrastate as well as interstate activities, with an object in view which could not be attained through the regulation of interstate relationships alone. Hence it appears affirmatively that Congress would never have passed the Statute to regulate the few remaining lines of interstate activity if it could not constitutionally regulate labor relations in intrastate industry as well."[61] Relying on the *Carter* and *Alton* cases, Lynch argued that the act's separability clause could not save it from total invalidation.[62] In answer, the government reiterated its contention that the act was incontestably valid and that the only question was its application to particular enterprises which if erroneous could be corrected by the courts "by holding that the order exceeded the Act, not that the Act exceeded the commerce power."[63]

The oral argument in the *Virginian Railroad* case, with the United States appearing as *amicus curiae,* was held on February 8, and the Wagner Act cases were argued before the Court February 9 through 11.[64] As the *United States Law Week* pointed out, the argument of the cases "was marked by unusually few questions from the bench."[65] The government's arguments were made by Solicitor General Stanley Reed, Special Assistant to the Attorney General Charles Wyzanski, Jr., NLRB General Counsel Charles Fahy, and NLRB Chairman Warren Madden, while Senator Robert Wagner joined the government counsel in the section of the courtroom reserved for lawyers.[66] The government's arguments closely followed the points made in its briefs.

Warren Madden, arguing that the Wagner Act's regulation of labor relations was similar to the regulation of packers and stockyards sustained by the Court in the *Stafford* case, asked, "Can there be any doubt that labor troubles in a stockyard, which stopped the flow of commerce through that stockyard, would constitutionally be a proper subject of control by the National Government?"[67] At this point, however, Madden was interrupted by Justices McReynolds and Sutherland.

> McReynolds: If the men in that stockyard were employed at something which may not interfere with interstate commerce, how far would you go?

[61] Brief on behalf of the Washington, Virginia and Maryland Coach Co., *Washington, Virginia and Maryland Coach Co. v. NLRB*, p. 43.

[62] *Ibid.,* pp. 44–47.

[63] Brief of the National Labor Relations Board, *Washington, Virginia and Maryland Coach Co. v. NLRB*, p. 10.

[64] Oral Arguments in the Cases arising under the Railway Labor Act and the National Labor Relations Act before the Supreme Court of the United States, February 8–11, 1937, Senate Document No. 52, 75th Cong., 1st sess. (Hereinafter cited as Arguments.)

[65] *United States Law Week*, Vol. 4, No. 5 (Feb. 16, 1937), p. 3.

[66] *Editor & Publisher*, Vol. 70 (Feb. 13, 1937), p. 7.

[67] Arguments, p. 115.

Madden: There is always, of course, in considering these problems, just as there has been when this Court considered the labor cases under the Sherman Act, not merely the constitutional question of the limitation but the question of the wisdom and practicality of it.

McReynolds: I am asking about power. Does Congress have the power to say to these men—

Madden: I should say that if they said to a man there, "You cannot quit your job," you would be in difficulties there with the thirteenth amendment to the Constitution. I should say that if you said to a group of men there, "You cannot enter into an agreement to quit your jobs, although individually you may quit them," there you would face no problem of constitutional power at all, but merely a problem of the wisdom of its exercise.

McReynolds: We are not going to decide the wisdom of Congress . . .

Sutherland: So far as cattle are concerned, how far could you go? You say that is an analogous situation?

Madden: That is right.

Sutherland: Taking it back, for instance, to the herder, suppose herders raising cattle organized a union. Could Congress regulate that?

Madden: I should say not, your Honor.[68]

Solicitor General Stanley Reed pointed out that the government was not arguing "contrary to the *Carter* case." "For the purpose of this argument we feel that the *Carter* case may be taken, as stated by the Court," he said, "to be directed at the control of labor conditions and prices. We submit that when you considered the *Carter* case you considered it from the standpoint of the power of Congress to reach in and control a wage or a labor condition as a part of the scheme of stabilizing the industry which was undertaken by Congress." But again, Justice Sutherland interrupted to question the Solicitor General on "direct" and "indirect" effects.

Sutherland: . . . what is the primary effect of a strike in a steel mill? Is it not to simply curtail production?

Reed: Certainly; that is one of its effects.

Sutherland: Isn't that the primary effect; the immediate effect?

Reed: Well, I should say it was the first effect. I do not mean to split hairs. Of course, that is one of the primary effects of it.

Sutherland: That is the primary effect, to curtail production, and then the curtailment of production in its turn has an effect upon interstate commerce; isn't that true?

Reed: As I understand it, no. The strike is not something that is a

[68] Arguments, pp. 115–16. The herders analogy was of course the analogy used by Sutherland in his opinion in the *Carter* case to distinguish the *Olsen* and *Stafford* cases. 297 U.S. 238, at 305–306.

momentary change of, but instantaneously and at the same time that it stops production stops interstate commerce. It is a single thing that happens, and that stoppage of work stops interstate commerce right at that instant.

Sutherland: It affects interstate commerce just as the cessation of work in a coal mine. The primary effect of that, as suggested in the *Carter* case, was to curtail the production, and then the secondary effect which came from the curtailment of production was the effect upon interstate commerce.[69]

John W. Davis asserted that the Wagner Act as applied to the Associated Press was "a direct, palpable, undisguised attack upon the freedom of the press," and he brought a smile from the press gallery when he argued that editorial writers must have contented minds in order to do their work properly.[70] Morris Watson, Davis said, "may have a heart as pure as Galahad and be as wise as Solomon, but if he is forced upon us by law to formulate and write what we must publish, we are no longer free insofar as the outgivings of the Associated Press are concerned." The reasoning of the Court in the *Schechter* and *Carter* cases, he said, "dooms this statute beyond all reasonable hope of recovery."[71]

In behalf of the Jones & Laughlin Steel Corporation, Earl F. Reed told the Court that if it were announced to the company's 22,000 employees that the discharged men would have to be rehired, "and could not be discharged except upon a hearing before the Labor Board, all freedom of contract, all right to manage your own business, is gone. Those men, if that is the law, if they can come back into this organization and go back to work for us, have a civil service status."[72] Counsel for the Fruehauf Trailer Company argued that the state of Michigan's right to allow the automobile industry to develop as it saw fit was violated by the application of the Wagner Act to the industry. "The State of Michigan," he said, "has permitted the automobile industry to develop and it has developed. . . . It has been the outstanding example of good employer-employee relations, with wages the highest of any business, and there has never been any trouble."[73]

In view of the sit-down strikes then in progress in the automobile industry, this statement was a blunder that Charles Wyzanski, in summing up the government's argument, could not overlook. "I thought the argument of the respondent in the *Fruehauf* case was a rather in-

[69] Arguments, p. 128.
[70] *Ibid.*, p. 65. *Editor & Publisher*, Vol. 70 (Feb. 13, 1937), p. 7.
[71] Arguments, p. 93.
[72] *Ibid.*, p. 141.
[73] *Ibid.*, p. 149.

teresting one," Wyzanski said, "in which he pointed out that in the State of Michigan were almost all the automobile factories, and it was only necessary for the State of Michigan to determine the policy in order to have the commerce of the country protected. I am not going to refer to facts which all of us know at the present day. I merely point out that it is well recognized that there is a national public interest in this subject, so great that no dispute of the character which he envisages could possibly be adjusted without the cooperation both of the parties themselves and of public authorities, and that in the past on many occasions the Federal authorities have found it necessary to intervene." "I contend," Wyzanski closed, "that where two colossal forces are standing astride the stream of commerce threatening to disrupt it, it cannot be that this Government is without power to provide for the orderly procedure by which the dispute may be adjusted without interruption to the stream of commerce."[74]

The time for oral arguments had now ended. The fate of the Wagner Act lay in the hands of the Court.

[74] *Ibid.,* pp. 173–74.

# 9

## VICTORY FOR THE WAGNER ACT

□ □ □ □ □ □ □ □ □ □ □ □ □ □ □ □ □ □ □ □ □ □ □ □ □ □ □ □ □ □ □ □ □ □ □ □ □ □ □ □ □ □ □

FOLLOWING THE ORAL ARGUMENTS, THERE WAS A DELAY OF TWO months while the Court digested the briefs and arguments in the Wagner Act cases. On March 29, reporters and spectators packed the courtroom hoping to hear the opinions in these cases but instead heard the Court's opinions in *West Coast Hotel* v. *Parrish*[1] and in the *Virginian Railroad* case.[2] The *Parrish* case involved the constitutionality of a Washington minimum wage statute almost identical with the New York law held invalid by the Court a year previously in the *Morehead* case. The appeal in the case had been filed in August, 1936, and the Court had considered the question of whether to grant a hearing in the week of October 5. In conference, Justices Van Devanter, Sutherland, Butler, and McReynolds voted to reverse the case summarily on the basis of the *Adkins* and *Morehead* decisions, but since the Court was now asked to overrule the *Adkins* case, Justice Roberts voted for the notation of probable jurisdiction. "I am not sure I gave my reason," he wrote later, "but it was that in the appeal in the *Parrish* case the authority of *Adkins* was definitely assailed and the Court was asked to reconsider and overrule it. Thus, for the first time, I was confronted with the necessity of facing the soundness of the *Adkins* case." The Four Horsemen expressed their surprise at Roberts' action and someone asked, "What is the matter with Roberts?" The case was argued before the Court on December 16 and 17, and when it was taken up in conference on December 19, Roberts voted to uphold the statute. Because of the illness of Justice Stone, the vote was four to four, but Stone returned to the Court and voted to uphold the statute on February 6, the day following Roosevelt's attack on the Court.[3]

[1] 300 U.S. 379 (1937).
[2] 300 U.S. 515 (1937).
[3] Felix Frankfurter, "Mr. Justice Roberts," 104 *University of Pennsylvania Law Review* 311, 315 (Dec., 1955).

Thus the Court announced its five-to-four decision in the *Parrish* case on March 29. Abandoning the narrow ground upon which he had dissented in the *Morehead* case, Chief Justice Hughes overruled the *Adkins* case in a strong opinion. "In each case," he said, "the violation alleged by those attacking minimum wage regulation for women is deprivation of freedom of contract. What is this freedom? The Constitution does not speak of freedom of contract. It speaks of liberty and prohibits deprivation of liberty without due process of law. In prohibiting that deprivation, the Constitution does not recognize an absolute and uncontrollable liberty."[4] The exploitation of workers because of their unequal bargaining power, Hughes said, was "not only detrimental to their health and well-being, but casts a direct burden for their support on the community." "The community is not bound," he declared, "to provide what is in effect a subsidy for unconscionable employers. The community may direct its law-making powers to correct the abuse which springs from the selfish disregard of the public interest."[5] The conservative four, however, charged in dissent that the majority had amended the Constitution by judicial decree. To say, Sutherland wrote, "that the words of the Constitution mean today what they did not mean when written—that is, that they do not apply to a situation now to which they would have applied then—is to rob that instrument of the essential element which continues it in force as the people have made it until they, and not their official agents, have made it otherwise."[6]

The furor over the switch of Roberts in the *Parrish* case, and the speculation that it was due to the introduction of Roosevelt's court plan, obscured the importance of the ruling in the *Virginian* case to the outcome of the Wagner Act cases. The Court was unanimous in this case in upholding the 1934 amendments to the Railway Labor Act. Writing the Court's opinion, Justice Stone upheld the amendments' requirement of collective bargaining by employers with their employees' representatives on the grounds that experience had shown that "when there was willingness of the employer to meet such representatives for a discussion of their grievances, amicable adjustment of differences had generally followed and strikes had been avoided."[7] Labor disputes could be shown to affect interstate railroad service substantially, Stone said, and this was even the case in disputes involving back shop employees, since "the cause is not remote from the effect. The relation between them is not tenuous. The effect on commerce cannot be re-

---

[4] 300 U.S. at 391.
[5] *Ibid.* at 399–400.
[6] 300 U.S. at 403.
[7] *Ibid.* at 545.

garded as negligible."[8] Finally, relying on the *Texas and New Orleans* and *Parrish* cases, Stone sustained the majority rule provision and pointed out that the fifth amendment was not a "guarantee of untrammeled freedom of action and of contract." "In the exercise of its power to regulate commerce," he said, "Congress can subject both to restraints not shown to be unreasonable."[9]

The Court's rejection of liberty of contract objections in the *Parrish* case, and its rejection of such arguments plus its flexible interpretation of the commerce power in the *Virginian* case, augured well for the fate of the Wagner Act cases. In addition, Stone's opinion in the *Virginian* case gave substantial reason for close observers to anticipate the Court's upholding of the Wagner Act, since he had made use of statistics and testimony from the government's briefs and the records in the Wagner Act cases to bolster his opinion at key points. Thus, following his argument that experience demonstrated that collective bargaining resulted in more peaceful labor relations, Stone cited the NLRB's summary of the expert testimony in the *Jones & Laughlin* case, *Governmental Protection of the Right to Organize.*[10] Later he cited statistics included in the government's Associated Press brief demonstrating that there had been fewer labor disputes on railroads under the Railway Labor Act than in other forms of transportation.[11]

Doubt about the Wagner Act's fate still predominated, however, when at twelve noon on April 12, Chief Justice Hughes parted the curtains behind the bench and led the Justices into the courtroom. After the Court was seated, the Chief Justice gave a slight nod to Justice Roberts, and Roberts began reading the opinion in the *Associated Press* case.[12] "The silent intake of spectators' breaths," it was reported, "all but caused a vacuum in the courtroom."[13]

After reciting the facts of the case and describing the nature of the AP's operations, Roberts declared that these "operations involve the constant use of channels of interstate and foreign communication." "They amount to commercial intercourse," he said, "and such intercourse is commerce within the meaning of the Constitution. Interstate communication of a business nature, whatever the means of such communication, is interstate commerce regulable by Congress under the Constitution."[14] To the AP's contention that its editorial employees

[8] 300 U.S. at 556.
[9] *Ibid.* at 558.
[10] 300 U.S. at 546, note 4.
[11] *Ibid.* at 553, note 7.
[12] *Associated Press* v. *NLRB*, 301 U.S. 103 (1937).
[13] *Time* (April 19, 1937), p. 14.
[14] 301 U.S. at 128.

were not engaged in commerce, Roberts, citing the *Texas and New Orleans* and *Virginian* cases, replied that "it is obvious that strikes or labor disturbances amongst this class of employees would have as direct an effect upon the activities of petitioner as similar disturbances amongst those who operate the teletype machines or as a strike amongst the employees of telegraph lines over which petitioner's messages travel."[15]

Having completely sustained the government's position on the commerce question, Roberts then proceeded to deny the claim that the act violated the freedom of the press. "We think," he said, "the contention not only has no relevance to the circumstances of the instant case but is an unsound generalization. The ostensible reason for Watson's discharge, as embodied in the records of the petitioner, is 'solely on the grounds of his work not being on a basis for which he has shown capability.' The petitioner did not assert and does not claim that he had shown bias in the past. It does not claim that by reason of his connection with the union he will be likely, as the petitioner honestly believes, to show bias in the future. The actual reason for his discharge, as shown by the unattacked finding of the Board, was his Guild activity and his agitation for collective bargaining. The statute does not preclude a discharge on the ostensible grounds for the petitioner's action; it forbids discharge for what has been found to be the real motive of petitioner." "The restoration of Watson to his former position," Roberts concluded, "in no sense guarantees his continuance in petitioner's employ. The petitioner is at liberty, whenever occasion may arise, to exercise its undoubted right to sever his relationship for any cause that seems to it proper save only as a punishment for, or discouragement of, such activities as the act declares permissible."[16]

Following the reading of his opinion in the *Associated Press* case, Roberts read the Court's brief, unanimous opinion upholding the Act as applied to the Washington, Virginia and Maryland Coach Company on the basis of the *Texas and New Orleans* and *Virginian* cases.[17] Justice Sutherland, joined by Van Devanter, McReynolds, and Butler, dissented from the majority opinion in the *Associated Press* case on the grounds that the act's application to news services violated the freedom of the press. "If the freedom of the press does not include the right to adopt and pursue a policy without government restriction," Sutherland said, "it is a misnomer to call it freedom."[18] The majority's decision,

---

[15] *Ibid.* at 129.
[16] 301 U.S. at 132.
[17] *Washington, Virginia and Maryland Coach Co.* v. *NLRB*, 301 U.S. 142 (1937).
[18] 301 U.S. at 137.

he contended, if pushed to its logical extreme, would give the American Newspaper Guild opportunity "to exercise a high degree of control over the character of the news service. Due regard for the constitutional guaranty requires that the publisher or agency of the publisher of news shall be free from restraint in respect to employment in the editorial force."[19] In conclusion, Sutherland asked, "Do the people of this land— in the providence of God, favored, as they sometimes boast, above all others in the plenitude of their liberties—desire to preserve those so carefully protected by the First Amendment . . . ? If so, let them withstand all *beginnings* of encroachment. For the saddest epitaph which can be carved in memory of a vanished liberty is that it was lost because its possessors failed to stretch forth a saving hand while yet there was time."[20]

It was a beautifully expressed dissent, but the government had been sustained in its two interstate commerce cases, and Chief Justice Hughes now took the lead from Roberts and read the opinions in the crucial manufacturing cases from the center chair. His opinion in the *Jones & Laughlin* case[21] was a full affirmation of the NLRB's approach to its manufacturing jurisdiction and the government's position in its brief. The Wagner Act's grant of authority to the Board, Hughes said, "purports to reach only what may be deemed to burden or obstruct . . . commerce and, thus qualified, it must be construed as contemplating the exercise of control within constitutional bounds. It is a familiar principle that acts which directly burden or obstruct interstate or foreign commerce, or its free flow, are within the reach of the congressional power. Acts having that effect are not rendered immune because they grow out of labor disputes."[22]

The right of employees to organize, the Chief Justice said, was a "fundamental right" equal to that of employers to organize their businesses. "Long ago," he continued, "we stated the reason for labor organizations. We said they were organized out of the necessities of the situation; that a single employee was helpless in dealing with an employer; that he was dependent ordinarily on his daily wage for the maintenance of himself and family; that if the employer refused to pay him the wages that he thought fair, he was nevertheless unable to leave the employ and resist arbitrary and unfair treatment; that union was essential to give laborers opportunity to deal on an equality with their employer."[23]

[19] *Ibid.* at 140.
[20] 301 U.S. at 141.
[21] 301 U.S. 1 (1937).
[22] *Ibid.* at 31–32.
[23] 301 U.S. at 33.

Hughes then considered whether, given the general validity of the Act, it had been validly applied to Jones & Laughlin and whether a labor dispute at its Aliquippa plant could reasonably be said to affect commerce. The answer, Hughes declared, was that in "view of respondent's far-flung activities, it is idle to say that the effect would be indirect or remote. It is obvious that it would be immediate and might be catastrophic." Abandoning his declaration in the *Schechter* case that the principle of "direct" and "indirect" effects was fundamental, and perhaps reflecting the effect of the sit-down strikes on the Court's thinking, Hughes declared that the Court was "asked to shut our eyes to the plainest facts of our national life and deal with the question of direct and indirect effects in an intellectual vacuum." "Because there may be but indirect and remote effects upon interstate commerce in connection with a host of local enterprises throughout the country," he continued, "it does not follow that other industrial activities do not have such a close and intimate relation to interstate commerce as to make the presence of industrial strife a matter of the most urgent national concern. When industries organize themselves on a national scale, making their relation to interstate commerce the dominant factor in their activities, how can it be maintained that their industrial labor relations constitute a forbidden field into which Congress may not enter when it is necessary to protect interstate commerce from the paralyzing consequences of industrial war? We have often said that interstate commerce itself is a practical conception. It is equally true that interferences with that commerce must be appraised by a judgment that does not ignore experience."[24]

The final hurdle for the Wagner Act, the fifth amendment liberty of contract issue, was scaled on the basis of the *Texas and New Orleans* and *Virginian* cases. The Chief Justice pointed out that the *Adair* and *Coppage* cases were not controlling. "The Act does not interfere with the normal exercise of the employer to select its employees or to discharge them," he said. "The employer may not, under cover of that right, intimidate or coerce its employees with respect to their self-organization and representation, and, on the other hand, the Board is not entitled to make its authority a pretext for interference with the right of discharge when that right is exercised for other reasons than such intimidation and coercion."[25] In addition, the objections to the Board's procedure on due process and seventh amendment grounds were brushed aside by the Court.

In brief opinions, the Chief Justice also sustained the Board's author-

[24] 301 U.S. at 41–42.
[25] 301 U.S. at 45–46.

ity in the *Fruehauf*[26] and *Friedman–Harry Marks* cases[27] on the basis of the *Jones & Laughlin* decision. As in the *Associated Press* case, Justices Sutherland, Butler, McReynolds, and Van Devanter dissented, this time on both commerce and due process grounds. Attacking the reasoning by which unfair labor practices in manufacturing enterprises were held by the majority to affect commerce, Justice McReynolds declared that by this "chain of indirect and progressively remote events we finally reach the evil with which it is said the legislation under consideration undertakes to deal." "A more remote and indirect interference with interstate commerce," he said, "or a more definite invasion of the powers reserved to the states is difficult, if not impossible, to imagine."[28] Relying on the *Adair* and *Coppage* cases, McReynolds described the right to contract as one which is "fundamental and includes the privilege of selecting those with whom one is willing to assume contractual relations. This right is unduly abridged by the Act now upheld. A private owner is deprived of power to manage his own property by freely selecting those to whom his manufacturing operations are to be entrusted. We think this cannot lawfully be done in circumstances like those here disclosed."[29]

Following the Court's announcement of these historic decisions, Senator Robert Wagner broadcast a radio speech on their significance. Characterizing them as deserving to be ranked "alongside the work done in the days of John Marshall," he asserted that had the act been sustained earlier the sit-down strikes would never have occurred. "Let no one any longer take the law in his own hands," Wagner said, "through self-appointed interpreters of what the Constitution means, through hired police or spies. . . ."[30] The liberals on the Court were also delighted. "Of course," Justice Stone wrote privately, "in order to reach the result which was reached in these cases last Monday, it was necessary for six members of the Court either to be overruled or to take back some things they subscribed to in the Guffey Coal Act case. But as I did not join in those statements, I had nothing to take back."[31]

Chief Justice Hughes and Justice Roberts had indeed "taken back" some of their earlier views. Only a year previously, Roberts had joined the majority in the *Carter* case and Hughes had declared in his partial dissent in the case that "if the people desire to give Congress the power

[26] *NLRB* v. *Fruehauf Trailer Co.*, 301 U.S. 49 (1937).
[27] *NLRB* v. *Friedman–Harry Marks Clothing Co.*, 301 U.S. 58 (1937).
[28] 301 U.S. at 97.
[29] *Ibid.* at 103.
[30] *Time* (April 19, 1937), p. 15.
[31] Alpheus T. Mason, *Harlan Fiske Stone: Pillar of the Law* (New York: The Viking Press, 1956), p. 459.

to regulate industries within the States, and the relations of employers and employees in those industries, they are at liberty to declare their will in the appropriate manner, but it is not for the Court to amend the Constitution by judicial decree."[32] The Constitution remained un-amended in April of 1937, but the Court in the Wagner Act cases had sustained the power of Congress "to regulate industries within the States, and the relations of employers and employees in those industries . . ." It is to both Hughes' and Roberts' credit, however, that, when the forces of political and social unrest beat upon the Court in the spring of 1937, they did not feel bound to a rigid adherence to previous utterances in the hope of maintaining reputations for constitutional consistency. Despite his questionable constitutional wavering, it is to the credit of Hughes especially that when the Court met its most serious modern challenge, he possessed the ability, both political and legal, to guide through the storm the institution which he headed.

The decisions in the Wagner Act cases were the turning point in the court fight, and the events that followed, according to Alsop and Catledge, "were the purest weariest anticlimax."[33] Informed of the decisions by Jim Farley, however, Roosevelt exclaimed, "We did it." "I am very, very pleased. You ought to see Homer Cummings, who's sitting with me now. He looks like the Cheshire cat that swallowed the canary. It's wonderful. I am convinced more than ever that the proposals for reform of the Court are warranted. It's the same four justices who have dissented all along that are against me this time—McReynolds, Butler, Sutherland and Van Devanter."[34]

Although the Gallup poll indicated a slight rise in the percentage of persons favorable to the President's plan following the Wagner Act decisions, by May 12 the poll indicated that only thirty-one per cent of the public then favored the plan.[35] Farley warned Roosevelt that the court bill could not pass as it stood and that unless a compromise was reached the Democratic party might be badly split. The President was determined to push the bill through, however, and refused to compromise. "This comes from telling them I would not be candidate again," he said.[36] But Congress had passed a new retirement plan for the Justices in March which allowed them to retire, rather than resign,

---

[32] *Carter v. Carter Coal Co.,* 298 U.S. 238, at 317–18.

[33] Stewart Alsop and Turner Catledge, *The 168 Days* (Garden City: Doubleday, Doran & Co., 1938), p. 147.

[34] James A. Farley, *Jim Farley's Story: The Roosevelt Years* (New York: McGraw-Hill Book Co., 1948), pp. 78–79.

[35] Frank V. Cantwell, "Public Opinion and the Legislative Process," *American Political Science Review,* Vol. 40, No. 5 (Oct., 1946), pp. 928–29.

[36] Farley *op. cit.,* pp. 81–82.

and to continue at full salary,[37] and Justice Van Devanter announced his retirement under its terms on May 18. Roosevelt had promised the first appointment to the Senate majority leader, Joseph Robinson of Arkansas, as a reward for pushing the bill through the Senate. Now he sought a compromise which would allow the President to appoint only one Justice per year for each one who had reached the retirement age but failed to retire, and he relied on the Senate's loyalty to Robinson for passage of the new plan.

On July 14, however, this hope also vanished when Robinson was found dead of a heart attack in his hotel room, and it was then obvious that the bill could not pass. The Congress finally passed a bill making minor judicial reforms,[38] the most important of which was to require a three-judge district court to be convened in cases involving the enjoining of federal laws and allowing direct appeal from such courts to the Supreme Court. Thus the court fight ended, and with its termination, the coalition which had pushed through the domestic New Deal began to crack. Only one further major piece of New Deal domestic legislation, the Fair Labor Standards Act,[39] would be passed, and it would have to be forced out of a committee in the House by discharge petition. The court fight had seen the beginning of the re-establishment of the conservative coalition in Congress which would mean the end of domestic reform.[40]

## THE SETTLEMENTS

For the National Labor Relations Board, the decisions in the Wagner Act cases meant the end of a period of almost two years during which the very existence of the agency could not be assured. That this condition had produced a problem for the Board's personnel was demonstrated by the resignation on March 12 of A. L. Wirin, who had prepared the *Friedman-Harry Marks* case at the hearing stage. In a letter to Chairman Madden on July 23, after the Wagner Act had been upheld, however, Wirin asked to be reinstated. "First," he said, "I have a confession to make. I guessed wrong on the Supreme Court and the NLRB. Others did too, I know; but I *acted* on my guess. Others were more patient. I saw the NLRB as a shell, after the Supreme Court finished it off. . . . It is now obvious to me that I made a serious mis-

[37] 50 Stat. 24 (1937).
[38] 50 Stat. 751 (1937).
[39] 52 Stat. 1060 (1938).
[40] James MacGregor Burns, *Roosevelt: The Lion and the Fox* (New York: Harcourt, Brace and Co., 1956), pp. 303–309.

take."[41] On a more important front, the injunctive attack on the Board was reported to have almost completely subsided by November, 1937, due to the Supreme Court's decisions, but the agency was now overwhelmed by complaints which had been held in abeyance until the constitutionality of the Act had been determined.[42] The number of complaints rose by about one thousand per cent and became more than the Board's staff was able to handle.[43]

When word of the Court's decision in the *Associated Press* case reached New York, representatives of the AP immediately notified the Board of the AP's willingness to reinstate Morris Watson. Thus, on Tuesday, April 13, Watson returned to the AP offices and was greeted by reporters and photographers. "We are willing to accept the ruling of the Court and stand by it," an AP spokesman said. "There will be nothing unpleasant in the office with the return of Mr. Watson. We welcome him back with the same feeling that we could greet a man who had been away on leave. He will return to his former job as reporter and rewrite man on the city staff."[44] In a statement to the press, Watson pointed out that the Supreme Court's decision meant that no one "need have any fear of joining the American Newspaper Guild and being active in it." "It does not mean, however," he said, "that we workers can turn our problems over to the government. We must work

[41] Hearings before a Special Committee to Investigate the NLRB, House of Representatives, 76th Cong., 3rd sess., Vol. 24, pp. 5098–99.

[42] National Labor Relations Board, *Second Annual Report* (1937), p. 31.

[43] *Ibid.*, p. 1. One of the NLRB's staff found sufficient time, however, to prepare the following humorous account of the Wagner Act cases:

IN THE SUPREME COURT OF THE UNITED STATES

Joe Madden and his Boys *vs.* American Liberty League, NAM, GOP, and the Constitution, Nos. 16–37–18–4 (Shift).

Batteries: For the Rights (vested or without vests)
"Call me John" Davis,
"Roughrider" Reed,
For the Lefts,
"Jumping Joe" Madden,
"Eat 'em Alive" Fahy.

Score: By "Flying Trapeze" Hughes: We think it's all bunk, but we don't want to be shot in the revolution. My brothers-in-law, Brandeis, Cardozo, and Stone, concur. So does Roberts, but we had an awful time with him.

Dissent: By "Romeo" McReynolds: We're practically dead anyhow, so why worry about a Lewis machine gun? Sutherland and Van Devanter concur. Butler says he still has enough drag with the railroads to make his escape, so he sticks. 5–4.

McReynolds: There never was any Constitution!

From Hearings, *op. cit.*, Vol. 24, pp. 5003–04.

[44] *Editor & Publisher*, Vol. 70 (April 17, 1937), p. 12.

them out for ourselves through disciplined and progressive trade union organization capable of real collective bargaining." "I should like to reassure the four Justices who worried about the freedom of the press," Watson added, "and to say that I subscribe wholeheartedly to the purposes of the American Newspaper Guild, one of which is 'to guarantee, as far as it is able, constant honesty in the news.' "[45]

Heywood Broun, speaking for the Guild, reflected Watson's sentiments and pointed out that the Guild "could hardly forget that eighteen months elapsed before a man who was unjustly dismissed was restored to his job. In its most immediate sense, the 5–4 decision of the Court will stimulate the Guild in perfecting its organization for all wire services, and bringing about contracts through collective bargaining."[46] The AP's counsel in the case, John W. Davis, also accepted the decision cheerfully, saying that "when a majority of the Supreme Court has spoken on a constitutional question, it is the duty of every citizen to accept the result. That is the sort of government we have. It is the sort of government we ought to have."[47] The only sour note was sounded by the American Newspaper Publishers' Association counsel, Elisha Hanson, who called the language of Justice Roberts "unfortunate." "I believe that if any agency of the government is given the power to say to a newspaper publisher that he must or must not employ an individual in his news and editorial departments," he said, "then the freedom of the press as guaranteed by the First Amendment to the Constitution has been destroyed."[48]

On April 15, Watson submitted a statement demanding $2,175.41 in back pay from the AP,[49] but even the Board objected to this amount as being too high.[50] Finally, after paying back to the government the salary he had earned as a director in the Federal Theater Project while his case was being litigated, Watson received $1,562.41 in back pay.[51]

The news of the Court's decision in the *Jones & Laughlin* case was received uproariously in Aliquippa. Asked what he thought of the decision, a Jones & Laughlin steel worker said, "When I hear Wagner bill went constitutional I happy like anything. I say, good, now Aliquippa become part of the United States."[52] A parade of steel workers cele-

[45] *Ibid.*

[46] *Ibid.*

[47] *Ibid.*

[48] *Ibid.* (April 24, 1937), p. 7.

[49] NA–Case No. C-84, Associated Press, Folder No. 2, Letter from Watson to L. F. Curtis, Treasurer of the AP, April 15, 1937.

[50] Memorandum from Elinore Herrick to NLRB, April 16, 1937.

[51] Memorandum by E. S. Frankfurter, Nov. 7, 1938.

[52] Rose M. Stein, "Aliquippa Celebrates," *The Nation,* Vol. 144 (April 24, 1937), p. 466.

brating the decision proceeded up the main street of the city, with the ten discharged employees in the first two cars bearing signs reading, "We Are the Ten Men Fired for Union Activity by J & L, We Are Ordered Back to Work by the Supreme Court" and "The Workers of Aliquippa Are Now Free Men."[53] The Court's decision also came as the steel industry was staggering under the drive of the CIO's Steel Workers Organizing Committee. Faced with the capture of the leaders of its company unions by the SWOC, U.S. Steel had begun negotiations with John L. Lewis in January, 1937, and an agreement had been signed on March 3, which established the eight-hour day and forty-hour week and granted recognition to the SWOC.[54]

This action of U.S. Steel was regarded as a sell-out by the heads of many steel corporations, and Myron R. Taylor, the chairman of the board of U.S. Steel who had negotiated with Lewis, was ousted as chairman of the Iron & Steel Institute and replaced by Tom R. Girdler, head of Republic Steel. Thus "Little Steel," composed of Republic and other moderate-sized corporations, decided on a continued resistance to the SWOC,[55] while Jones & Laughlin became a key target of the SWOC's organizational efforts. By May, Jones & Laughlin began negotiations with Phillip Murray, but these broke down and on May 12 a strike was called by the SWOC. This strike in Aliquippa was described as being "virtually a civil upheaval" and more "a demonstration of political and economic independence on the part of the workers than a labor dispute."[56]

On May 13, a leader of the Aliquippa strikers telegraphed President Roosevelt that unless an NLRB election was held, "we will take the law into our own hands at ten a.m., Saturday, May 15, 1937. You as President of these United States may be responsible for loss of life and property if you do not do your duty."[57] The seriousness of the situation was not helped by reports that Tom Girdler's Republic Steel had sent its gas pipe gang and almost all of its company police into Aliquippa during the crisis.[58] The strike at Aliquippa had lasted only thirty-six hours, however, when Jones & Laughlin signed a contract with the

---

[53] *Ibid.*, p. 466.

[54] Walter Galenson, "The Unionization of the American Steel Industry," *International Review of Social History*, Vol. 1, pt. 1, pp. 19–23.

[55] Edward Levinson, *Labor on the March* (New York: Harper & Brothers, 1938), p. 201.

[56] Galenson, *loc. cit.*, p. 29. See also Robert R. R. Brooks, *As Steel Goes . . . Unionism in a Basic Industry* (New Haven: Yale University Press, 1940), pp. 122–29.

[57] NA–Case No. C-57, Jones & Laughlin Steel Corp., Folder No. 1, Telegram from William H. Turner to President Roosevelt, May 13, 1937.

[58] NLRB Memorandum, May 19, 1937.

SWOC, and on May 20, in an NLRB election, the SWOC received 17,028 votes out of a total of 24,412 votes cast and became the exclusive bargaining agent of Jones & Laughlin's employees.[59] Asked what he thought of the SWOC's organization of Jones & Laughlin, a steel worker replied that it was "worth twelve dollars a year to be able to walk down the main street of Aliquippa, talk to anyone you want about anything you like, and feel that you are a citizen."[60]

The Sixth Circuit Court of Appeals entered its decree ordering the reinstatement of the six discharged employees of the Fruehauf Trailer Company on June 28, 1937.[61] Almost a month later, however, the company had still failed to comply with the order, and the Board informed it that "unless we can promptly obtain compliance with this decree, we shall petition the court for an appropriate citation for contempt."[62] The company then sent letters to the men offering reinstatement on August 11,[63] and in September the Board was informed that the men had been reinstated and had received a total of over four thousand dollars in back pay.[64] The regional director in Detroit informed the Board that he had been advised "that all the men have received their checks in this case and that the company has fully complied with the order of the Board. . . . there is no reason why the case should not be closed."[65]

In Richmond, Virginia, the Friedman–Harry Marks Clothing Company had offered reinstatement and back pay to its discharged employees by September, the back pay settlement totaling over thirty-eight hundred dollars.[66] On September 21, 1937, Jacob S. Potofsky, the assistant general president of the Amalgamated Clothing Workers, informed the NLRB regional director that the ACW had "entered into an agreement with the Friedman–Harry Marks Clothing Company, and there has been full compliance with the decision of the Labor Relations Board." "This has been an epoch-making case," he said, "and you and the Board have earned the gratitude of all those who were in any way connected with it. I want to take this opportunity to express my appreciation."[67]

[59] NLRB Memorandum, May 24, 1937.
[60] Brooks, *op. cit.*, p. 129.
[61] NA–Case No. C-2, Fruehauf Trailer Co., Folder No. 1, Memorandum from Robert Watts to Charles Fahy, June 28, 1937.
[62] Memorandum from Watts to Harold Cranefield, July 26, 1937.
[63] Memorandum from Cranefield to Malcolm Halliday, Aug. 12, 1937.
[64] Letter from Victor W. Klein to Frank H. Bowen, Sept. 8, 1937.
[65] Memorandum from Bowen to B. S. Stern, Oct. 8, 1937.
[66] NA–Case No. C-40, Friedman–Harry Marks Clothing Co., Correspondence Folder, Memorandum from W. M. Aicher to E. S. Frankfurter, Dec. 3, 1938.
[67] Letter from Potofsky to Bennett Schauffler, Sept. 21, 1937.

The final settlement of the fifth and last of the Wagner Act cases points up rather vividly how the individuals in such cases often are obscured by the great issues of public policy involved and are almost lost from sight. On April 14, Charlton Ogburn, counsel for the A.F. of L., informed the counsel of the Washington, Virginia and Maryland Coach Company that the discharged men were "ready to report to work at the time and place designated by your client. Will you kindly advise me this afternoon when and where they report to resume work?"[68] Counsel for the company, however, wrote to Charles Fahy requesting a conference on the question of back pay. The company, he said, "is not desirous of litigating if it can avoid it. However, it is a small Company, and if the back pay provision is going to run for fifty-eight weeks, and cost the Company around $15,000.00, the Company literally will not know where to get the money. I would not like to be compelled to file an application in the court below for construction and modification of the order. Still less would I like to be compelled to undertake a re-organization proceeding under Section 77B of the Bankruptcy Act. . . ."[69]

Fahy advised a conference with the regional director and regional attorney,[70] but the Board then apparently lost track of the case, since when the central office requested information on its settlement from the regional director in December of 1938, he replied that the information was unavailable and that the request, therefore, "embarrasses us into further attempts."[71] After several weeks, the Board again asked the regional director for information. "Since we have had no communication from you since December 8 on this case," it said, "we conclude that you are too much embarrassed or not embarrassed enough. Which is it?"[72] The Board was finally informed in January of 1939 that all but two of the discharged employees had accepted reinstatement and had received over eight thousand dollars in back pay.[73] Writing its regional director, the Board expressed the hope "that never again will the Board be put in the position of not knowing whether there has been compliance with its order or with the court order enforcing its order." "It makes one wonder," it closed, "what price victory."[74]

[68] NA–Case No. C-63, Washington, Virginia and Maryland Coach Co., Folder No. 1, Letter from Ogburn to Robert E. Lynch, April 14, 1937.
[69] Letter from William Hughes to Charles Fahy, April 21, 1937.
[70] Letter from Fahy to Hughes, April 24, 1937.
[71] Memorandum from William M. Aicher to E. S. Frankfurter, Dec. 8, 1938.
[72] Memorandum from B. M. Stern to Aicher, Dec. 23, 1938.
[73] Letter from Robert Lynch to NLRB, Jan. 20, 1939.
[74] Memorandum from Stern to Aicher, Feb. 14, 1939.

# 10

## THE CASES IN PERSPECTIVE

□ □ □ □ □ □ □ □ □ □ □ □ □ □ □ □ □ □ □ □ □ □ □ □ □ □ □ □ □ □ □ □ □ □ □ □ □ □ □ □ □ □

BY THE 1930'S, THE STATE OF CONSTITUTIONAL DEVELOPMENT PRE-
sented the Supreme Court the opportunity of choosing between signifi-
cantly different doctrines in both commerce and due process cases. On
questions of interstate commerce, the Court could choose to sustain
national power, and amply support its choice by reference to the precedents supplied by the "flow of commerce" cases, principally the *Swift*,[1]
*Stafford*,[2] and *Olsen*[3] cases, or it could resort to the "direct-indirect"
effects formula and the tenth amendment and invalidate the exercise of national power, again being supplied with sufficient precedents
from the *Knight*[4] and *Hammer* v. *Dagenhart*[5] line of cases. In due
process cases, the Court could uphold interferences with the liberty
of contract on the basis of such precedents as the *Muller* case,[6] or it
could deny the validity of regulation of the contractual relationship on
the basis of the *Adair-Coppage* line of cases.[7] The decision of the
*Texas and New Orleans* case[8] in 1930 seemed to portend a liberal
trend in the Court's decisions, but as the New Deal years wore on, the
Court committed itself ever more completely to the "direct-indirect"
effects formula and the line of cases which restricted national power,
and with its decision in the *Carter* case,[9] this commitment seemed
almost irreversible.

The pressure for the enactment of the Wagner Act, admirably ma-
nipulated by Senator Wagner, could not, however, be immobilized by

[1] *Swift & Co.* v. *United States,* 196 U.S. 375 (1905).
[2] *Stafford* v. *Wallace,* 258 U.S. 495 (1922).
[3] *Chicago Board of Trade* v. *Olsen,* 262 U.S. 1 (1923).
[4] *United States* v. *E. C. Knight Co.,* 156 U.S. 1 (1895).
[5] 247 U.S. 251 (1918).
[6] *Muller* v. *Oregon,* 208 U.S. 412 (1908).
[7] *Adair* v. *United States,* 208 U.S. 161 (1908); *Coppage* v. *Kansas,* 236 U.S. 1
(1915).
[8] *Texas & New Orleans Railroad* v. *Brotherhood,* 281 U.S. 548 (1930).
[9] *Carter* v. *Carter Coal Co.,* 298 U.S. 238 (1936).

the array of precedents against such an exercise of national power nor by the massive opposition of business and the initial indifference from the White House. The authors of the act were essentially betting on the viability of the "flow of commerce" cases, and the care with which the constitutional basis of the act was drafted demonstrates the awareness on the part of its proponents that legislative victory would merely create the necessity for final victory in constitutional adjudication. Business, on the other hand, was betting on the continuation of the Court's adherence to the "direct-indirect" effects formula, and the confidence business groups placed in constitutional protection could be seen by the emphasis they placed on the fixity and immutability of constitutional principles. The New Deal was blocked, a writer in a business journal said, because "the Constitution and the Supreme Court stand in the way. Not because of the wills of the Justices of the Court, but because the Constitution was written as the code of a society of free individuals, and as a compact between states having sovereign powers. So long as the Constitution stands, and so long as the Supreme Court interprets it as its words mean, the New Deal cannot come to fruit."[10]

The use of public and semi-public briefs by the Liberty League, NAM, and ANPA asserting the Wagner Act's unconstitutionality under the "direct-indirect" effects formula was undoubtedly an attempt to influence the courts indirectly on the issue of the act's validity. This tactic in constitutional litigation was not without historical precedent, since a similar device had been utilized by the possessors of the disputed Yazoo land claims as early as the 1790's. Then, a public opinion had been secured from Alexander Hamilton expressing the view that the Georgia legislature's revocation of the land grants was invalid under the contract clause of the Constitution. This tactic had been crowned with success when John Marshall sanctioned the Hamiltonian view in his opinion in *Fletcher* v. *Peck*.[11]

Such maneuvers may be classified with the advantageously timed law review or magazine article as tactics by which interested parties or groups may attempt, in a socially condoned manner, to influence judicial decision-making indirectly.[12] In addition, however, the employer groups' briefs asserting the invalidity of the Wagner Act undoubtedly contributed to business resistance to the NLRB, but insofar as they

[10] Mark Sullivan, "The Unfinished Business of the New Deal," *Nation's Business*, Vol. 24 (Aug., 1936), pp. 15, 60.

[11] 6 Cranch 87 (1810). Benjamin F. Wright, *The Contract Clause of the Constitution* (Cambridge: Harvard University Press, 1938), pp. 21–22, 30–31.

[12] On the influence of law review articles on the Supreme Court's behavior, see Chester A. Newland, "Legal Periodicals and the United States Supreme Court," *Midwest Journal of Political Science*, Vol. III (Feb., 1959), p. 58.

encouraged business to refuse to participate in NLRB hearings, they were misguided, since participation in the hearings would have allowed an opportunity to rebut the Board's evidence. Here the NAM's brief, with its emphasis on the importance of the hearing records, was the best guide for business. The most serious consequence to the Board of business' use of the public and semi-public brief as a tactic was the threat of injunctive paralysis of its activities and the possibility that the act might have been tested on the basis of injunction litigation. Had the act been so tested, the Board would have been forced to defend the validity of the act in a case not of its own choosing and without the benefit of hearing testimony and supplementary evidence to bolster its cause. The uniformity of the injunction pleadings and, on the whole, the successful defense of the act's procedures in the courts enabled the Board to retain the strategically important control of litigation which the procedures established by the act conferred upon it.

This control of litigation by the Board forced the labor movement to be dependent upon it for the initiation of cases, and labor's cooperation with the Board seems to have been generally good, despite the growing split within its ranks and some evidence of pressure to proceed less cautiously in the initial cases. The Board was further aided by the publicity accorded the proceedings of the LaFollette Committee, which acted as a counter to the publicity accompanying business's constitutional attack on the Board and the act.

As far as legal factors were concerned, it is difficult to overestimate the importance of the accompaniment of the *Virginian Railroad* case[13] with the Wagner Act cases to the Supreme Court. This case provided a bolstering argument for the Board at the circuit court level and was cited by the Board particularly in the two interstate commerce cases. In addition, congressional authority over labor relations in the railroad industry had long been received generously by the Supreme Court, as in the *Texas and New Orleans* case, and the provisions of the Railway Labor Act[14] were similar enough to those of the Wagner Act to provide for the government a good argument by analogy for the validity of the latter at the Supreme Court level.

The NLRB performed in the Wagner Act litigation in much the same manner as interest groups involved in constitutional litigation. Thus, in attempting to overcome the impressive array of precedents against the validity of its manufacturing jurisdiction, the Board resorted to extra-legal materials to justify its position before the Court. It first selected those cases in which the evidence of unfair labor practices was

[13] *Virginian Railroad Co.* v. *System Federation,* 300 U.S. 515 (1937).
[14] 44 Stat. 577.

above reproach and then introduced into the hearing records, particularly in the *Jones & Laughlin*[15] and *Friedman–Harry Marks*[16] cases, testimony from labor relations experts on the social and economic desirability of governmental protection of the right to organize, despite the legal precedents which denied the constitutional validity of such protection in manufacturing enterprises. By using such extra-legal materials, the Board adopted a tactic which appears to be the tactic of most parties or groups which are at a disadvantage in relation to legal precedent in the process of adjudication.[17]

The initial strategy of the Board, which entailed the securing of an early test of the Act's validity in a strong interstate commerce case, was obviously the strategy which promised the best chance of success, given the prevailing constitutional doctrine. The Board's failure to carry this strategy through successfully could have resulted in serious consequences, since under the doctrine of the *Texas and New Orleans* case, and ultimately the *Virginian* case, the Board's jurisdiction over clearly interstate enterprises seemed assured, while by bringing the manufacturing cases as well as the interstate commerce cases to the Court at the same time, the Board ran the risk of tempting the Court to extend a ruling of invalidity in the manufacturing cases to the interstate commerce cases as well.

Nevertheless, in their final posture before the Court, the Board's cases presented the Court with a broad range of policy alternatives. The *Associated Press* and *Washington, Virginia and Maryland Bus Co.* cases would have allowed the Court to adhere to the "direct-indirect" effects formula and still sustain the act as narrowly applied to interstate commerce businesses. In the manufacturing area of the Board's jurisdiction, the *Jones & Laughlin, Fruehauf,* and *Friedman–Harry Marks* cases presented the Court with examples of, respectively, large, medium, and small businesses and allowed it to choose as to whether labor relations in each affected commerce to the extent necessary for federal regulation under the commerce clause. Thus, the Court had three alternatives in dealing with the Board's manufacturing jurisdiction and could make significant choices as to how far it desired to extend the scope of the commerce power. With its five test cases, therefore, the Board presented to the Court the broadest possible range of alternatives within the scope of the then prevailing constitutional doctrines.

It now seems apparent that the Board was due to win in the two

---

[15] *NLRB* v. *Jones & Laughlin Steel Corp.,* 301 U.S. 1 (1937).

[16] *NLRB* v. *Friedman–Harry Marks Clothing Co.,* 301 U.S. 58 (1937).

[17] Clement E. Vose, *Caucasians Only* (Berkeley: University of California Press, 1959), pp. 64–65.

interstate commerce cases on the basis of the *Texas and New Orleans* case and that validation of the use of the Wagner Act in these two cases alone would have been the alternative upon which a majority of the Justices would have agreed had other factors not entered the picture. There seems to be little doubt that the views of Chief Justice Hughes and Justice Roberts on the power of Congress to regulate labor relations were affected by three major factors—the overwhelming re-election of Roosevelt in 1936, the sit-down strikes, and the attack on the Court, with the latter probably being the most important. Finally, by its involved argument for distinguishing the *Carter* case, the Board presented to Hughes and Roberts the means by which the shift in their views in the Wagner Act cases could be rationalized with at least a vestige of grace. As a result, the upholding of the Wagner Act as a whole, which had for so long seemed so improbable, became a reality.

The Wagner Act cases mark the end of the "old Constitution" which was composed largely of doctrines protective of property rights as defined by classical economic theory and which had been erected through the reshaping of constitutional law by the forces of industrialism following the Civil War. After 1937, business groups placed on the defensive in the political process could no longer retreat to this body of law as a final refuge, as they had following the passage of the Wagner Act. The Wagner Act cases opened the floodgates of national power and henceforth the conflict over its exercise would generally be resolved in the legislative and administrative processes.

The Wagner Act cases were followed by Supreme Court decisions sustaining federal regulation of wages and hours[18] and of agriculture[19] and the establishment of social security.[20] These decisions together resulted in greatly expanded commerce and taxing power and a virtual surrender of the Court's veto in these areas. The evidence of the Court's retreat and the consequences resulting therefrom are perhaps best illustrated by the interaction between the courts and the National Labor Relations Board on the question of the Board's jurisdiction since the decision of the Wagner Act cases. In the *Jones & Laughlin* case, the Court had accepted the Board's theory of NLRB jurisdiction which had maintained that the Wagner Act was valid and the only question was whether it had been validly applied to unfair labor practices which would "burden" or "affect" commerce. Thus, Chief Justice Hughes had

[18] *United States* v. *Darby Lumber Co.*, 312 U.S. 100 (1941).
[19] *Wickard* v. *Filburn*, 317 U.S. 111 (1942).
[20] *Steward Machine Co.* v. *Davis*, 301 U.S. 548 (1937); *Helvering* v. *Davis*, 301 U.S. 619 (1937).

held that the act purported "to reach only what may be deemed to burden or obstruct that commerce and, thus qualified, it must be construed as contemplating the exercises of control within constitutional bounds." Whether or not "particular action does affect commerce in such a close and intimate fashion to be subject to federal control, and hence to lie within the authority conferred upon the Board," Hughes continued, "is left by the statute to be determined as individual cases arise."[21]

While this language seemed to portend a rather careful supervision by the courts of the Board's assertion of jurisdiction, the lower federal courts generally refused to limit its assertion of jurisdiction following the Wagner Act cases,[22] and in a series of cases in 1938 and 1939, the Supreme Court sustained the assertion of jurisdiction by the Board over enterprises which engaged in only very limited business in interstate commerce, with the result that the Board's jurisdiction was enormously expanded.[23] In the last of these cases, *NLRB v. Fainblatt,*[24] the Court said that the Wagner Act did not place restrictions "upon the jurisdiction of the Board to be determined or fixed exclusively by reference to the volume of interstate commerce involved." "Examining the Act in the light of its purpose and the circumstances in which it must be applied," the Court continued, "we can perceive no basis for inferring an intention of Congress to make the operation of the Act depend on any particular volume of commerce affected more than that to which courts would apply the maxim *de minimis.*"[25]

Referring to the apparent disappearance of the line between interstate and local commerce which this increase of the NLRB's jurisdiction entailed, one federal judge remarked that perhaps "the cackle of the farmer's hen as she announces completion of her daily chore, or the squeal of the pig in its struggle to become a porker, are not beyond this boundary line, but in this we can give no assurance."[26] The Court's abdication of its power to check the exercise of federal power, which was signaled by the Wagner Act cases and the decisions following in their wake, meant that the resolution of conflict in this area would almost completely pass from the Court to the Congress, and more importantly, to the administrative agencies. Thus the problem of the extension of federal power, which formed the basis of the greatest

[21] 301 U.S. at 31–32.
[22] *Monthly Labor Review,* Vol. 80 (July, 1957), p. 829.
[23] See *Santa Cruz Co.* v. *NLRB,* 303 U.S. 453 (1938); *Consolidated Edison Co.* v. *NLRB,* 304 U.S. 197 (1938).
[24] 306 U.S. 601 (1939).
[25] *Ibid.* at 606.
[26] *Polish National Alliance* v. *NLRB,* 136 F.2d 175, at 180 (CCA 7th, 1943).

conflicts and most important constitutional problems before the Court in the 1930's, is now often consigned to the less obtrusive processes of administration.

The NLRB, for example, decided the question of its jurisdiction on a case by case basis until 1950, when for the first time it announced standards by which enterprises would come within its jurisdiction.[27] These standards were based on the dollar volume of business which a firm directly or indirectly derived from or contributed to interstate commerce.[28] As a result of the Eisenhower victory in 1952, however, the Board for the first time since its creation came under the control of a Republican-appointed majority whose announced objective was to "roll back" the reach of the federal bureaucracy. Thus the Board's new Chairman had, previous to his appointment, announced his belief that the "one thing this nation needs more than anything else to maintain its vigor and strength is a revival of interest by local government in tackling and solving the problems of their local people. That is why I strongly advocate a gradual but nevertheless marked withdrawal of the hand of the NLRB from strictly local disputes."[29] Despite the vigorous objections of the Democrat-appointed members, the majority of the Board drastically curtailed its jurisdiction in 1954.[30]

The ultimate effect of this action by the NLRB was to create another "no man's land" in which the federal government would not act and the states could not act, almost twenty years after the Court had created a constitutional "no man's land" in the *Morehead*[31] and *Carter* cases. The NLRB, which was now limiting its own powers, was the only agency of the federal government which could protect the right to organize because, in interpreting the Wagner Act, the courts had held that the right to organize free from employer interference was not conferred upon employees as an individual, private right, but was instead conferred in the public interest as a public right and that as such it was enforceable exclusively by the NLRB.[32] In addition, the Supreme Court had held that the states could not assert jurisdiction

[27] See "The Jurisdictional Standards of the National Labor Relations Board," A Report prepared for the Committee on Labor and Public Welfare, U.S. Senate, by the Legislative Reference Service of the Library of Congress (March 19, 1957).

[28] In the Matter of Hollow Tree Lumber Co., 91 NLRB 635 (1950).

[29] 110 NLRB at 502–503.

[30] In the Matter of Breeding Transfer Co., 110 NLRB 493 (1954).

[31] *Morehead* v. *New York,* 298 U.S. 587 (1936).

[32] *Amalgamated Workers* v. *Consolidated Edison Co.,* 309 U.S. 261 (1940). See also Louis L. Jaffe, "The Public Right Dogma in Labor Board Cases," 59 *Harvard Law Review* 720 (May, 1946) and "The Individual Right to Initiate Administrative Process: The Relation between Public and Private Rights," 25 *Iowa Law Review* 485 (May, 1940).

over labor relations even in enterprises over which the NLRB declined to assert jurisdiction, since Congress had pre-empted this field by the passage of the Wagner Act and the Taft-Hartley amendments.[33] Under these rulings, therefore, labor unions—and also businesses, since the Taft-Hartley amendments had created employer rights against alleged labor abuses—could not seek enforcement of federal prohibitions of unfair labor practices in the courts because of the public right doctrine, while they were at the same time denied remedy under state labor laws because of the doctrine of federal pre-emption.[34]

This problem of a "no-man's-land" in labor relations, and its ultimate solution, demonstrates graphically the constitutional readjustment which has followed the decision of the Wagner Act cases and the crisis of the 1930's. Then the Court had been an active arbiter between the claims of business and labor groups, claims which had been expressed in constitutional terminology as choices between state or federal power and as determinations as to whether an action affected interstate commerce "directly" or "indirectly." Having retreated fully from this role when the problem of the "no-man's-land" occurred in the late 1950's, however, the Court merely pointed out that "Congress is free to correct the situation at will."[35] The problem of drawing the line between state and federal power was now consigned by the Court to the legislative and administrative processes, and to affect the determination of the issue, business and labor now were forced to resort to them. Accordingly, Congress increased the NLRB's appropriation in 1958, urging it to increase its jurisdiction above the 1954 standards, and the agency soon complied.[36] In 1959, Congress determined by statute that the Board should assert jurisdiction over all cases falling within these new standards, and the states were empowered to assert jurisdiction over cases arising outside the Board's standards.[37] A problem similar to the problem which had formed a substantial part of the constitutional crisis of the 1930's was thus resolved in the 1950's by largely unheralded actions by Congress and an administrative agency.

The effect of the Court's retreat on the tactics of interest groups when questions of social and economic policy arise is also demonstrated by the business pressure on Congress which resulted in the passage of

[33] *Guss* v. *Utah Labor Relations Board,* 353 U.S. 51 (1957). See also Harry Brody, "Federal Pre-emption Comes of Age in Labor Relations," 5 *Labor Law Journal* 43 (Nov., 1954).

[34] Fred Witney, "NLRB Jurisdiction Policies and the Federal-State Relationship," 6 *Labor Law Journal* 3 (Jan., 1955).

[35] 353 U.S. 1, at 11.

[36] In the Matter of Siemans Mailing Service, 122 NLRB 81 (1958).

[37] 73 Stat. 541.

the Taft-Hartley amendments in 1947.[38] Increasingly after the Civil War and especially in the 1930's, business groups could depend on the protection of certain of their interests by constitutional doctrines which prevented many questions affecting property rights from being finally determined by the elective branches of the government. The National Association of Manufacturers, for example, could regard the passage of the Wagner Act as only a loss in a preliminary battle which it could confidently expect to win in the judicial process. Following 1937, however, the NAM gradually came to accept the Wagner Act as being above constitutional objection, and its tactical efforts were then focused on Congress in an attempt to procure amendments to the act which would restrict union activities. Its efforts were successful when the Taft-Hartley amendments were enacted by Congress in 1947.[39]

Although it opposed these amendments with a bitterness comparable to that of business groups opposing the Wagner Act in 1935, labor could not, given the Court's retreat, simply carry the fight over the Taft-Hartley amendments into the process of constitutional adjudication and expect protection, as business had done following the passage of the Wagner Act. This is clearly shown by labor's attempt to assert the right of liberty of contract to procure constitutional protection from state "right-to-work" laws which the Taft-Hartley amendments allowed to take precedence over federal regulation of union security.[40] In answer to labor's reliance on its pre–1937 decisions affirming the liberty of contract, the Court pointed out that it had "rejected the due process philosophy enunciated in the Adair-Coppage line of cases." In doing so, the Court declared, "it has consciously returned closer and closer to the earlier constitutional principle that states have power to legislate against what are found to be injurious practices in their internal commercial and business affairs, so long as their laws do not run afoul of some specific constitutional prohibition. . . . Under this constitutional doctrine the due process clause is no longer to be so broadly construed that the Congress and state legislatures are put in a strait jacket when they attempt to suppress business and industrial conditions which they regard as offensive to the public welfare. . . . Just as we have held that the due process clause erects no obstacles to block legislative protection of union members, we now hold that legislative protection can be afforded nonunion workers."[41]

[38] 61 Stat. 136.
[39] Richard W. Gable, "NAM: Influential Lobby or Kiss of Death?" *Journal of Politics,* Vol. 15 (May, 1953), pp. 254, 271.
[40] Section 14 (b).
[41] *Lincoln Federal Labor Union* v. *Northwestern Iron & Metal Co.,* 335 U.S. 525, at 535–37.

Accompanying this retreat by the Court from the old doctrines has also been a breakdown of the traditional theory of the role and nature of judicial power in the United States. The doctrine that the Court was not a policy-making body but simply a discoverer of principles embodied in the Constitution by the people for the purpose of controlling their own excesses had formed a significant part of the politics of business defense from the 1870's to the final battle over the Wagner Act. The critique of this theory by Holmes, Brandeis, Stone, Cardozo, and the judicial realists in the legal profession, which was in a sense practically implemented when Roosevelt launched his attack on the Court, must be counted as a major determining factor in the Court's reversal of its role which began with the Wagner Act cases.

The realists had pointed out, first, that the Court was a policy-making body, and secondly, that the laissez-faire doctrines of constitutional law were not dictated by the Constitution, but were merely the personal preferences of a majority of the Court. Their remedy, especially insofar as social and economic policy was concerned, was for the Court to adopt a policy of self-restraint and to refuse to invalidate the reasonable demands of legislative majorities for legal change, a policy which has been substantially implemented by the post-1937 Court. In undermining the traditional conception of judicial power, however, the realists also focused attention on the fact that the Court existed as a non-elective policy-making institution in a society otherwise considered to base the legitimacy of policy-making on the elective principle, and they offered no new conception of democratic theory or of the role of the Court by which this situation could be reconciled.[42]

As the Court has become responsive to the claims of new and different groups seeking constitutional protections, and as decision-making by the Court has continued to be an important part of the political process in the United States, the lack of an integrating theory by which the exercise of the Court's power may be justified in conformity with democratic principles has become a problem of major concern. Thus Justice Frankfurter, following what he considered to be the Holmesian tradition, referred to the Court as "the non-democratic organ of our Government" whose powers are "inherently oligarchic,"[43] and a student of judicial review has pointed out that a "theme of uneasiness, and even of guilt, colors the literature of judicial review," that it is widely felt that it "is an undemocratic shoot on an otherwise respectable tree," and that many feel that it "should be cut off, or at

---

[42] Fred V. Cahill, Jr., *Judicial Legislation* (New York: The Ronald Press Co., 1952), pp. 150–51.

[43] *A.F. of L.* v. *American Sash & Door Co.,* 335 U.S. 538, at 555–56 (1949).

least kept pruned and inconspicuous."[44] This theoretical problem of the role of the Court as a political institution is undoubtedly one of the most important legacies of the constitutional crisis of the 1930's, and because doubt on the question continues in the legal profession and among the Justices themselves, it remains a crucial factor in constitutional adjudication.

[44] Eugene V. Rostow, "The Democratic Character of Judicial Review," 66 *Harvard Law Review* 193 (Dec., 1952).

# BIBLIOGRAPHY

## BOOKS

Alinsky, Saul, *John L. Lewis* (New York: G. P. Putnam's Sons, 1949).

Alsop, Joseph, and Catledge, Turner, *The 168 Days* (Garden City: Doubleday, Doran and Co., 1938).

Berman, Edward, *Labor and the Sherman Act* (New York: W. W. Norton & Co., 1949).

Bernstein, Irving, *The New Deal Collective Bargaining Policy* (Berkeley: University of California Press, 1950).

Blaisdell, Doris Arlene, "The Constitutional Law of Mr. Justice McReynolds" (Madison: Unpublished Ph.D. Dissertation, University of Wisconsin, 1952).

Bonnett, Clarence E., *Employers' Associations in the United States* (New York: The Macmillan Co., 1922).

Brooks, Robert R. R., *As Steel Goes . . . Unionism in a Basic Industry* (New Haven: Yale University Press, 1940).

————, *When Labor Organizes* (New Haven: Yale University Press, 1938).

Burns, James MacGregor, *Roosevelt: The Lion and the Fox* (New York: Harcourt, Brace and Co., 1956).

Cahill, Fred V., *Judicial Legislation* (New York: The Ronald Press Co., 1952).

Cohen, Morris R., *Law and the Social Order* (New York: Harcourt, Brace and Co., 1933).

Commons, John R., *History of Labour in the United States,* Vol. III (New York: The Macmillan Co., 1922).

Corwin, Edward S., *Constitutional Revolution Ltd.* (Claremont, Calif.: Claremont College, 1941).

Daugherty, Carroll R., DeChazeau, Melvin G., and Stratton, Samuel S., *The Economics of the Iron and Steel Industry,* 2 vols. (New York: McGraw-Hill Book Co., 1937).

Derber, Milton, and Young, Edwin (eds.), *Labor and the New Deal* (Madison: University of Wisconsin Press, 1957).

Farley, James A., *Jim Farley's Story: The Roosevelt Years* (New York: McGraw-Hill Book Co., 1948).

Gerhart, Eugene C., *America's Advocate: Robert H. Jackson* (New York: The Bobbs-Merrill Co., Inc., 1958).

Girdler, Tom M., *Boot Straps: The Autobiography of Tom M. Girdler* (New York: Charles Scribner's Sons, 1943).

Goldman, Eric F., *Rendezvous with Destiny* (New York: Vintage Books, 1956).

Gregory, Charles O., *Labor and the Law* (New York: W. W. Norton & Co., 1949).

Harris, Herbert, *Labor's Civil War* (New York: Alfred A. Knopf, 1940).

Harris, Joseph P., *The Advice and Consent of the Senate* (Berkeley: University of California Press, 1953).

Hellman, George S., *Benjamin N. Cardozo: American Judge* (New York: McGraw-Hill Book Co., 1940).

Holmes, Oliver Wendell, Jr., *The Common Law* (Boston: Little, Brown and Co., 1888).

————, *Collected Legal Papers* (New York: Harcourt, Brace and Co., 1920).

Howell, Ronald F., "Conservative Influence on Constitutional Development, 1923–1937: The Constitutional Theory of Justices Van Devanter, McReynolds, Sutherland and Butler" (Baltimore: Unpublished Ph.D. Dissertation, The Johns Hopkins University, 1952).

Ickes, Harold L., *The Secret Diary of Harold L. Ickes: The Inside Struggle, 1936–1939,* Vol. II (New York: Simon and Schuster, 1954).

Jackson, Robert H., *The Struggle for Judicial Supremacy* (New York: Alfred A. Knopf, 1941).

Jacobs, Clyde E., *Law Writers and the Courts* (Berkeley: University of California Press, 1954).

Josephson, Matthew, *Sidney Hillman: Statesman of American Labor* (Garden City: Doubleday & Co., 1952).

Levinson, Edward, *Labor on the March* (New York: Harper & Brothers, 1938).

Lorwin, Lewis L., and Wubnig, Arthur, *Labor Relations Boards* (Washington: The Brookings Institution, 1935).

McPherson, William Heston, *Labor Relations in the Automobile Industry* (Washington: The Brookings Institution, 1940).

Mason, Alpheus T., *Harlan Fiske Stone: Pillar of the Law* (New York: The Viking Press, 1956).

————, *The Supreme Court from Taft to Warren* (Baton Rouge: Louisiana State University Press, 1958).

————, *Brandeis: A Free Man's Life* (New York: The Viking Press, 1946).

Miller, Glenn, *American Labor and the Government* (New York: Prentice-Hall, Inc., 1948).

Millis, Harry A., and Brown, Emily C., *From the Wagner Act to Taft-Hartley* (Chicago: University of Chicago Press, 1950).

Mowry, George E., *Theodore Roosevelt and the Progressive Movement* (Madison: University of Wisconsin Press, 1946).

Paschal, Joel Francis, *Mr. Justice Sutherland: A Man Against the State* (Princeton: Princeton University Press, 1951).

Paul, Arnold M., *Conservative Crisis and the Rule of Law: Attitudes of Bar and Bench, 1887–1895* (Ithaca: Cornell University Press, 1960).

Perkins, Frances, *The Roosevelt I Knew* (New York: The Viking Press, 1946).

Pringle, Henry F., *The Life and Times of William Howard Taft,* 2 vols. (New York: Farrar & Rinehart, Inc., 1939).

Pritchett, C. Herman, *The Roosevelt Court: A Study in Judicial Politics and Values, 1937–1947* (New York: The Macmillan Co., 1948).

Pusey, Merlo J., *Charles Evans Hughes* (New York: The Macmillan Co., 1951), 2 vols.

Rosenman, Samuel (ed.), *The Public Papers and Addresses of Franklin D. Roosevelt,* 1937 vol. (New York: The Macmillan Co., 1941).

Rutherford, M. Louise, "The Influence of the American Bar Association on Public Opinion and Legislation" (Phila.: Ph.D. Dissertation, University of Pennsylvania, 1937).

Schubert, Glendon A., *Quantitative Analysis of Judicial Behavior* (Glencoe: The Free Press and the Michigan State University Bureau of Social and Political Research, 1959).

Seidman, Joel, *The Needle Trades* (New York: Farrar & Rinehart, Inc., 1942).

Silverberg, Louis G. (ed.), *The Wagner Act: After Ten Years* (Washington: The Bureau of National Affairs, 1945).

Tugwell, Rexford, *The Democratic Roosevelt* (Garden City: Doubleday & Co., Inc., 1957).

Twiss, Benjamin R., *Lawyers and the Constitution* (Princeton: Princeton University Press, 1942).

Vose, Clement E., *Caucasians Only* (Berkeley: University of California Press, 1959).

White, Morton, *Social Thought in America: The Revolt Against Formalism* (Boston: Beacon Press, 1957).

Wolfskill, George, *The Revolt of the Conservatives, A History of the American Liberty League, 1934–1940* (Boston: Houghton Mifflin Co., 1962).

## PERIODICALS

Bates, Ernest Sutherland, "The Diehard Justices," *New Republic,* Vol. 87, p. 166 (June, 1936).

Brady, Harry, "Federal Pre-emption Comes of Age in Labor Relations," 5 *Labor Law Journal* 43 (Nov., 1954).

Cantwell, Frank V., "Public Opinion and the Legislative Process," *American Political Science Review,* Vol. 40, p. 924 (Oct., 1946).

Carey, Homer, and Oliphant, Herman, "The Present Status of the Hitchman Doctrine," 29 *Columbia Law Review* 441 (1929).

Cohen, Morris R., "Justice Holmes and the Nature of Law," 31 *Columbia Law Review* 352 (1931).

———, "The Process of Judicial Legislation," 48 *American Law Review* 161 (1914).

Detroit *Times,* Oct. 24, 1935.

*Editor & Publisher,* Vols. 66–70.

Frankfurter, Felix, "Mr. Justice Roberts," 104 *University of Pennsylvania Law Review* 311 (1955).

Gable, Richard W., "NAM: Influential Lobby or Kiss of Death?" *Journal of Politics,* Vol. 15, p. 254 (May, 1953).

Galenson, Walter, "The Unionization of the American Steel Industry," *International Review of Social History,* Vol. 1, pt. 1 (1956).

Garrison, Lloyd K., "The Constitution and the Future," *New Republic,* Vol. 85, p. 328 (Dec., 1936).

———, "7 (a) and the Future," *Survey Graphic,* Vol. 24, No. 2, p. 53 (Feb., 1935).

"Goodbye Section 7(a)," *New Republic,* Vol. 80, p. 325 (Oct., 1934).

Hamilton, Walton H., "Property—According to Locke," 41 *Yale Law Journal* 879 (1933).

"It Happened in Steel," *Fortune,* Vol. 15, p. 91 (May, 1937).

Jaffe, Louis L., "The Public Right Dogma in Labor Board Cases," 59 *Harvard Law Review* 720 (1946).

———, "The Individual Right to Initiate Administrative Process: The Relation between Public and Private Rights," 25 *Iowa Law Review* 485 (1940).

*Monthly Labor Review,* Vol. 80, p. 829 (July, 1957).

Pound, Roscoe, "Liberty of Contract," 18 *Yale Law Journal* 454 (1908).

———, "Mechanical Jurisprudence," 8 *Columbia Law Review* 605 (1908).

Powell, Thomas Reed, "Fifty-eight Lawyers Report," *New Republic,* Vol. 85, p. 120 (Dec., 1935).

Richmond *News Leader,* July 30, 1935.

Richmond *Times Dispatch,* July 6, 1935.

Rostow, Eugene V., "The Democratic Character of Judicial Review," 66 *Harvard Law Review* 193 (1952).

Rudolph, Frederick, "The American Liberty League, 1934–1940," *American Historical Review,* Vol. 55, No. 1, p. 19 (Oct., 1950).

Sayre, Francis B., "Labor and the Courts," 39 *Yale Law Journal* 682 (1930).

Schmidhauser, John R., "The Justices of the Supreme Court: A Collective Portrait," *Midwest Journal of Political Science,* Vol. III, p. 32 (Feb., 1954).

Severance, Cordenio A., "The Constitution and Individualism," 8 *American Bar Association Journal* 535 (1922).
Stanley, Louis, "The Collapse of the A.F. of L.," *The Nation,* Vol. 131, p. 367 (Oct., 1930).
Stein, Rose M., "Aliquippa Celebrates," *The Nation,* Vol. 144, p. 466 (April, 1937).
Stone, I. F., "Robert F. Wagner," *The Nation,* Vol. 159, p. 507 (Oct., 1944).
Sullivan, Mark, "The Unfinished Business of the New Deal," *Nation's Business,* Vol. 24, p. 15 (Aug., 1936).
Villard, Oswald G., "Pillars of Government: Robert F. Wagner," *Forum and Century,* Vol. 96, p. 124 (Sept., 1936).
Vose, Clement E., "The National Consumers' League and the Brandeis Brief," *Midwest Journal of Political Science,* Vol. I, p. 274 (Nov., 1957).
"Weirton and 7(a)," *New Republic,* Vol. 77, p. 183 (Dec., 1933).
White, Owen P., "When the Public Needs a Friend," *Colliers,* Vol. 93, p. 18 (June, 1934).
Witney, Fred, "NLRB Jurisdictional Policies and the Federal-State Relationship," 6 *Labor Law Journal* 3 (Jan., 1955).

## CASES CITED

*Adair* v. *United States,* 208 U.S. 161 (1908).
*Adkins* v. *Childrens' Hospital,* 261 U.S. 525 (1923).
*A.F. of L.* v. *American Sash & Door Co.,* 334 U.S. 538 (1949).
*Allgeyer* v. *Louisiana,* 165 U.S. 578 (1897).
*Amalgamated Workers* v. *Consolidated Edison Co.,* 309 U.S. 261 (1940).
*Anderson* v. *United States,* 171 U.S. 604 (1898).
*Associated Press* v. *NLRB,* 301 U.S. 103 (1937).
*Atkin* v. *Kansas,* 191 U.S. 207 (1903).
*Bailey* v. *Drexel Furniture Co.,* 259 U.S. 20 (1922).
*Baltimore & Ohio Ry. Co.* v. *ICC,* 221 U.S. 612 (1911).
*Bedford Cut Stone Co.* v. *Journeymen Stone Cutters,* 274 U.S. 37 (1927).
*Braceville Coal Co.* v. *People,* 147 Ill. 66, 35 N.E. 62 (1893).
*Bradley Lumber Co.* v. *NLRB,* 299 U.S. 559 (1936).
*Bunting* v. *Oregon,* 243 U.S. 426 (1917).
*Butcher's Union* v. *Crescent City Co.,* 111 U.S. 746 (1884).
*Carter* v. *Carter Coal Co.,* 298 U.S. 238 (1936).
*Chicago Board of Trade* v. *Olsen,* 262 U.S. 1 (1923).
*Commonwealth* v. *Perry,* 155 Mass. 117, 28 N.E. 1126 (1891).
*Consolidated Edison Co.* v. *NLRB,* 304 U.S. 197 (1938).
*Coppage* v. *Kansas,* 236 U.S. 1 (1915).
*Coronado Coal Co.* v. *United Mine Workers,* 268 U.S. 295 (1925).
*Donham* v. *West-Nelson Mfg. Co.,* 273 U.S. 657 (1927).
*Duplex Printing Co.* v. *Deering,* 254 U.S. 443 (1921).
*Employers' Liability Case,* 207 U.S. 463 (1908).
*Erie Ry. Co.* v. *Williams,* 233 U.S. 685 (1914).
*Ex parte Hawley,* 85 Ohio 494, 98 N.E. 1126 (1911).
*Ex parte Kubach,* 85 Cal. 274, 24 P. 737 (1890).
*Federal Radio Commission* v. *Nelson Brothers,* 209 U.S. 266 (1933).
*Frisbie* v. *United States,* 157 U.S. 160 (1895).
*Frorer* v. *People,* 141 Ill. 171, 31 N.E. 395 (1892).
*Gillespie* v. *People,* 188 Ill. 176, 58 N.E. 1007 (1900).
*Godcharles* v. *Wigeman,* 113 Pa. 431, 6 A. 354 (1886).
*Guss* v. *Utah Labor Relations Board,* 353 U.S. 51 (1957).
*Hammer* v. *Dagnehart,* 247 U.S. 251 (1918).
*Harding* v. *People,* 160 Ill. 459, 43 N.E. 624 (1896).
*Hawley* v. *Walker,* 232 U.S. 716 (1914).

*Helvering* v. *Davis*, 301 U.S. 619 (1937).
*Hill* v. *Wallace*, 259 U.S. 44 (1922).
*Hitchman Coal Co.* v. *Mitchell*, 245 U.S. 225 (1917).
*Holden* v. *Hardy*, 169 U.S. 366 (1898).
*Home Building and Loan Association* v. *Blaisdell*, 290 U.S. 398 (1934).
*Hopkins* v. *United States*, 171 U.S. 578 (1898).
*Houston E. & W. T. R. Co.* v. *United States*, 234 U.S. 342 (1914).
*Humphrey's Executor* v. *United States*, 297 U.S. 602 (1935).
*Industrial Association* v. *United States*, 268 U.S. 64 (1925).
*In re Eight Hour Law*, 21 Col. 29, 39 P. 328 (1895).
*In re House Bill*, 21 Col. 27, 39 P. 431 (1895).
*In re Jacobs*, 98 N.Y. 98, 50 Am. Rep. 637 (1885).
*In re Miller*, 162 Cal. 687, 124 P. 427 (1912).
*In re Morgan*, 26 Col. 415, 58 P. 1071 (1895).
*In re Preston*, 63 Ohio 352, 59 N.E. 101 (1900).
*International Organization* v. *Red Jacket* C.C. & C. Co., 18 F.2d 839 (CCA 4th, 1927).
*Int. Textbook* v. *Pigg*, 217 U.S. 91 (1910).
*Ives* v. *South Buffalo Ry. Co.*, 201 N.Y. 271, 94 N.E. 431 (1911).
*Johnson* v. *Goodyear Mining Co.*, 127 Cal. 4, 59 P. 304 (1899).
*Keokee Coke Co.* v. *Taylor*, 234 U.S. 227 (1914).
*Knoxville Iron Co.* v. *Harbison*, 183 U.S. 513 (1901).
*Leep* v. *St. Louis I.M. & S. Ry.* 58 Ark. 407, 25 S.W. 75 (1894).
*Lincoln Federal Labor Union* v. *Northwestern Iron & Metal Co.*, 335 U.S. 525 (1949).
*Local 167* v. *United States*, 291 U.S. 293 (1934).
*Lochner* v. *New York*, 198 U.S. 45 (1905).
*Loewe* v. *Lawler*, 208 U.S. 274 (1908).
*Louisville Bank* v. *Radford*, 295 U.S. 555 (1935).
*Low* v. *Rees Printing Co.*, 41 Neb. 127, 59 N.W. 362 (1894).
*McLean* v. *Arkansas*, 211 U.S. 539 (1909).
*Miller* v. *Wilson*, 236 U.S. 373 (1915).
*Millett* v. *People*, 117 Ill. 294, 7 N.E. 631 (1886).
*Morehead* v. *New York*, 298 U.S. 587 (1936).
*Muller* v. *Oregon*, 208 U.S. 412 (1908).
*Munn* v. *Illinois*, 94 U.S. 113 (1877).
*Murphy* v. *Sardell*, 269 U.S. 530 (1925).
*Nashville & St. Louis Ry. Co.* v. *Alabama*, 128 U.S. 96 (1905).
*Near* v. *Minnesota*, 283 U.S. 697 (1931).
*Nebbia* v. *New York*, 291 U.S. 502 (1934).
*NLRB* v. *Associated Press*, 85 F.2d 56 (CCA 2d, 1936).
*NLRB* v. *Bemis Bag Co.* (Unreported).
*NLRB* v. *Fainblatt*, 306 U.S. 601 (1939).
*NLRB* v. *Friedman–Harry Marks Clothing Co.*, 85 F.2d 1 (CCA 2d, 1936).
*NLRB* v. *Friedman–Harry Marks Clothing Co.*, 301 U.S. 58 (1937).
*NLRB* v. *Fruehauf Trailer Co.*, 85 F.2d 391 (CCA 6th, 1936).
*NLRB* v. *Fruehauf Trailer Co.*, 301 U.S. 49 (1937).
*NLRB* v. *Jones & Laughlin Steel Corp.*, 83 F.2d 998 (CCA 5th, 1936).
*NLRB* v. *Jones & Laughlin Steel Corp.*, 301 U.S. 1 (1937).
*NLRB* v. *Washington, Virginia and Maryland Coach Co.*, 85 F.2d 990 (CCA 4th, 1936).
*Ogden* v. *Saunders*, 12 Wheat. 213 (1827).
*Penn. Ry. Co.* v. *U.S. Railway Labor Board*, 261 U.S. 72 (1923).
*Pensacola Tel.* v. *Western Union*, 96 U.S. 1 (1878).
*People* v. *Beck*, 144 N.Y. 225, 39 N.E. 80 (1894).
*People* v. *Coler*, 166 N.Y. 1, 59 N.E. 716 (1901).

*People* v. *Kreutzberg*, 114 Wis. 530, 90 N.W. 1098 (1902).
*People* v. *Marx*, 99 N.Y. 377, 2 N.E. 29 (1885).
*Phila., Balt., Wash., Ry. Co.* v. *Schubert*, 224 U.S. 603 (1912).
*Polish National Alliance* v. *NLRB*, 136 F.2d 175 (CCA 7th, 1943).
*Powell* v. *Pennsylvania*, 127 U.S. 678 (1888).
*Radice* v. *New York*, 264 U.S. 292 (1924).
*Railroad Retirement Board* v. *Alton*, 295 U.S. 330 (1935).
*Ramsey* v. *People*, 142 Ill. 380, 32 N.E. 364 (1892).
*Ritchie* v. *People*, 115 Ill. 98, 40 N.E. 454 (1897).
*St. Louis Ry. Co.* v. *Paul*, 173 U.S. 404 (1899).
*Santa Clara County* v. *Southern Pacific Ry. Co.*, 118 U.S. 394 (1886).
*Santa Cruz Co.* v. *NLRB*, 303 U.S. 453 (1938).
*Schechter Poultry Corp.* v. *United States*, 295 U.S. 495 (1935).
*Second Employers' Liability Case*, 223 U.S. 1 (1912).
*Slaughter House Cases*, 16 Wall. 36 (1872).
*Southern Ry. Co.* v. *United States*, 222 U.S. 20 (1911).
*Stafford* v. *Wallace*, 258 U.S. 495 (1922).
*State* v. *Fire Creek Coal Co.*, 33 W.Va. 188, 10 S.E. 288 (1899).
*State* v. *Goodwill*, 33 W.Va. 179, 10 S.E. 285 (1899).
*State* v. *Haun*, 61 Kans. 146, 59 P. 340 (1900).
*State* v. *Julow*, 129 Mo. 163, 31 S.W. 781 (1895).
*State* v. *Loomis*, 115 Mo. 307, 22 S.W. 350 (1893).
*State* v. *Mo. Tie & Timber Co.*, 181 Mo. 536, 30 S.W. 933 (1904).
*Stettler* v. *O'Hara*, 243 U.S. 426 (1917).
*Steward Machine Co.* v. *Davis*, 301 U.S. 548 (1937).
*Stout* v. *Pratt*, 12 F. Supp. 864 (W.D. Mo., 1935).
*Stout* v. *Pratt*, 85 F.2d 172 (CCA 8th, 1935).
*Street* v. *Varney Electrical Supply Co.*, 160 Ind. 338, 65 N.E. 895 (1903).
*Swift & Company* v. *United States*, 196 U.S. 375 (1905).
*System Federation* v. *Penn Ry. Co.*, 267 U.S. 188 (1925).
*System Federation* v. *Virginian Railroad Co.*, 11 F. Supp. 621 (D.C., ED Va., 1935).
*Table Supply Stores* v. *Hawking*, 9 F. Supp. 888 (S.D. Fla., 1935).
*Texas & New Orleans Ry. Co.* v. *Brotherhood*, 24 F.2d 426 (N.D. Tex., 1928).
*Texas & New Orleans Ry. Co.* v. *Brotherhood*, 25 F.2d 873 (N.D. Tex., 1928).
*Texas & New Orleans Ry. Co.* v. *Brotherhood*, 33 F.2d 13 (CCA 5th, 1929).
*Texas & New Orleans Ry. Co.* v. *Brotherhood*, 281 U.S. 548 (1930).
*Truax* v. *Corrigan*, 257 U.S. 312 (1921).
*United Mine Workers* v. *Coronado Coal Co.*, 258 F. 829 (CCA 8th, 1919).
*United Mine Workers* v. *Coronado Coal Co.*, 259 U.S. 344 (1922).
*United States* v. *American Tobacco Co.*, 221 U.S. 106 (1911).
*United States* v. *Darby Lumber Co.*, 312 U.S. 100 (1941).
*United States* v. *E. C. Knight Co.*, 156 U.S. 1 (1895).
*United States* v. *Patten*, 226 U.S. 525 (1913).
*United States* v. *Weirton Steel Co.*, 10 F. Supp. 55 (D.C. Del., 1935).
*Virginian Railroad Co.*, v. *System Federation*, 300 U.S. 515 (1937).
*Wallace* v. *Georgia*, 97 Ga. 213, 22 S.E. 529 (1894).
*Washington, Virginia and Maryland Coach Co.* v. *NLRB*, 301 U.S. 142 (1937).
*West Coast Hotel* v. *Parrish*, 300 U.S. 379 (1937).
*Wickard* v. *Filburn*, 317 U.S. 111 (1942).
*Wolff Packing Co.* v. *Industrial Court*, 262 U.S. 522 (1923).
*Wolff Packing Co.* v. *Industrial Court*, 267 U.S. 552 (1925).

## NLRB CASES CITED

In the Matter of the Associated Press, 1 NLRB 788 (1935).
In the Matter of Breeding Transfer Co., 110 NLRB 493 (1954).

In the Matter of Friedman–Harry Marks Clothing Co., 1 NLRB 411 (1935).
In the Matter of Fruehauf Trailer Co., 1 NLRB 68 (1935).
In the Matter of Hollow Tree Lumber Co., 91 NLRB 635 (1950).
In the Matter of Jones & Laughlin Steel Corp., 1 NLRB 503 (1935).
In the Matter of MacKay Radio & Telegraph Co., 1 NLRB 201 (1935).
In the Matter of Pennsylvania Greyhound Lines, 1 NLRB 1 (1935).
In the Matter of the San Francisco Call-Bulletin, 2 NLRB 1 (1934).
In the Matter of Siemans Mailing Service, 122 NLRB 81 (1958).
In the Matter of Washington, Virginia and Maryland Coach Co., 1 NLRB 769 (1935).

## STATUTES CITED

Adamson Act of 1916, 39 Stat. 721.
Arbitration Act of 1888, 25 Stat. 501.
Economy Act of 1933, 48 Stat. 8.
Erdman Act of 1898, 30 Stat. 424.
Fair Labor Standards Act of 1938, 52 Stat. 1060.
Federal Employers' Liability Act of 1906, 34 Stat. 232.
Grain Futures Act of 1922, 42 Stat. 998.
Hours of Service Act of 1907, 34 Stat. 1415.
Judiciary Act of 1914, 38 Stat. 790.
Judiciary Act of 1937, 50 Stat. 24.
Mann Act of 1910, 36 Stat. 825.
National Industrial Recovery Act of 1933, 49 Stat. 195.
Norris–LaGuardia Act of 1932, 47 Stat. 70.
Packers and Stockyards Act of 1921, 42 Stat. 159.
Railway Labor Act of 1926, 44 Stat. 577.
Railway Labor Act of 1926, as amended, 1934, 48 Stat. 1185.
Retirement Act of 1869, 16 Stat. 45.

## DOCUMENTS

BRIEFS

NLRB, *Associated Press* v. *NLRB.*
Associated Press, *Associated Press* v. *NLRB.*
American Newspaper Publishers' Association as *Amicus Curiae, Associated Press* v. *NLRB.*
Commercial Telegraphers' Union as *Amicus Curiae, Associated Press* v. *NLRB.*
American Newspaper Guild as *Amicus Curiae, Associated Press* v. *NLRB.*
NLRB, *NLRB* v. *Friedman–Harry Marks Clothing Co.*
Friedman–Harry Marks Clothing Co., *NLRB* v. *Friedman–Harry Marks Clothing Co.*
NLRB, *NLRB* v. *Fruehauf Trailer Co.*
Fruehauf Trailer Co., *NLRB* v. *Fruehauf Trailer Co.*
American Federation of Labor as *Amicus Curiae, NLRB* v. *Fruehauf Trailer Co.*
NLRB, *NLRB* v. *Jones & Laughlin Steel Corp.*
Jones & Laughlin Steel Corp., *NLRB* v. *Jones & Laughlin Steel Corp.*
NLRB, *Washington, Virginia and Maryland Coach Co.* v. *NLRB.*
Washington, Virginia and Maryland Coach Co., *Washington, Virginia and Maryland Coach Co.* v. *NLRB.*
American Federation of Labor and the Amalgamated Association of Street, Electric Railway and Motor Coach Employees of America as *Amici Curiae, Washington, Virginia and Maryland Coach Co.* v. *NLRB.*
Pennsylvania Greyhound Lines as *Amicus Curiae, Washington, Virginia and Maryland Coach Co.* v. *NLRB.*

HEARINGS AND OTHER DOCUMENTS

Hearings before a Subcommittee of the Committee on Education and Labor, U.S. Senate, 75th Cong., 2nd sess. (LaFollette Committee).

Hearings on S. 1392, Judiciary Committee, U.S. Senate, 75th Cong., 1st sess.

Hearings before the Committee on Education and Labor on S. 2926, U.S. Senate, 73rd Cong., 2nd sess.

Hearings before the Committee on Education and Labor on S. 1958, U.S. Senate, 74th Cong., 1st sess.

Hearings before a Special Committee to Investigate the NLRB, House of Representatives, 76th Cong., 3rd sess.

National Industrial Recovery, Hearings on S. 1712 and HR 5755, Senate Committee on Finance, 73rd Cong., 1st sess.

National Labor Relations Board, *First Annual Report* (1936).

National Labor Relations Board, *Second Annual Report* (1937).

National Labor Relations Board, *Legislative History of the National Labor Relations Act.*

National Labor Relations Board, Division of Economic Research, *Collective Bargaining in the Newspaper Industry,* Bulletin No. 3 (Oct., 1936).

National Labor Relations Board, Division of Economic Research, *Written Trade Agreements in Collective Bargaining,* Bulletin No. 4 (Nov., 1939).

National Labor Relations Board, Report No. 1371, House of Representatives 74th Cong., 1st sess.

National Lawyers Committee of the American Liberty League, *Report on the Constitutionality of the National Labor Relations Act* (Sept., 1935).

National Lawyers Committee of the American Liberty League, *Report on the Constitutionality of the Bituminous Coal Conservation Act of 1935* (Dec., 1935).

Official Report of the Proceedings before the NLRB, In the Matter of Associated Press; Jones & Laughlin Steel Corp.; Friedman–Harry Marks Clothing Co.; Fruehauf Trailer Co.; Washington, Virginia and Maryland Coach Co.

Oral Arguments in the Cases arising under the Railway Labor Act and the National Labor Relations Act before the Supreme Court of the United States, February 8–11, 1937, Senate Document No. 52, 75th Cong., 1st sess.

Report of the Pennsylvania Department on Labor and Industry on the Relations between the Jones & Laughlin Steel Corp. and its Workers, Submitted at the request of the National Steel Labor Relations Board, Charlotte E. Carr, Sec. of Labor and Industry, Commonwealth of Pennsylvania (Nov. 10, 1934).

Senate Report No. 573, Committee on Education and Labor, 74th Cong., 1st sess.

# INDEX

Acheson, Dean, 67
Acheson, M. W., 115
Aliquippa, Pa., 69, 77, 114
  conditions in, 58–60
  establishment, 58
  reaction to Wagner Act cases in,
    180–82
Amalgamated Association of Iron,
  Steel, and Tin Workers, 57–58,
  90, 92
Amalgamated Association of Street,
  Electric Railway and Motor
  Coach Employees
  *amicus curiae* brief filed by, 139
  brief of, 165
  organizing activities, 134
Amalgamated Clothing Workers, 123
  contract with Friedman–Harry
    Marks Clothing Co., 182
  cooperation with NLRB, 122
  effect on NIRA code hearings, 48–
    49
  organizing activities, 70, 87–88,
    119–21
  pressure on NLRB exerted by, 121
American Bar Association
  committee on citizenship created by,
    23–24
  committee to oppose judicial recall
    created by, 12
  concern over attacks on judiciary, 23
American Civil Liberties Union, 54
American Federation of Labor, 47–48,
  74, 77, 183
  *amicus curiae* brief filed by, 139
  brief of, 165
  intervention in *Washington, Virginia
    and Maryland Coach Co.* case,
    135
  lobbying activities, 78
  opposition to changes in section
    7(a), 46
  opposition to John J. Parker, 36–37

American Federation of Labor
  (*Continued*)
  position in 1933, 44
  split within, 90–92
American Liberty League, 88, 105, 117,
  121, 150
  attack on Guffey Act, 100
  composition and finances, 94–95
  formation and tactics, 73
  purpose of public briefs issued by,
    185–86
  report on constitutionality of Wag-
    ner Act, 93–95
American Newspaper Guild, 131, 179
  activities in *AP* case, 126–30
  *amicus curiae* brief filed by, 132, 139
  brief of, 160–61
  creation of, 52–55
  involvement in Jennings case, 65–66
  opposition to free press amendment,
    84
  reaction to Wagner Act cases, 180
American Newspaper Publishers' Association
  *amicus curiae* brief filed by, 139
  attitude toward NIRA, 51–54
  brief of, 160
  Free Press Committee of, 53
  involvement in *AP* case, 128, 132
  opinion of Wagner Act, 96–97
  opposition to NLRB, 65–66
  opposition to Wagner Act, 78, 81
  purpose of public brief issued by,
    185–86
  reaction to Wagner Act cases, 180
Arkansas Supreme Court, 4
Associated Industries of Cleveland, 72
Associated Press, 52, 140, 156–57, 161
  appeal to Supreme Court, 138–39
  argument of, 168
  brief of, 158–60
  coercion of Morris Watson, 55–56
  NLRB proceedings against, 126–33

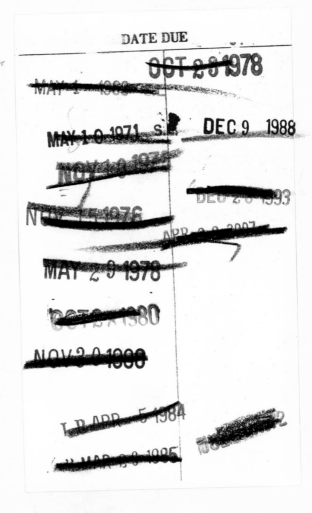